MW01406192

Praise for *The Mystified Letter*

Stemming from a profound sense that reading is in crisis, Craig Tichelkamp's splendid new volume offers a creative, novel, and persuasive constructive proposal rooted in the Middle Ages and, more precisely, in the sacralization and enchantment of reading in the monasteries and schools of the high Middle Ages. Deeply informed historically and written with elegance, Tichelkamp's work proposes practices of mystical reading that address contemporary maladies in academic and ecclesiastical reading cultures in ways captivating not only to medievalists but to all who find the notion of the "mystified letter," be they religious or not, profoundly right and compelling. Highly recommended.
—Kevin Madigan, Winn Professor of Ecclesiastical History, Harvard Divinity School; author of *Medieval Christianity: A New History*

Craig Tichelkamp offers a trenchant diagnosis of the weariness, aridity, and incomprehension that too often attend reading today, both in our churches and at the university. Like the educational reformer Ivan Illich, Tichelkamp turns to the medieval school of St. Victor to remind us that the experience of reading was once charged with mystery. He offers hope that reading can again prove to be rejuvenating, personally transformative, and communally rich. Reading Tichelkamp's own stirring book proves the point.
—Ann W. Astell, professor of theology, University of Notre Dame

Tichelkamp's study triumphs as an invaluable contribution to the field of medieval Victorine studies. More broadly considered, his adept treatment of the Victorine inheritance of Dionysian mysticism, as it pertains to the school's development of a theology of the "letter," will be useful for historical and systematic theologians alike for years to come. Within this broader project, moreover, *The Mystified Letter* will also serve as an important resource for those who are specifically interested in the thought of Thomas Gallus, whose contributions to the development of a theology of reading within that context are here introduced by Tichelkamp with exquisite clarity and captivating prose.
—Katherine Wrisley Shelby, author of *Spiraling into God: Bonaventure on Grace, Hierarchy, and Holiness*

In *The Mystified Letter*, Tichelkamp succeeds in making a persuasive, accurate, and quite worthy case for a "re-enchantment" of the practice of reading by retrieving the mystical ethos of reading that existed in monastic communities during the Middle Ages, specifically within the culture of the Victorine School in twelfth-century Paris. Such a retrieval, as Tichelkamp correctly explains, is not the imposition of a more "traditional" set of values onto the effects of contemporary culture; rather, it is the distilling of essential ideas and practices for the "radical" renewal of understanding: here, the author utilizes the medieval monastic understanding of reading as a sacred, potentially mystical relationship between the text and the reader and among a community of readers. Tichelkamp rightly reminds us that in medieval schools, reading both sacred and secular literature was a practice that allowed spaces of mystery and incomprehensibility, that welcomed communion and conversation, but that did not always seek—as we do now—the absolute surety of specific interpretation, forms of analyses that tend to incite division and disagreement. The medieval world regarded the text as sacred and capable of spiritual inspiration as well as moral transformation, which depth of thinking about reading, Tichelkamp argues, we must attempt to recover. Reading, he enthuses, must again become an imaginative as well as cognitive experience, the occasion for wonder and awe and delight, and not only, as happens now too often, simply for technical and perfunctory purposes.

For Tichelkamp, the generally medieval but specifically Victorine ease with a mystical sensibility in all matters of life—that is, beginning with the mundane and literal but then seeking and looking beyond the apparent to the unseen and the ineffable—is an attitude that must again be cultivated not just in churches and schools but in contemporary culture altogether. He wants to shock contemporary culture out of its apathy, indifference, and sullen antagonism toward reading and to regain the sense of mystery and wonder that has always been present in the written word, at least as medieval thinkers argued. As the Victorines taught and Tichelkamp recommends, readers should again "ramble" and "wander" along literary paths—fiction, poetry, drama, and all other forms—not always seeking an "answer" or the correct "interpretation" but rather allowing the dignity and the phenomenon of the text to be present before the reader, salvaging the text from constant deconstruction and destabilization. Reading need not always have just the goal of completion in mind: sometimes, as the Victorines taught, it is sufficient just to linger over a verse or a phrase or a description and revel in that singular moment.

This is a worthy text not only for educators and institutional leaders who have been frustrated with the disaffection with reading that has pervaded current mores, especially among the young, but for anyone who hopes to (re)gain the mystical wonder of the text and the transformative power of reading.

—June-Ann Greeley, professor of languages and literature,
Sacred Heart University

The MYSTIFIED LETTER

The
MYSTIFIED LETTER

How Medieval Theology
Can Reenchant the
Practice of Reading

Craig Tichelkamp

Fortress Press
Minneapolis

THE MYSTIFIED LETTER
How Medieval Theology Can Reenchant the Practice of Reading

Copyright © 2023 by Fortress Press, an imprint of 1517 Media. All rights reserved. Except for brief quotations in critical articles or reviews, no part of this book may be reproduced in any manner without prior written permission from the publisher. Email copyright@1517.media or write to Permissions, Fortress Press, PO Box 1209, Minneapolis, MN 55440-1209.

Library of Congress Control Number: 2023012810 (print)

Cover image: Manuscript Leaf with the Celebration of a Mass in an Initial S, from an Antiphonary, Italian, second half 15th century, from the Metropolitan Museum of Art
Cover design: Kristin Miller

Print ISBN: 978-1-5064-8673-4
eBook ISBN: 978-1-5064-8674-1

CONTENTS

Acknowledgments	vii
1. Introduction: Reading Now and Then	1
2. Theology of the Letter	25
3. Mystical Theology: The Letter as God's Veil	51
4. Mystical Theology: The Letter and the Word of God	83
5. The Letter and Experience	127
6. Conclusion: Reading Then and Now	177
Bibliography	187
Index	195

ACKNOWLEDGMENTS

This book on the enchantment of reading would not be possible without a community of enchanting readers. My profound gratitude goes out to my teachers, colleagues, students, family, and friends. Those who set me on the path of the mystified letter are Jennifer Jesse, Medi Volpe, Boyd Taylor Coolman, Charles Stang, and Amy Hollywood. More recently, Mary Joan Leith has been a treasured mentor and conversation partner. My students at Stonehill College, Harvard Divinity School, and Tufts University have generously joined me on the journey.

My family has picked me up along the way toward my "book on reading." Thanks to my parents, Gwen and John Pelzer and Neal and Cynthia Tichelkamp. I also owe much to Alan Lankford and the late Laura Lankford (who was always reading). I am especially thankful to my sister, Kate Tichelkamp, who supports me unfailingly. My partner, David Lankford, deserves the most thanks. Those who have met him will recognize when I invoke his generosity, steadfastness, and good humor, but they do not know the extent of the goodness he is capable of, a knowledge I treasure immensely. I dedicate this book to David.

1

INTRODUCTION: READING NOW AND THEN

This field in which you labor, having been well plowed with your exegetical pen, will yield a manifold harvest for you.

—Hugh of St. Victor, *Didascalicon on the Study of Reading*, VI.III

Our Reading Culture

Reading is a drag. The two institutional pillars of our reading culture, the Church and the academy, struggle to reckon with the fact that reading has become divisive and dull. Both extol reading, and yet within their doors reading is in crisis. In the Church, sacred writings like the Scriptures have become objects of division, harm, and apathy. When Christians muster the energy to read in community, the exhaustingly familiar outcome is disagreement, division, and even formal splits over *the text* and its ostensible instructions on the full inclusion of LGBTQ+ persons or the ordination of women. Sacred writings become instruments for harm, and reading becomes little more than a strategy for survival. As divisions harden in reading cultures, readers suffer. In this environment, it becomes difficult to foster a reading culture, to instill the love of reading, and to experience the Word as transformative.

Consider also the academy. Reading is a common habit of education and research, and the university provides a place and a time for it to occur. At the same time, the modern academy deprives readers of its pleasure and potential as pressures toward technocratic-meritocratic forms of education and research instrumentalize reading, turning it into a skill to be mastered or tool to be leveraged—hardly a practice of spiritual formation. With all their anxious attention on securing status and a financial future, students (and their parents, university administrators, and even their professors) see little intrinsic value in close, communal reading. Reading becomes yet another task to be speedily completed, exhausting the reader and sapping literature of its transformative potential. Of course, ingenious professors and curious students know the hidden depth of reading's transformative possibility, but they too often lack the cultural conditions and institutional support to realize it. Without adequate habits of imagination fostered by a healthy reading culture in the academy, readers suffer.

We are left to read alone. It is no wonder that many of us experience reading primarily as a diversion, an escape from division and apathy. We retreat with a good book to enjoy a solitary pleasure. Of course, these private experiences are wonderful, but they presume a reading culture where reading is not especially serious or transformative, and where it has few personal or social effects. Diversionary reading may achieve modest forms of personal transformation—"Habitual readers are more empathetic," we're assured—but it's difficult to say it creates effective social change or spiritual transformation. It certainly does not meet the lofty ambitions of the Church and the academy, which promise that personal and social transformation occurs when we read together.

Given such a state of our reading cultures, there's little impetus to theorize reading, to imagine what it is or might be, much less to theologize it, to construct an account of its role in determining our relation to God, our spiritual development, and our social transformation. While we all recognize that the experience of reading has been changing with new technologies and mediums over the last few years, some long-standing pieties have us half-heartedly supporting, but not really thinking about, reading. Perhaps reading plays a role in the established institutions of the Church and the academy, but does it really have the potential to transform us?[1]

---

1   A related question is whether these institutions themselves have the potential to transform us at a time when there is a large amount of disaffection, apathy, and division marking our attitudes toward the Church, the academy, and institutions generally. Recognizing the serious causes for this disaffection, there is no getting around the fact that churches and classrooms are where many of us learn to read. They are pillars of our reading culture. If a sensible realism urges caution in our capacity to transform these institutions, a hope in the possibility of reading to transform persons and societies leads me to imagine their transformation or renewal.

This book begins with the admission that connecting reading to God or spirituality, to social or personal transformation, appears quaint. But appearances can deceive. To address the way our reading cultures inculcate division and harm, apathy and triviality, and to construct a new theology of reading, this book will perform an act of theological retrieval, drawing from sources of the Christian past to renew our reading cultures in the present and future. Why should we care about reading? And what can be done to revive or reform the ailing reading cultures of the Church and the academy?

By a *reading culture*, I refer to a community that makes reading possible through what it says and does, its imagination and its practical habits. As such, a reading culture is a world in which we read and thus have a worldview that integrates reading into our broader living. A reading culture encompasses the social, imaginary, and disciplinary conditions for making reading real. According to this definition, the Church and the academy are both reading cultures. They have habits of reading, and they inculcate ways of thinking and feeling about reading. They see reading as central to their identity and mission, to the forms of personal and social transformation they claim to facilitate. And yet these reading cultures are not doing well. This book means to put theology to work imagining an alternative reading culture, renewing our imagination about and habits of reading.

The Mystified Letter

This book develops a renewed theology of reading and imagines an alternative reading culture, one centered on the theological concept of *the mystified letter*. The central diagnostic argument I make in this book is that our reading cultures of the Church and the academy are ailing because they struggle to reckon with the mystical condition of reading—they fail to *mystify the letter*. The terms *mystical*, *mystify*, and *mystification* can be fuzzy and difficult to define. In modern and common parlance, to *mystify* often has a nefarious connotation—it means to make something obscure in order to mislead or oppress. However, my use of the term is more morally neutral. By *mystification*, I refer to the aesthetic, rhetorical, liturgical, or theological techniques that invest something with a sense of ineffability and unintelligibility, wonder and awe, and that inculcate humility or reverence for the mystified object. For something to be *mystified*, it must be imbued with a sense of hard-to-grasp extraordinary potential, of an unspeakable capacity to inspire and transform. A mystified object incites passion and curiosity. In this book, I will focus on the mystification of literature (or "the letter" as I'll often refer to it here, a translation of the Latin term *littera*). I've begun this book by arguing that the Church and the academy today struggle to mystify the letter. Why and how might our churches, academic communities, and classrooms inculcate a sense of literature's abundant potential and inarticulable mystery, its capacity for spiritual and social transformation? If the letter has largely been demystified in these contexts, if reading the letter has little capacity to inspire and transform, what role might theology play in mystifying the letter anew?

To probe these questions and construct a potential response, this book will engage in an act of theological analysis and retrieval. Though there have been many remarkable reading cultures, this book turns its attention to a twelfth- and thirteenth-century school called St. Victor, where the letter once became mystified. The Abbey of St. Victor was founded by William of Champeaux in 1113. Although William retreated from the cathedral school in Paris to found the abbey on the outskirts of the city, it would be wrong to assume the Victorines—as the scholar-monk-priests at the abbey came to be known—were removed from the intellectual and religious life of the city. In fact, St. Victor became not only a place of retreat for students in Paris (the Victorines serving as confessors or spiritual advisers at times) but also an influential hub of scholarship. The twelfth- and thirteenth-century Victorines became well known for their writings on Scripture and theology, producing volumes and volumes of commentaries, treatises, poetry, sermons, and liturgical sequences. These Latin writings cover many topics but especially pedagogy in the school's early days, mystical theology in its later days, and biblical interpretation throughout. These theological writings provide a window into the abbey school's reading culture, and their analysis is central to this book.

Life at the abbey was lived according to a rule (*regula*), as was characteristic of medieval religious communities. The Victorines were "regular" canons or, more specifically, Augustinian canons since they followed the *Rule of Augustine*. As monks following a rule, they engaged in ritual prayer at prescribed times and ate, worked, conversed, and slept according to a prescribed order. As canons, they also had responsibilities of priestly ministry, administering sacraments and preaching (both duties reflected prominently in their writings). As scholars, they not only read and wrote but also educated both novices (those preparing for life in the abbey) and outside students. Reading was done together in the context of the cloister as the "brothers" at St. Victor read, lived, and worked in the community. Indeed, among all the religious disciplines practiced by the Victorines, reading seems to have played the central role. Reading had the incalculable capacity to transform soul, body, and society. The Victorines' writings all center on reading, with commentaries and translations being especially prominent. Even their theological treatises, poetry, and liturgical compositions are rooted in the experience of reading literature (both secular and sacred).

Though the Abbey of St. Victor is long gone, the historical archive has been generous, leaving us many of these writings. Some had robust readerships during their own time and in the centuries to follow. For example, the number of late medieval manuscripts containing the writings of Hugh of St. Victor, the school's early and premiere pedagogue, is staggering.[2] The mystical writings of Richard of St. Victor (who became prior in 1162) were also beloved. Others produced less popular but more practical writings, like the historical or literal (*ad litteram*) biblical commentaries of Andrew of St. Victor. In the twentieth century, a reappraisal of Andrew led to considerable enthusiasm among scholars for his contributions to biblical exegesis, especially his use of Jewish sources.[3] Still other Victorines have been more recently rediscovered, like Thomas Gallus, the last great Victorine. Gallus's commentaries on the Old Testament's Song of Songs and the writings of Pseudo-Dionysius are insightful works of mystical theology that reflect and refract the reading culture of the school.[4] Finally, there are also extant

---

2   See Torsten Edstam, "From Twelfth-Century Renaissance to Fifteenth-Century Reform: The Reception of Hugh of St. Victor in the Later Middle Ages" (PhD diss., University of Chicago, 2014).
3   See Beryl Smalley, *The Study of the Bible in the Middle Ages*, 2nd ed. (Notre Dame, IN: University of Notre Dame Press, 1964), 112–72.
4   See Boyd Taylor Coolman, *Eternally Spiraling into God: Knowledge, Love, and Ecstasy in the Theology of Thomas Gallus* (Oxford: Oxford University Press, 2017). All recent work on Thomas Gallus is indebted to the critical editions of his commentaries on

writings from a slew of other Victorines and enthusiasts for St. Victor like John Saracen, about whom we know little but whose translations of the writings of Pseudo-Dionysius are central to the emergence of the mystified letter at the school, or James of Vitry, who admiringly characterized St. Victor (where he likely visited as a student in Paris) as a "tranquil harbor," a telling metaphor for a bishop of Acre in the crusader states who must have spent considerable time at sea. While this book draws especially on the theologies of the framing figures of Hugh and Thomas Gallus (the school's first and last great readers), it strives to exhibit some of the theological plurality and plenitude that emerged from this remarkable reading culture.

Given such a vast and intellectually diverse community, it is striking that a singular vision for reading at St. Victor cohered across the twelfth and thirteenth centuries. The Victorines read in community, and I take this to be a function of the letter's mystery at the school. In this book, I talk about the emergence of the mystified letter at St. Victor to encapsulate the unique ways I see distinct strands of theology coming together at the school to inculcate a sense of the letter's mystery within the Victorine reading culture. This established vision is apparent in the culminating thirteenth-century figure of Thomas Gallus, whose writings are major sources in the latter part of this book. This book will trace out how the mystified letter came into being at the school in order to consider how the letter's mystery functions within a reading culture. As such, the book highlights primarily theological concepts and habits and only secondarily the material and practical contexts of reading.[5]

Pseudo-Dionysius prepared by Declan Lawell for the series *Corpus Christianorum Continuatio Mediaevalis*.

5   Undoubtedly it took much more than theology—habits of reasoning or writing about God—to mystify the letter at the school. It is beyond the purview of this book to explore how, for instance, aesthetic or liturgical techniques were integral to the process of mystification. These extratextual techniques of mystification go beyond my scholarly competency and beyond what the historical archive leaves us from St. Victor. While this study focuses on the role theology had in mystifying the letter, it could be complemented by studies of art and liturgy as well.

Margot E. Fassler's book *Gothic Song: Victorine Sequences and Augustinian Reform in Twelfth-Century Paris*, 2nd ed. (Notre Dame, IN: University of Notre Dame Press, 2011), while not using mystification as a theoretical framework, analyzes and contextualizes Victorine liturgical sequences. Fassler's use of Hugh of St. Victor's theology to contextualize

Ultimately, this book is interested in the techniques of mystifying literature at the school, especially those developed by the school's changing theology. How did literature—the letter, or *littera*—become mystified? Among the canons of St. Victor, what about their theology invested literature with unintelligibility and ineffability? What made it awesome and wonderful, full of potential and possibility? Why did those at the school treat it with humility and reverence, passion and curiosity? How did it draw together a vast community of diverse readers confident in its capacity to transform them personally and socially? I want to emphasize that a sense of literature's mystery is not inevitable or natural but has to be enculturated through habits of thought and action and explore the ways theology contributed to the mystification of reading at the medieval school of St. Victor. Doing so will allow this book to engage in an act of theological retrieval, analyzing and evaluating the theology of the twelfth- and thirteenth-century school of St. Victor, where the reading culture came to revolve around the mystified letter.

What Is Retrieval?

The central task of this book is to *retrieve* a theology of the mystified letter. As a modern *mode* of theology, retrieval has a recent history. While modern theologies of retrieval are too diverse to constitute a movement or school, they are distinguished by an instinct to return to sources of Christian theology for constructive work in the present.[6] In mid-twentieth-century

---

her analysis of liturgical sequences encourages me to consider that liturgical music played a considerable role in mystifying the letter, especially sacred Scriptures, at the school. While this study focuses on theology's role in mystifying the letter, it makes no special claim for the primacy of theological techniques for doing so.

    For an excellent example of a study of aesthetic techniques of mystification in a context far from the medieval abbey school, see Jeffrey L. Kosky, *Arts of Wonder: Enchanting Secularity—Walter De maria, Diller + Scofidio, James Turrell, Andy Goldsworthy* (Chicago: University of Chicago Press, 2013). Kosky plumbs the theoretical potential of mystical theologies like that of the Victorine Thomas Gallus (80–81), arguing convincingly that scholars of both religious and secular cultures benefit from theorizing techniques of mystification.

6   John Webster, "Theologies of Retrieval," in *The Oxford Handbook of Systematic Theology*, ed. Kathryn Tanner, John Webster, and Iain Torrance (Oxford: Oxford University Press, 2007), 584, 589.

Catholic theologies of retrieval (known as *ressourcement* through the influence of leading French theologians), "sources" was a key metaphor for the inherited theological literature from which retrieval occurs—the Scriptures and other sacred writings. These writings serve as "living fountains" (*fontes* in Latin) that continually renew communities of readers in the present.[7] These "sources" of faith, then, are not just "resources" for theological research or even scripts for creed and worship but renewing wellsprings of life fed by the Source of life Itself.

A theologian engaging in retrieval sees intellectual, moral, and spiritual potential or possibility in the habits of speech and thought exhibited in these sources. However, retrieval is not a repetition. The goal is to retrieve these habits to construct a formative theological proposal in the present. In this way, the theological mode of retrieval, which looks to the past to discern renewing habits of thought and practice for spiritual transformation in and beyond the present, downplays some of the priorities of other subfields of theology. It is not primarily concerned with the conceptual coherence of theological *loci* (systematic theology), the persuasiveness of Christian doctrine in stark contrast with other worldviews (apologetics), the interpretation of the Bible as the sole or primary normative guide of faith (exegetical theology), or even an account of the development of Christian doctrine over time (historical theology). Though, as a *mode* of theology, retrieval can be found within and across all subfields of theology as it aspires toward renewal of thought and practice in the present.

What potential could there be in retrieving the theological habits of the past if our problems have to do with present reading cultures? What can premodern sources of Christian theology possibly say about our divisive and uninspiring reading cultures today? In short, the value of theological retrieval is most often paradoxically in reading the past to look *beyond* the present. Theologies of retrieval attempt to "transcend the restraints of modern theology."[8] Often responding to a genealogy of theology that sees a decline in

---

[7] Jennifer Newsome Martin, "Only What Is Rooted Is Living: A Roman Catholic Theology of *Ressourcement*," in *Theologies of Retrieval: An Exploration and an Appraisal*, ed. Darren Sarisky (London: Bloomsbury T&T Clark, 2017), 91, 96.

[8] Webster, "Theologies of Retrieval," 589. This does not mean they transcend the restraints of time itself as theology is a temporal enterprise—whatever its claims about the

the modern period (diagnosed variously), theologies of retrieval enable "a certain liberty in relation to the present" or "exceed the possibilities of the present" with their "capacity to expose and pass beyond its limitations."[9] That is, while retrieval sounds traditional or conservative in its enthusiasm for the analysis of premodern theological literature, its engagement with premodern sources actually shocks modern theology out of its ineffective habits of God talk by confronting it with the strangeness or otherness of past habits. Put more simply, theologies of retrieval find new wisdom for our common future in the (often rediscovered) sources of theology. Like scouts of a nomadic people, theologians engaged in retrieval continually search out, find, return to, and rediscover sources of renewal for their community. This book does some scouting for our contemporary reading cultures of Church and academy.

A primary criticism of retrieval reduces it to nostalgia for the Christian past. This is undoubtedly a danger to be avoided as the attempt to establish the historical unity and continuity of the Christian tradition has both ignored the insights of critical history and, worse, absolutized and universalized Christian thought in order to downplay or repress cultural and

---

eternal, it is bound by its temporal condition. Retrieval as a theological habit respects the temporal condition of theology, looking for living sources of reflection within history.

9   Webster, "Theologies of Retrieval," 585, 590. This decline has been understood in too many ways to recount. One might, for instance, point to the ways Enlightenment philosophy reduces God talk to a rationalistic theism, minimizing central Christian doctrines like the Trinity and the incarnation. One might focus on modern theology's embrace and exaltation of "the subject" as the starting point of theological reflection. One might object to the loss of a participatory and teleological metaphysics that fosters a sense of the created human being's dependence on and direction toward their Creator. Whether the culprit is fourteenth-century nominalism, the sixteenth-century Protestant "crisis," or eighteenth-century Enlightenment critical rationalism (among the most often cited), theologians involved in retrieval often go in search of alternatives to what modern theology has produced. Whatever the view of theology's decline, these theologians seek not so much to redress the past as to retrieve an alternative set of theological habits in the present. They share the view of the medievalist Alistair Minnis, who, in writing on the potential of studying medieval literary theory, suggests that its "strangeness" or "alterity" might "serve as a stimulus" to think beyond our "blind modernism." *Medieval Theory of Authorship: Scholastic Literary Attitudes in the Later Middle Ages*, 3rd ed. (Philadelphia: University of Pennsylvania Press, 2010), 7.

historical difference. Retrieval valorizes and celebrates historical and cultural difference, seeing in the historical and cultural diversity of Christian traditions the potential for present and local renewal. Returning to or rediscovering the *fontes* once again, the theological mode of retrieval embraced in this book works toward a "creative appropriation of the past that simultaneously enlivens the present."[10] That is, its work is what Rowan Williams calls "creative archaeology."[11] When theologians of retrieval attend to both the past theological source and the contemporary situation, they engage in "correlation" or "mutually hospitable conversation" that genuinely thinks anew in the present.[12] Thus, while retrieval is often misunderstood as conservative or traditionalist, it is more radically new (or renewing) than the established, often invisible habits of modern theology.[13]

While it would be impossible here to review all the theological foundations on which retrieval has rested, consider a couple of theological concepts that have inspired this mode of theology. First, theologies of retrieval have often drawn on the concept of the communion of saints, living and

---

10   Newsome Martin, "Only What Is Rooted," 90.
11   Rowan Williams, *Why Study the Past? The Quest for the Historical Church* (Grand Rapids, MI: Eerdmans, 2005), 100. While theologies of retrieval are often rooted in narratives of the decline of modern theology as it contends with critical philosophy, I see little tension between retrieval and the modern academic philosophical habit of critique. If critique is something like the examination and evaluation of the categories by which we think (originally and paradigmatically critical philosophers interrogated the categories of early modern confessional theologies), then retrieval shares an instinct with critique. They both strive to make visible and therefore critique-able the established habits of thought reflected in contemporary society.
12   Webster, "Theologies of Retrieval," 593.
13   Consider two very different examples of modern theological habits. First, the theological habit of absolutizing Christian truth is one that historians of religion increasingly identify as having developed through the emergence of Christian fundamentalisms and colonialisms in the modern period. Second, the systematization of theology is an ideal that flourished in the modern period and is mostly foreign to the theological habits of earlier eras. Theologies of retrieval often note how premodern theological habits were more literary and liturgical, for instance, than either absolutizing or systematizing. Does the modern fundamentalist theological habit of absolutization or the modern liberal theological habit of systematization renew the communities that rely on theology? Or should we look for alternatives to these modern habits?

dead.[14] The belief in the unity of diverse Christians through and beyond time effected by the Spirit they share has encouraged theologians to retrieve the wisdom of the saints. Relatedly, theologians of retrieval have tended to trust in the Spirit's operation throughout history, unifying Christians but also being "supple enough (Jn 3:8) to speak to different situations differently."[15] Confident that the Spirit guides their reading in Christian theologies of the past, theologians of retrieval take on a different theological style. Rather than engaging in modern apologetics or systematization, they tend to celebrate the formative potential of their historically distant "sources" to renew their readers in the present. In other words, they see the reading of (often premodern) theological literature as potentially transformative today.[16]

This book uses this mode of theological retrieval, returning to the school of St. Victor to renew our reading cultures today. It draws on the abbey school's theology of reading to slake our thirst for the mystified letter and revivify the reading cultures of the Church and the academy during a time of division and dryness. It looks to the communion of saints to celebrate a theological vision for reading together, engaging in a renewed account of why and how we might read. By moving from past to present, from the living sources to the cup we share, the book offers a renewed theology of reading.

What Is Mystical Theology?

Retrieving the mystified letter from St. Victor, this book enters into a conversation with the established field of scholarship known as mystical theology. Simply put, mystical theology reflects on the hiddenness of God and its implications for the human experience of and theological discourse about God. Though mystical theologies are diverse, their habits of reflection attend to God's ineffability and unintelligibility, often theorizing the search for, manifestation of, and union with the God *beyond*. Although all theology

---

14 Webster, "Theologies of Retrieval," 590.
15 Newsome Martin, "Only What Is Rooted," 89. See also Webster, "Theologies of Retrieval," 590.
16 In short, theologians engaged in retrieval are devotees of the mystified letter. Their faith is in the capacity of reading sacred literature to transform individuals and societies in and beyond the present.

reckons with language to express the reality of God (or God's actions), mystical theologies are especially attuned to the use of language given the complications introduced by God's ineffability. In short, mystical theology involves habits of thinking and writing about the mystery of God.

Scholars in the contemporary field of mystical theology have engaged in much methodological reflection in the century since mysticism became a primary object of analysis for the field of religious studies. The Latin theological writings from the school of St. Victor draw on a number of terms related to mysticism that have been the subject of debate more recently—*experience, ecstasy, affect*—even *mystical* and *theology* themselves. A fundamental methodological instinct of this book (and of the theological mode of retrieval generally) is that there is much to learn from the Victorines' attempts to theorize these terms, and so part of my task will be to illuminate their use at the school. The unfamiliarity of these terms in the Victorine context may spark a rethinking of our own critical perspectives on reading. For this reason, until chapter 6, I will try to allow the texts to speak for themselves. What I consider my commitment to Victorine theology on its own terms in this study is born from my encounter with larger methodological concerns in the contemporary academic field of mystical theology. Because it would be impossible to recount every way that debates within the field have come to affect my approach to Victorine theology, I will highlight just three major developments in the last few decades that I recognize as having formed my thinking and guided this book's analysis and retrieval of the mystified letter.

Mysticism: From Mystical Experience to Mystical Theology

Recent scholarship on Victorine mystical theology owes much to the school's prominent place in Bernard McGinn's magisterial *The Presence of God* series, a field-defining history of Western Christian mysticism. McGinn includes the Victorines alongside the Franciscans and other "new religious movements" of the twelfth and thirteenth centuries in the second and third volumes of his series, titled *The Growth of Mysticism* and *The Flowering of Mysticism*. In the same series, he set the methodological agenda for the field of mystical theology. At the time of the release of his first volume a few decades ago (*The Foundations of Mysticism*), McGinn addressed a concept that had a long pedigree in religious studies but was roiling the study of mysticism: religious experience.[17]

The study of mysticism, argued McGinn, had suffered from a misunderstanding about the nature of religious experience. McGinn argues for the historian's methodological agnosticism toward the *experience* of the mystic. Religious experience was *not* the object of his analysis primarily because it was not available for analysis by the historian. In the decades since, scholars of Christian mysticism have shifted away from the study of mystical *experience* to the study of mystical *theology*, reflecting the concerns McGinn spells out. Mystical theology, according to McGinn's early volumes, is a variant or branch of historical theology, which identifies and analyzes the development of Christian teaching, taking into account the historical, social, and linguistic contexts out of which particular systems of doctrine arise. Medieval mystical texts of whatever genre, it is presumed, are not so different from modern systematic theological treatises. They provide the coherent conceptual and symbolic apparatuses (the discourse or theological "systems") of mysticism—but not the mystic's experience itself. This discursive or conceptual system is all the historian of religion or historical theologian has access to as it is all that is provided by the texts in the historical archive, like the extant writings from St. Victor.[18]

---

[17] A number of scholars of history and philosophy of religion in the 1980s and 1990s critiqued the concept: Wayne Proudfoot, *Religious Experience* (Berkeley: University of California Press, 1985); Joan Scott, "The Evidence of Experience," *Critical Inquiry* 17, no. 4 (Summer 1991): 773–97; Robert H. Scharf, "The Rhetoric of Experience and the Study of Religion," in *Critical Terms for Religious Studies*, ed. Mark C. Taylor (Chicago: University of Chicago Press, 1998), 94–116; Matthew C. Bagger, *Religious Experience, Justification, and History* (Cambridge: Cambridge University Press, 1999); and David C. Lamberth, "Putting 'Experience' to the Test in Theological Reflection," *Harvard Theological Review* 93, no. 1 (2000): 67–77.

[18] To be more specific, McGinn and others argued that one cannot analyze a religious experience apart from the symbolic, linguistic, or ritual context in which it occurs. This is because there is no such thing as a nonlinguistic experience, a position put forth by George A. Lindbeck in his influential work *The Nature of Doctrine: Religion and Theology in a Postliberal Age* (Louisville, KY: Westminster John Knox Press, 1984). The cultural-linguistic or contextualist concerns at the center of these debates are in the background of McGinn's contribution to the study of mysticism. The proper object of study is the theological system, language, or discourse of a particular mystic in their cultural context, the set

The salutary effect of McGinn's methodological reflections was that the study of mysticism or mystical theology could be approached with the disciplinary rigor that was already applied in the more established fields of historical and systematic theology. Authors of mystical literature, McGinn revealed, could be as systematic and coherent as other theologians, though they perhaps worked with a different set of theological *loci*—for example, contemplation and union rather than sin and salvation. In addition, their theological systems could be analyzed in terms of the historical development of doctrines. In effect, McGinn and like-minded scholars accomplished the monumental task of translating premodern mystical theology into a field approachable by the contemporary theological researcher inclined toward systematic coherence and sympathetic to critical history rather than just the spiritual director or contemplative seeker. As religious experience waned in theological and religious studies, mystical theology waxed.

In so many ways, this book's retrieval of the mystified letter would not be possible without these achievements. However, there are limits to treating mystical theology like a branch of historical or systematic theology. Theology (discourse or reasoning about God), especially mystical theology, is not always systematic or coherent, as McGinn himself often notes. As this study will argue (relying on one of McGinn's own helpful formulations), Victorine theology of the letter depended on a set of "dialectical tensions," along with other literary and rhetorical features.[19] Following the example of their favorite mystical theologian, Dionysius, the Victorines were, if sophisticated and imaginative thinkers, not always systematic ones.[20] More importantly,

---

of symbols and concepts delimited by the author's cultural belonging and typically having a rational and affective order to them. Indeed, for many of his readers, McGinn opened up mystical theology as an overlooked undercurrent or tributary (or sometimes central waterway) of historical Christian theology, with its own cultural-linguistic system of theological *loci* (for example, union, indwelling, and eschaton).

19   Bernard McGinn, *The Foundations of Mysticism: Origins to the Fifth Century* (New York: Crossroad Publishing, 1991), 157–82.

20   And certainly not ones who write in the mode of modern systematic theology. McGinn's early work, for instance, tends to systematize mystical literature by looking for the theological *loci* characteristic of modern theology. For example, of Dionysius, he writes, "There is little theological anthropology as such in his surviving writings, though one is surely implied." *Foundations of Mysticism*, 161.

applying the model of systematic theology or historical theology to texts of mystical theology can obfuscate the way literary form and spiritual, liturgical, embodied practice are central to (even indistinguishable from) the theorization of the mystical. In ways not always noticed by the systematic or historical theologian, whose attention is often directed to conceptual doctrine, mystical theology relied on, or was disciplined by, religious practice.[21] This book argues, for instance, that Victorine mystical theology can be understood only if due attention is paid to practices of reading and writing.

Transformative Language in Mystical Theology

Another of the most significant developments made in the study of mysticism in the last few decades has been the attention paid to the diverse operations of language in mystical theological literature.[22] If the ascendant field of mystical theology redefined the traditional study of mysticism by adapting the methods of systematic and historical theology, the study of mystical language has focused more on how mystical literature is distinct from other modes of theological writing, especially in its use of rhetoric, form, and structure. One of the most striking features of mystical theological literature is the multivalent manner in which it uses language. Analyzing the literary or rhetorical devices used in mystical literature attends to how mystical language stylizes that which is extralinguistic or exists at the limits of language; that is, it analyzes how mystical language "mystifies." For instance, Dionysius famously advocates for and performs the use of both *cataphatic* (affirmative) and *apophatic* (negative) statements about God (i.e., "God is life," "God is not life"). Attending to the use of mystifying language, one can ask: What

---

21   This insight is especially clear in the work of Amy Hollywood, for instance, "Song, Experience, and the Book in Benedictine Monasticism," in *The Cambridge Companion to Christian Mysticism*, ed. Amy Hollywood and Patricia Z. Beckman (Cambridge: Cambridge University Press, 2012), 59–79, where she treats "the transformation of the monk's or nun's experience through his or her engagement with the Psalms and other texts performed—chanted or sung—during the Divine Office" (71).

22   For example, the influential work by Michael A. Sells, *Mystical Languages of Unsaying* (Chicago: University of Chicago Press, 1994). Also, Matthew C. Bagger, *The Uses of Paradox: Religion, Self-Transformation, and the Absurd* (New York: Columbia University Press, 2007); Kerylin Harkaway-Krieger, "Mysticism and Materiality: *Pearl* and the Theology of Metaphor," *Exemplaria* 28, no. 2 (2016): 161–80.

does such a technique accomplish? How is it related to Dionysius's conceptual theology? What effect does it have on the reader? One might conclude that the technique of *cataphasis-apophasis* inculcates a sense in the reader of God's transcending abundance and ineffability, aspects of Dionysius's theology that are not as effectively rendered with simple propositional statements. Simply saying "God is transcendent" does not move the mind of the reader affectively and intellectually in the same way that the sustained use of *cataphasis* and *apophasis* does. The former *says* that God is mystery; the latter *mystifies* God.

Yet mystical language is not simply persuasive. The important thing that distinguishes much critical study of mystical language from rhetorical analysis is that religious studies scholars emphasize a more diverse range of transformative effects of these literary techniques. Mystical language is transformative. Or, to adapt a felicitous expression from the scholar of late ancient philosophy Pierre Hadot, mystical writings not only *inform* but *form* their readers (and perhaps their writers).[23] That is, if McGinn's contextual approach advocated a scholarly remove from mystical "experience" as an object of analysis—at least insofar as that experience was held to be a prelinguistic first-order phenomenon from which doctrines and symbols emerge only secondarily—attention to the performative quality of language has begun to return to experience in a new way. Analyses of performative language consider how special uses of language transform the consciousness, mind, or even (as many mystical theologians might say) soul of the reader.

One important qualification of this approach has come from those working with critical gender theory. Patricia Dailey, for instance, has recently shown that the transformation rendered by the language of medieval mystical literature is not only of the soul but also of the body (Dailey stresses that in Christian mystical literature, body and soul are seldom rendered dualistically).[24] Dailey traces "the relationship of embodiment to poetics and literary

---

23   See the essays on philosophy as a "spiritual exercise" in Pierre Hadot, *Philosophy as a Way of Life*, trans. Michael Chase (New York: Blackwell, 1995). For an account of writing as a spiritual exercise that engages with McGinn and Hadot, see Charles Stang, "Writing," in *The Cambridge Companion to Christian Mysticism*, ed. Amy Hollywood and Patricia Z. Beckman (Cambridge: Cambridge University Press, 2012), 252–63.
24   Patricia Dailey, *Promised Bodies: Time, Language, and Corporeality in Medieval Women's Mystical Texts* (New York: Columbia University Press, 2013).

form" in Paul, Augustine, Hadewijch of Brabant, Julian of Norwich, and others to show how their texts construct Christian bodies as eschatologically charged and transformed by the reception of divine grace. If earlier critical approaches to mystical language focused on how the language of mystical literature transforms the mind, soul, or consciousness, Dailey's study argues that it could also have an effect on bodies.[25]

At times, McGinn himself takes a critical approach to mystical language, as when he emphasizes the importance of incoherence, paradox, or dialectical tension in inculcating mystical modes of consciousness. This approach mitigates a limit of McGinn's own influential early approach to mystical theology described above. It sees mystical theology not as a set of propositional doctrines about mystical presence or other theological *loci* but as a discipline that shapes or forms those engaged in it. This is much more in line with how medieval mystical theologians describe their own practice. For the Victorine Thomas Gallus, for instance, writing commentaries on the sacred writings of Dionysius and Solomon (the traditional author of the Song of Songs) is not just a pedagogical practicality making the theological systems of these texts accessible (a common way of describing the genre of

---

25   It strikes me that some difficult questions arise here. Does the literary or poetic construction of Christian bodies have the kind of transformative effect corporeally or materially that mystical discourse on the soul has intellectually or affectively? Or does this kind of dualistic thinking cause more problems than it solves? Processes of affection and intellection are discernable in reading and writing that seem to account for how reading shapes or forms the mind. The relationship between text and body seems more tenuous and socially mediated—recognizable in the ways poetic construction determines the cultural habitus in which one's own materiality is experienced but not as connected to the forms of cogitation and affection that seem the more immediate processes that engage texts. If reading transforms bodies, how does it do so?

While this study largely sidesteps these questions, it may provide tools for thinking through them. The Victorines' own rhetoric of practice, experience, exercise, and discipline never discriminates between soul and body. For them, reading, writing, and contemplation itself—all textual or linguistic activities—exercise (*exercere*), discipline (*disciplinare*), and adapt (*apto*) the mind in the way physical activity disciplines and transforms the body. For accounts of Christian mystical literature that emphasize the continuity between intellectual effort and embodied practice in Christian mysticism, see the essays in *The Cambridge Companion to Christian Mysticism*, especially Hollywood, "Song, Experience, and the Book."

commentary) but a spiritual practice meant to transform the soul of the commentator by engaging with the mystified letter.

Though methodological differences remain in the study of mysticism, what unites many of the scholars from McGinn to Dailey is that they try to allow mystical theologians themselves to theorize their own texts by considering the value of their own critical terms for describing mystical theory and practice. That is, they see mystical theology as reasoning or writing about and/or with God, a discipline inscribed linguistically and textually, that should be considered from a number of angles but presuming the theologian has something valuable to say about their own practice. One limitation of this approach is that one can become lost in this act of translation—losing one's own present critical concerns that drew one to the texts in the first place and lapsing into a valueless antiquarianism or repetitive nostalgia. Yet if this danger exists, this study nevertheless presumes such a historiographical and theological practice is critical to the project of retrieval.[26] Here I develop an interpretive apparatus drawn largely from the Victorines' own theology, showcasing the coherence of theory and practice in their writings.

Intimacy, Relations, and Experience

The focus on the transformative capacity of mystical language (whether that transformation is of consciousness, soul, or body) has sometimes led scholars to interpret premodern mystical theology in a modern, individualist way. The loss of a critical language of experience in the study of mystical theology has contributed to this state of the field—an impoverishment that the Victorines (especially the later ones like Thomas Gallus) invite us to reconsider. As we've seen, the language used in mystical theology is often taken to form the consciousness, the soul, or the self of the individual reader (or perhaps at times the writer)—or even their body.[27]

---

26   On these dangers, and some thoughts on why nevertheless to pursue a historiographical approach that attends generously to the theoretical integrity of one's historical subject, see the essay by Amy Hollywood, "Gender, Agency, and the Divine in Religious Historiography," in *Acute Melancholia and Other Essays: Mysticism, History, and the Study of Religion* (New York: Columbia University Press, 2016), 117–27.

27   Just as a representative sample: Stephen Greenblatt, *Renaissance Self-Fashioning: From More to Shakespeare* (Chicago: University of Chicago Press, 1980); Caroline Walker

Constance Furey, a scholar of early modern religion, calls attention to the way these objects of analysis (consciousness, soul, self, body) fall under what might be characterized as a recent fashionable concern for *subjectivization*. In Furey's view, the "turn to the body" in religious and theological studies is just the latest example of this scholarly trend toward subjectivization, that is, attention to the religious practitioner as a subject on the analogy of a grammatical subject. Put simply, a religious subject is the "I" of an experience, thought, or consciousness of a religious object. Subjectivization in religious studies refers to the ways texts and traditions shape, form, or render an individual subject distinct from their social reality (like a grammatical subject who acts or is acted on). This scholarly tendency is the product of a laudable goal: analysis of subjectivization illuminates how religious practitioners have modes of agency that do not demand strict autonomy from religious discourses and rituals. In fact, subjectivization is predicated on such discourses and rituals. ("I" experience God, for instance, when given the language and practices that foster such an experience.) Yet, argues Furey, too much attention to the religious subject (and the practices that form it) obfuscates the way the aims of religion (including religious texts) are often less individual than relational. Furey advocates attention to an overlooked object of analysis for scholars of religion—social relationships and intimacies.[28] What would it look like for scholars of mystical theology to shift their

---

Bynum, *Fragmentation and Redemption: Essays on Gender and the Human Body in Medieval Religion* (New York: Zone Books, 1991); Paul A. Olson, *The Journey to Wisdom: Self-Education in Patristic and Medieval Literature* (Lincoln: University of Nebraska Press, 1995); Margaret R. Miles, *A Complex Delight: The Secularization of the Breast: 1350–1750* (Berkeley: University of California Press, 2008); Bernard McGinn, "Mystical Consciousness: A Modest Proposal," *Spiritus* 8, no. 1 (2008): 44–63; Jennifer Bryan, *Looking Inward: Devotional Reading and the Private Self in Late Medieval England* (Philadelphia: University of Pennsylvania Press, 2008); Brian Stock, *The Integrated Self: Augustine, the Bible, and Ancient Thought* (Philadelphia: University of Pennsylvania Press, 2017).

28 "Our scholarly turn to embodiment has undermined simplistic notions of rational choice, along with the assumption that liberty entails autonomy, or that virtue requires solitary self-formation. Still, all too often in our work, the religious subject stands alone in a crowd. Yes, we find that subject participating in communal rituals, subject to religious authorities and disciplinary practices, a pious supplicant or abject lover of the divine. But few studies of religion track this subject as a participant in intimate relationships, defined by

attention slightly from the religious "subject" to religious relations and intimacies? This book will analyze and commend the experience of the mystified letter inscribed in the writings from St. Victor. Its theology of reading will attend to the experience and transformed relations—with God, self, and community—that emerge through engagement with the mystified letter. It will be concerned with the readerly community as much as the reader.

While Furey's studies focus on social relations between human beings (found in Puritan marriage poetry, for instance),[29] I am applying her insight to a relationship "less easily named."[30] The Victorines were most concerned with the mystical relationship between the soul and the eternal Word of God. What I am *not* asking is: How do the Victorines' writings stylize the soul as the subject of a mystical practice or construct a self as a reader or commentator? While Thomas Gallus famously proffers what contemporary scholars have called a "hierarchical anthropology," dividing the soul into nine angelic orders, each with its particular role in mystical progress, his underlying concern is not subjectivization in an individualist mode. He does not give an account of how the Christian becomes a subject who knows or loves God's Word.[31] Rather, the soul's mental hierarchy, as I will show, is indecipherable apart from Gallus's equally complex theology of the eternal Word, which actively engages

---

the problems and pleasures of kinship, friendship, patronage, marriage, and *other relationships less easily named*. In our quest to better understand subjectivity, we have isolated the subject." Constance Furey, "Body, Society, and Subjectivity in Religious Studies," *Journal of the American Academy of Religion* 80, no. 1 (2012): 10 (emphasis mine).

29 Constance Furey, "Relational Virtue: Anne Bradstreet, Edward Taylor, and Puritan Marriage," *Journal of Medieval and Early Modern Studies* 42, no. 1 (2012): 201–24.

30 See quote above, 19–20n28.

31 For a detailed account of Gallus's "hierarchical anthropology," see Coolman, *Eternally Spiraling into God*, 74–100, 236–44. I have reservations about the imposition of the category of theological anthropology as an interpretive tool for Victorine theology, although it is widely embraced by scholars of the Victorines and medieval theology generally. The best theological anthropology (a category invented in modern systematic theology especially prevalent in Catholic thought) theorizes the human person in *relation* to God, other human beings, and the created world, but I worry that the language of anthropology itself tends toward the conceptual reifying of the human person as a reality apart from those others. It may share with modern critical philosophy the privileging of the human subject in our theological analyses, a methodological instinct I see as at odds with that of the Victorine theology of reading retrieved in this book.

or affects the soul.[32] Instead of focusing on the soul or subjectivization, I ask, How does the Victorines' theology of the mystified letter (the theory and practice put forth in their writings) render an intimate or intersubjective experience of the soul's union with the Word? How do their theory and practice, mutually informing one another, perform an experience that is best described as happening *between* the soul and the Word? How does reading the letter involve and envelope the intellect and the affect in the Word's mystery?

To put it another way, in this book's study of Victorine theology, I return to experience as a helpful category for the study of mystical theology. Here I intend not to study special religious or mystical experiences themselves in the manner to which scholars a few decades ago rightly objected. Rather, I examine the experience (or, rather, *experientia*) of the mystified letter as constructed by and pursued in Victorine mystical theology, which can be embraced for its capacity to theorize the relational, excessive, super-intellectual, and ineffable aspects of Christian reading that are continuous with a larger pedagogical vision of Christian perfection as personal and social transformation. This vision puts a relation *between* the soul and the Word at the center of the Victorines' efforts. Reading the mystified letter becomes an experience of spiritual transformation, union with God, and renewal of social relations.

For the Victorines, as we will see, the experience of the mystified letter was awesome and wonderful, ineffable and unintelligible. In the reading culture of St. Victor, the soul was affected or re-formed by the eternal Word through reading the mystified letter. Encountering the theology of the Victorines shocks us from our apathy toward our divisive and uninspiring reading cultures. In the Church and the academy, too often the wonderful experience of being transformed by reading is lost. The Victorine theology of reading reminds us of the necessity to cultivate the reading cultures of the Church and the academy and gives us some helpful tools to do so.

An Itinerary for This Book

When a Victorine read anything—Scripture, philosophy, poetry, liturgical sequences—they followed the *cursus* laid out before them. The Latin term *cursus* had both a temporal and a spatial sense, meaning a "course" or a

---

32   See ch. 5.

"path," "progress" or a "journey." Literature (or the letter) always had such a *cursus*. Related terms in the Victorines' writings, like *series* and *sequentia* (the succession or sequence of the writing), as well as various metaphors of textual voyages and itineraries, suggest that a Victorine reader was attentive to the flow of a writing (and of the entirety of literature, or the letter, itself). In a prologue composed and placed before their commentary on a sacred writing, they would most often identify and preview this *cursus*, the specific path or flow the letter would take in the writing at hand.

This book has its own *cursus*. In fact, the path or flow of this book follows two interrelated courses, one chronological and one mystical. The chronological course traces the emergence and trajectory of the mystified letter at the school of St. Victor in the twelfth and thirteenth centuries. As a work of historical-theological analysis, this book argues that the Victorine approach to the mystified letter emerged as two strands of Christian theology—(1) a *theology of the letter* and (2) a *mystical theology*—slowly but steadily wove together at the school.

First, I sketch an early and medieval Christian *theology of the letter*, a strand of theology embraced and developed by the school's early luminary Hugh of St. Victor, who adopts and adapts the theologies of Paul and Augustine. Hugh reads these two as preeminent theologians of the letter, using their thought to establish that the Victorines' reading culture would revolve around the letter. I then outline a second strand of *mystical theology*, showing how the letter was mystified by the introduction of a new translation of the writings of Dionysius around 1167. The retranslated and reinterpreted theological corpus of Dionysius would theorize the letter anew, which was already at the center of religious life at St. Victor. Dionysius's mystical theology of God, language, and union would mystify the letter.

Having traced the historical development of St. Victor's theology of the mystified letter, I examine how the mystified letter functioned within the writings of the last great Victorine, Thomas Gallus, in the thirteenth century. Gallus would continue to engage with the mystified letter, producing two extant commentaries on the Song of Songs, an erotic love poem of the Old Testament that offered the "practice" to the Dionysian "theory." These central analytical studies show how the Victorines came to encounter the mystified letter in theory and in practice as the two strands of Christian theology came together. At the heart of the book, then, is a chronologically narrated theological history of the emergence of the mystified letter, the retrieval of which can serve as an antidote to our ailing reading cultures today. Just as the mystified letter emerged at St. Victor in the twelfth and thirteenth centuries, we can hope and work for its return and renewed application in our own day.

The second *cursus* of the book is its mystical course. Since theologies of retrieval try to mimic the mystical movement from time to eternity and back again, as one ascending and descending Jacob's ladder, this book has begun with a set of present challenges we face.[33] It will go on to analyze the theological wisdom of the mystified letter at St. Victor. Of course, however confident theologies of retrieval are in the communion of saints united by the Spirit, they do not presume that a particular theology from the Christian past (even that of Christianity's great luminaries) provides absolute or universal truth for the present. (The Spirit operates in a supple manner in distinct times and places.) Rather, having engaged in retrieval, they apply the insights of a past moment in theology to present circumstances. Therefore, at the end of the book, I develop a renewed constructive theology of reading. I will argue that the Church and the academy can learn from the Victorines' theology of the mystified letter to renew our ailing reading cultures today.

---

33   Newsome Martin, "Only What Is Rooted," 86.

2

THEOLOGY OF THE LETTER

The letter kills, but the spirit gives life.

—Paul, 2 Corinthians 3:6

The Holy Spirit arranged the sacred scriptures wonderfully and helpfully to satisfy our hunger in plainer passages and chase away our boredom in more complicated ones.

—Augustine, *On Christian Teaching* 2.6

The Abbey of St. Victor: A Reading Culture

The mystified letter drew many to the abbey school of St. Victor. Among the school's admirers was James of Vitry, a thirteenth-century bishop of Acre in the crusader states. James, a keen observer of the new religious movements of his day, was part of a vast network of lovers of the letter with connections to St. Victor.[1] During the twelfth century, St. Victor became well known for scriptural interpretation as enthusiastic readers soaked up the writings of its canons Hugh, Richard, and Andrew. By the time James wrote in the thirteenth century, St. Victor was a well-established and influential hub of Scripture reading. Although James's expansive *History of the West* crossed multiple centuries and continents, he singled out the school's twelfth-century abbot

---

1   A classic study of the new religious movements of the twelfth and early thirteenth centuries that relies heavily on James's observations of them is Herbert Grundmann, *Religious Movements in the Middle Ages: The Historical Links between Heresy, the Mendicant Orders, and the Women's Religious Movement in the Twelfth and Thirteenth Century, with the Historical Foundations of German Mysticism*, trans. Steven Rowan (Notre Dame, IN: Notre Dame University Press, 1995; 1st ed., 1935). Bernard McGinn explores the "new mysticism" associated with these movements in *The Flowering of Mysticism: Men and Women in the New Mysticism—1200–1350* (New York: Crossroad Publishing, 1998), 12–30.

Hugh of St. Victor, whose foundational writings on secular and sacred topics secured the school's prominence. With effusive praise that would be echoed again and again by Hugh's later medieval readers, James wrote:

> *Digging up many wells of living waters with his published books, which cover faith and habits subtly and sweetly, he unearthed difficult and hidden aspects of divine wisdom in many ways, leaving behind for his posteriors his immortal memory as if a carefully mixed perfume, a painter's work, or the sweet taste of honey over every part of the mouth, or even a party with the right mix of music and wine, or a fleet of ships bearing fruit.*[2]

James revels in the experience of reading Hugh's works. "Master Hugh" was like a "zither-player of the Lord (*citharista domini*), an instrument of the Holy Spirit (*organum spiritus sancti*)," a writer whose very "immortal memory" reflected the Word of God.[3] Why did James single out Hugh of St. Victor in his history of all of Western Christendom? James had studied at the University of Paris. Perhaps he even wandered to the outskirts of the city to visit his fellow Augustinian canons at the school of St. Victor during his time there (the canons sometimes served as confessors, or spiritual advisers, for Parisian scholars and students). He recorded that "for those who desire to empty themselves of the shipwreck of this world," St. Victor was "a most tranquil harbor" that "opens a way of mercy, and in its bosom it warms and feeds them like a holy mother."[4] In the early thirteenth century, then, the school of St. Victor was a point of pride for Augustinian canons like James, a refuge where the reading culture established many decades before by Hugh continued to renew the weary soul.

What attracted James and others to Hugh at St. Victor? What about the theological and literary culture at St. Victor was so compelling? If Hugh's "immortal memory" was the perfect repository of divine Wisdom and the abbey school a place of refuge and spiritual renewal, what made them so?

---

2   James of Vitry, *The Historia Occidentalis of Jacques de Vitry*, ed. John Frederick Hinnebusch, O.P. (Fribourg, Switzerland: University Press, 1972), XXIV.138 (my translation).
3   James of Vitry, *Historia Occidentalis*, XXIV.138.
4   James of Vitry, *Historia Occidentalis*, XXIV.138.

How did St. Victor attract enthusiasts to its reading culture centered on the mystified letter?

This chapter begins to address these questions by examining the *theological* foundations of the mystified letter at St. Victor, the theory of sacred reading that made the school a place of refuge and renewal. The mystical reading culture of Hugh and the Victorines was rooted in "the letter," especially—though not exclusively—the Scriptures and the Church Fathers. For this reason, it makes good sense to start with the theological foundation of the mystified letter at the school. This chapter traces how the Victorine approach to the letter comes from the apostle Paul and the fourth-century bishop Augustine of Hippo. The chapter focuses on Hugh's appropriation of Paul's distinction between *the letter* and *the spirit* and Augustine's theology of literature, especially his theory of signs. The next chapters build on this foundation by treating a third theologian beloved at the school, the mystical theologian Dionysius. The purpose of these chapters is not primarily to account for all the reasons for the school's success or attractiveness or even to trace definite lines of theological influence, though I hope these chapters offer welcome contributions to both. Instead, these chapters show how two strands of Christian theology could come together at St. Victor to mystify the letter and foster the abbey school's unique reading culture. Understanding how these strands of theology contributed to the mystification of the letter at St. Victor will spur us to consider whether and how we might mystify the letter today as we foster our own cultures of reading.

Littera, or "the Letter": Defining a Theological Concept

The Latin term *littera* has a broader semantic range than any of its traditional English translations, including "literature" or "letter." Throughout Christian Latin, *littera* can refer to everything from the smallest orthographical marking (such as the "letters" A, B, or C), to a coherent body of writings (what we call "a literature"), and to the whole of learning itself (a meaning somewhat preserved in the antiquated sense of "arts and letters"). It is fair to say that *littera,* or what I most often translate in this book as "the letter," is a theological concept, a term that governs the Christian imagination while always abounding or resonating with more meaning than any single translation, description, or example can get across. One of the goals of this book is to show how at St. Victor the letter was a theological concept like the Trinity, incarnation, or redemption and was central to the Christian imagination.

How did the letter become a central theological concept at St. Victor? How does the letter animate the theological imagination? Where did the letter come from? Though its important role in Christian theology has often been underappreciated, *littera* as a theological concept had roots in two of the theologians most responsible for the Christian theological imagination—Paul and Augustine. The rest of this chapter shows how Hugh of St. Victor adopted and adapted their thought to formulate a Victorine "theology of the letter."

The Letter and the Spirit

"The letter kills, but the spirit gives life" (2 Cor 3:6). This pithy phrase of Paul—"the Apostle," as the Victorines knew him—played an outsized role in establishing and mystifying the letter as a theological concept at St. Victor. This may be surprising given that the phrase sounds a clear warning about the letter. But the letter went through a series of transformations on its way to becoming a central theological concept for the Victorines. In his monumental *Didascalicon on the Study of Reading*, Hugh teases out Paul's distinction between letter (*littera*) and spirit (*spiritus*) directly. He explains that Paul distinguishes sharply between letter and spirit "because the reader of sacred writings needs to be grounded in the truth of spiritual understanding."[5] That is, the reader of Scripture should always be rooted in the more stable spiritual meaning beyond the letter. Hugh warns that "the one who follows *the letter alone* cannot go far without stumbling."[6] A good reader, seeking to be rooted in the Holy Spirit, is cautious about following *only* the letter. Those who have the Spirit or seek spiritual understanding while reading are sturdy and grounded, firmly making progress on the path, while those who attend only to the letter trip along the path and fall off course. Yet notice in these quotes, the entire life of spiritual progress or perfection proceeds along a path of letter and spirit. In Hugh's reading, there is no

---

5   Hugh of St. Victor, *Didascalicon de studio legendi: A Critical Text*, ed. C. H. Buttimer (Washington, DC: Catholic University of America Press, 1939), VI.121 (my translation).
6   Hugh, *Didascalicon*, VI.121 (my emphasis).

spirit or spiritual understanding without the letter. What does Hugh mean by "stumbling" over the "letter" and being "grounded" in the "spirit"? Consider the original rhetorical context of the phrase. In 2 Corinthians 3, Paul contrasts his own ministry among the churches in Corinth with the ministry performed by other Jewish-Christian missionaries whom he opposes. While these opposing missionaries offer a "ministry of death" (3:7) according to the letter "on tablets of stone" (3:3), Paul's ministry is of a "new covenant" (3:6), a "ministry of the Spirit" (3:8) written "on tablets of human hearts" (3:3). Paul distinguishes his own ministry in the Spirit from that of these other followers of Jesus who, in the manner of Moses (3:13), identify freedom with the "veil" of the written Law. By saying that it is the Spirit that gives life, Paul points to a new or renewed understanding of the Law, echoing both the recent teaching of Jesus and the long-standing teaching of the Prophets that God offers a new covenant and renewed heart, leading to righteous action centered on love of God and neighbor.[7] The Spirit renews one's disposition toward the Law, not rejecting but completing one's understanding and practice of the Law by transforming one's heart.

Thus, it is possible to delineate what the letter-spirit distinction is *not* for Paul. It is *not* a distinction between Scripture or the Old Testament and the Spirit. While it was tempting among some early Christians to contrast the Spirit with the Old Testament, this position was irreconcilable with Paul.[8] When Paul wrote 2 Corinthians, the issue was not with Scripture or the Old Testament as a "letter that kills" since Paul frequently appeals to the Scriptures containing the Law and the Prophets in his letters. Relatedly, the distinction between letter and spirit is also *not* a distinction between Law and Spirit. While Paul contrasts a death-dealing and hard-hearted way of approaching the Law as it was written on tablets of stone, he advocates for a Spirit-filled approach written on the heart. For Paul, it seems the

---

7 A helpful treatment of the issue, including the antecedents of Paul's call for a renewal of the heart in the Prophets, is James D. G. Dunn, "The Letter Kills, but the Spirit Gives Life (2 Cor. 3:6)," *Pneuma* 35, no. 2 (January 2013): 163–79.

8 For example, the early Christian Marcionite movement emphasized "release from the shackles of the Law," contrasting the vengeful Creator-God of the Old Testament with "'the saving spirit' Jesus Christ." W. H. C. Frend, *The Rise of Christianity* (Philadelphia: Fortress Press, 1984), 212.

letter that kills is a shorthand for a divisive approach or disposition toward the written framework of religio-legal observance, while the life-giving Spirit involves its renewed and unifying application given the coming of the Messiah.[9]

Paul's distinction between letter and spirit concerns moral renewal. It is not *directly* related to Scripture. But when Hugh and the Victorines read the Pauline letters in the twelfth century, they were far removed from Paul's context and the Corinthians' challenges. And yet the Victorines had a remarkably sophisticated understanding of the issues involved. They avoid any easy association of "letter" with Scripture, the Old Testament, or even the Law itself. In fact, their enthusiasm for reading the Old Testament may be unmatched among medieval Christian reading cultures.[10]

When Hugh treats the phrase "the letter kills, but the spirit gives life," he is not thinking of only a moral disposition in relation to the Law, the renewal of one's heart given the new indwelling of the Spirit, but also of the moral disposition of the reader of Scripture. For Hugh, the contemporary Christian reader can easily fail to embrace the Spirit's renewal of one's reading, or the way the Spirit vivifies the letter for intellectual and moral growth. Recall that the earlier quote by Hugh suggested that one "stumbles"

---

9   The pairing of letter and spirit was original to Paul. He writes of this moral renewal as a move from the written objects that kill (the opposing ministers' letters of recommendation, the Mosaic tablets of stone) to the Spirit's writing on the hearts of the Corinthians. Michael Wolter calls this a change of media in "'Spirit' and 'Letter' in the New Testament," in *The Spirit and the Letter: A Tradition and a Reversal*, ed. Paul S. Fiddes and Günther Bader (London: Bloomsbury T&T Clark, 2013), 31–46. The language of change in the medium will be helpful for understanding the Victorines' own approach as the experience of reading the letter involved a transformation into spiritual understanding that did not leave the letter behind but changed it as it changed the reader.

10   Classic and contemporary research on the Victorines reveals the considerable effort they expended in reading and commenting on the Old Testament, possibly even engaging with their neighboring Jewish exegetes. The classic study is by Beryl Smalley, which argues that Andrew, for example, "knew more about the Jews than he could have learnt from their books." *Study of the Bible*, 155. For an excellent and more recent study of Christian Hebraism at the school, especially in the works of Andrew, see Montse Leyra Curiá, *In Hebreo: The Victorine Commentaries on the Pentateuch and the Former Prophets in Light of Its Northern-French Jewish Sources* (Turnhout, Belgium: Brepols, 2017).

when one follows "the letter alone," when one misses "the truth of spiritual understanding." Hugh echoes the Pauline reservation about a narrow moral disposition that is directed toward the letter alone rather than open to the indwelling Spirit's transformation of both the reader-traveler and the letter-path.

Hugh uses the letter-spirit distinction to address the moral disposition of the reader in his *On the Sacraments*. In one passage, Hugh addresses a tough issue emerging from the reading of the letter of the Gospels. The Gospel narratives state that during his passion on the cross, Jesus exclaimed, "My God, my God, why have you abandoned me?"[11] Some wrongly conclude, Hugh warns, that at his death, the divinity of Jesus withdrew from his flesh since, according to the letter of the text—the very words of Jesus—God abandoned Jesus on the cross. Hugh does not deny the challenge the words pose to the reader, how easily the letter might cause them to stumble, but he contrasts those who read Jesus's words according to the letter with those who read in the Spirit. Those who separate Jesus's divinity from his flesh "come up with (*inveniunt*) certain verses where this seems to be said, and after they do, they cling to the letter (*litterae*) of this sort, and do not strive for the spirit (*spiritum*)."[12] Hugh does not deny that the letter alone seems to suggest divine abandonment, but his concern is with the reader who clings only to this letter, not striving to read it in the Spirit. The bad reader "invents," "finds," or "makes up" this letter. The Latin term *invenio* had long been used in rhetoric to describe how an orator will "devise" their speech from the facts and persuasive considerations before them.[13] Here the bad reader "devises"

---

11 Matt 27:46; Mark 15:34.

12 Hugh of St. Victor, *De sacramentis christianae fidei*, ed. J.-P. Migne, Patrologia Latina 176 (Paris: Migne, 1854), 339c (my translation).

13 Cf. Cicero, *De inventio*, ed. Jeffrey Henderson, trans. H. M. Hubbell (Cambridge, MA: Harvard University Press, 1949), VII: "The parts of [the art of rhetoric], as most authorities have stated, are Invention, Arrangement, Expression, Memory, Delivery. Invention is the discovery of valid or seemingly valid arguments to render one's cause plausible."

In his *On Christian Teaching*, Augustine Christianized classical Latin rhetoric, turning rhetorical "invention" into an act of hermeneutic discovery. He writes that the Christian interpreter of Scripture engages in an act of discovering, finding, or inventing (*inveniendi*) what ought to be understood before offering or preaching (*proferendi*) what has been understood. *De doctrina christiana*, ed. Joseph Martin, Corpus Christianorum

or "comes up with" a literal reading, sticking too closely to the letter and not remaining open to the Spirit's understanding of it. In contrast, a good reader does not "invent," "devise," or even—and perhaps most surprisingly—stick closely to the plain meaning of the letter. Following the letter alone, Hugh had told his readers in *Didascalicon*, will cause them to stumble. Instead, they should remain well established in the text's spiritual meaning. A good, Spirit-filled reader may even conclude what seems opposite to the plain meaning according to the letter: in the most important sense, God never abandons Jesus, who likewise never loses his divinity.[14]

Series Latina 32 (Turnhout, Belgium: Brepols, 1962), I.1, trans. R. P. H. Green. Notice that *invention* in both the classical and Christian cases carried the implications of an activity involving the intellectual agency of the reader, whether rhetorical or hermeneutical. Thus, Hugh's too-literal readers "invent" or "come up with" what they find in only the letter, lacking the Spirit, which makes for right reading.

14   Notice how this builds on the Pauline approach to "the letter" of the Law, even as it shifts these concerns to a more hermeneutical frame. Paul's teaching emphasized that all followers of Jesus, both Gentiles and Jews like himself and Peter, should act with renewed hearts in the Spirit. This may lead one to, because prioritizing spirit over letter, even act in apparent violation of the Law's written guidance. In fact, when Peter eats with Gentiles, or Paul encourages Gentile newcomers to the faith to avoid circumcision, they are acting according to the change of medium, the new covenant written on the tablet of human hearts. It is not that the Law is rejected or overcome but that moral renewal leads one to a new disposition toward the Law's observance, imitating Christ in his willingness to relativize Sabbath observance, for instance, in order to heal others (Mark 3:1–6). By relativizing the letter of the Law to the Spirit, one can most faithfully live in relation to the Law.

    Hugh's letter-spirit hermeneutics is just as radical. One should deny God's "abandonment" of Christ despite the bare letter of the Gospel because one has the Spirit or seeks spiritual understanding, which affirms the divinity of Christ and the Father's unity with and faithfulness to Christ. Just as Paul's teaching led the early Jewish and Gentile followers of Jesus to proceed with the Law according to their new life in the Spirit, so did Hugh teach good readers not to follow the letter alone but to seek spiritual understanding. In both cases, this could lead to a radically revised moral approach.

    In terms of a hermeneutic theory, the question remains of how to determine when a literal and a spiritual understanding are in opposition to one another. That is, when should the reader relativize the literal to the spiritual meaning, as they should in the case of Christ's cry of abandonment? Hugh's answer is deeply traditional and characteristically ecclesiastical, relying on the articles of faith established by the Church to guarantee the reader rightly relativizes letter to Spirit. As we will see, though, Hugh thought spiritual

Another example from *On the Sacraments* clarifies how one's thinking according to the letter should be transformed by spiritual understanding. Here, Hugh has in mind those who bring up difficulties related to Christ being God and human. His response is to challenge the approach of those who obsess over verbal definitions (such as "what is a person?") when such speech becomes less helpful the more we use it to speak of things "beyond us."

> *Those preoccupied with such questions often want to draw out the judgment of the Spirit from the letter, not draw out the judgment of the letter from the Spirit. For they don't know that the Spirit ought to judge the letter, and not the letter the Spirit. So, as it was written,* the spiritual person judges all things, and he is judged by no one *(1 Corinthians 2). For they labor in the judgment of speech, since they do not have the judgment of understanding. They want to have judgment, but they don't want to have that Spirit without which they can't judge rightly. Therefore, they labor in speech and they find so many things needing to be spoken about which have only one understanding.*[15]

The letter ought to be relativized to the Spirit. Rather than proceeding with the letter alone—through painstaking examination of definitions, a heaping up of words on words—the theologian should judge according to the Spirit. As valuable as the consideration of divine and human personhood may be, Hugh treats those who excessively verbalize about the issue in the same way as he treated those who too rigidly follow the literal meaning of Jesus's cry of abandonment: they fail to engage with the letter in a Spirit-filled manner. What these two examples show is that Hugh is devoted to a kind of reading and theology that prioritizes spiritual understanding, which may mean both drawing conclusions at odds with the plain meaning of Scripture and tempering one's use of excessive speech, avoiding over-literalization. The distinction between letter and spirit creates a moral situation where the Victorine reader stays grounded in and strives for spiritual understanding, engaging with but being careful not to get tripped up by the letter.

---

understanding would most often conform to or even be built on a foundation of literal understanding.

15   Hugh, *De sacramentis*, PL 176:405c-d (my translation).

What can we conclude about Paul's letter-spirit distinction at St. Victor? Paul's formulation provided a warning, and Hugh used the distinction between letter and Spirit to develop moral admonitions for the Victorine reader. Most importantly, when Paul warns that "the letter kills," it seems that Hugh took this to mean that "the letter *alone* kills." One who attends to the letter alone misses out on the life-giving Spirit and stumbles on the path of spiritual progress. When reading the letter, there is always a Spirit, which vivifies the letter itself and the reader who reads it. Hugh teaches that the Christian reader should always expect, strive for, and hope for as much. Staying grounded in spiritual understanding, the reader comes to appreciate the distance that can exist between the letter and its spiritual meaning, such as when Christ's claim of abandonment means its apparent opposite.

Yet while the Pauline distinction creates a distance between letter and spirit, it also weds the spirit intimately to the letter. Whereas the examples from *On the Sacraments* suggest how the letter-spirit distinction served as a warning to Victorine readers—stay grounded in the Spirit as you traverse the path of the letter—Hugh's *Didascalicon on the Study of Reading* develops a more integrated vision of how spiritual understanding relates to the letter. Said otherwise, in *Didascalicon*, the distinction between letter and spirit serves not only as an admonition but as the basis of a wider theory of reading. As we will see, the letter was a theological concept central to the path of spiritual progress. There was no encounter with the Spirit, no spiritual understanding, without the letter. The letter was the vehicle or medium of spiritual understanding. One of the greatest legacies of the Pauline distinction between letter and spirit at St. Victor was that it suggested that the meaning of the letter was something vivid and alive, dynamic and elusive, like the Spirit Itself. The sense that spiritual understanding should be distinguished from the letter and prioritized over it was a central contribution of Pauline theology to the reading culture at St. Victor, whatever the intention of Paul himself. Yet much of Hugh's understanding of this distinction was fleshed out through his reading of the fourth-century bishop Augustine of Hippo.

The Letter as Signs

The Victorines had a special reverence for Augustine. While many twelfth-century religious communities followed the monastic *Rule of Benedict* for guidance in their daily religious life, the canons at St. Victor instead followed a rule traditionally ascribed to Augustine.[16] Their writings, especially those of Hugh, evince Augustine's deep influence over their reading culture. Later medieval readers of Hugh's writings would recognize the Augustinian influence—they called Hugh "another Augustine" (*alter Augustinus*). Hugh's *Didascalicon on the Study of Reading* was in effect an Augustinian theology of reading. In it, Hugh describes how reading itself is the basis for contemplation (*contemplatio*) and perfection (*perfectio*), the ends of monastic life, so the *Didascalicon* is a curriculum of reading for the religious life of "scholar-monk-priests" like the Victorines.[17]

What did this curriculum look like? In the preface to *Didascalicon*, Hugh previews the organization of the treatise, writing that this book

> *instructs the reader of secular writings as much as the reader of divine writings. For this reason it is divided into two parts, each of*

---

[16] Juliet Mousseau posits the theory that this choice reflects the fact that the *Rule of Augustine* was less prescriptive about the traditional monastic ideal of stability than other rules. Since canons were clerics responsible for ministering to communities and needing to leave the cloister, it was helpful to not be so bound to one place. "Daily Life at the Abbey of St. Victor," in *A Companion to the Abbey of St. Victor in Paris*, ed. Hugh Feiss and Juliet Mousseau (Leiden: Brill Academic, 2018), 57.

[17] Hugh, *Didascalicon*, V.109: "*Quattuor sunt in quibus nunc exercetur uita iustorum et, quasi per quosdam gradus ad futuram perfectionem subleuatur, uidelicet lectio siue doctrina, meditatio, oratio, et operatio. Quinta deinde sequitur, contemplatio, in qua, quasi quodam precedentium fructu, in hac uita etiam que sit boni operis merces futura pregustatur. . . . De his quinque gradibus primus gradus, id est lectio, incipientium est, supremus, id est contemplatio, perfectorum.*"

Franklin T. Harkins, trans., *Didascalicon on the Study of Reading*, ed. Franklin T. Harkins and Frans van Liere (Turnhout, Belgium: Brepols, 2013), 161: "The life of a just person is trained in four things, which serve as certain stages through which he is raised to future protection: namely, reading or learning, meditation, prayer, and action. Then follows a fifth, contemplation, in which—as if a certain fruit of the preceding stages—the just person enjoys even in this life a foretaste of the future rewards of good work. . . . The first of these five stages, that is, reading, is for beginners; the last, that is, contemplation, is for the perfect."

Boyd Taylor Coolman describes the Victorines as "scholar-monk-priests" in "The Victorines," in *Wiley-Blackwell Companion to Christian Mysticism*, ed. Julia A. Lamm (Malden, MA: Wiley-Blackwell, 2013), 251.

which has three distinctions. In the first part it teaches the reader of the arts (lectorem artium), *and in the second part the reader of divine things* (lectorem divinum). *It teaches in this way: by showing first what* (quid) *should be read, and next in what order* (quo ordine), *and finally how* (quomodo) *it should be read.*[18]

These three—what to read, in what order to read, and how to read—are the underlying concerns of Hugh's study of reading. The passage above foreshadows Hugh's answer to the question of what to read: everything. The Victorine canon should read both secular literature ("the arts") and sacred literature ("divine things"). Reading, however, should not be haphazard. Rather, a careful course of reading can progressively restore or reform the soul from its fallen state if one understands how to do it. When it came to the letter (*littera*) at St. Victor, the canon should know what, in what order, and how to read it.

Hugh's pedagogical program—what, in what order, and how to read—was everywhere rooted in Augustine. In the following sections, I will first describe Hugh's vision of what one should read, focusing on his embrace of Augustine's positive estimation of secular literature. There is little concern here that the letter might kill. The Victorine should read, not just sacred literature but all literature, to begin to restore or reform their soul. Second, Hugh's curriculum was an integrated, orderly, and progressive one. He argues that, though the Victorine canon should study secular literature in preparation for the reading of sacred literature, they should also read the Scriptures in an orderly manner. For this reason, it is tempting to view the vast commentary literature produced by the Victorines as the project of a collective reading culture to enact Hugh's pedagogical vision of guiding readers through the entire "course" or "flow" (*cursus*) of literature. Finally—and most importantly—I rehearse Hugh's approach to scriptural interpretation and the Augustinian theory of signs that undergirds it. This theory teaches one how to read. Just as secular literature is a necessary preparation for sacred literature, the literal or historical interpretation of a sacred writing—its

---

18   Hugh, *Didascalicon*, Pref.2 (translation slightly modified from Harkins, 82): "*In prima parte docet lectorem artium, in secunda parte diuinum lectorem. Docet autem hoc modo, ostendendo primum quid legendum sit, deinde quo ordine et quomodo legendum sit.*"

letter—is the foundation for its spiritual understanding because it populates one's memory with God's "deeds done in time (*res in tempore gestae*)," the media of the Spirit's manifestation.[19] In turn, the good Victorine reader may come to know the Wisdom of God and have spiritual understanding of the letter. In sum, I suggest how Hugh's reading program illuminates the Victorine reading culture's approach to the letter—its attention to the value of all secular learning, the integrity and order of sacred writings themselves, and the method for striving for spiritual understanding.

What to Read

Despite Hugh's reservation about "the letter *alone*" in *On the Sacraments*, in *Didascalicon*, he shows no hesitation about engaging with the letter itself, whether sacred literature or secular literature. While Hugh advocated the reading of secular literature alongside sacred literature, the *Didascalicon* also carefully establishes the relationship between the two. The structure of the work itself suggests that secular literature complements sacred literature: the first half treats secular literature in three books, while the second half covers sacred literature in three more. In his composition of the *Didascalicon*, Hugh was deeply indebted to and builds on Augustine's *On Christian Teaching*. Augustine had famously described the place pagan—what Hugh would call "secular"—literature played in Christian teaching with an image drawn from the Exodus narrative. It is worth quoting at length:

> *Any statements by those who are called philosophers, especially the Platonists, which happen to be true and consistent with our faith should not cause alarm, but be claimed for our own use, as it were from owners who have no right to them. Like the treasures of the ancient Egyptians, who possessed not only idols and heavy burdens, which the people of Israel hated and shunned, but also vessels and ornaments of silver and gold, and clothes, which on leaving Egypt the people of Israel, in order to make better use of them surreptitiously claimed for themselves (they did this not on their own authority but at God's command, and the Egyptians in their ignorance actually gave them the things of which they had*

---

19   Hugh, *Didascalicon*, IV.70, trans. Harkins, 134.

> *made poor use)—similarly all the branches of pagan learning . . . these treasures . . . must be removed by Christians, as they separate themselves in spirit from the wretched company of pagans, and applied to their true function, that of preaching the gospel. As for their clothing—which corresponds to human institutions, but those appropriate to human society, which in this life we cannot do without—this may be accepted and kept for conversion to Christian purposes.*[20]

This image suggests that for Augustine, the Christian should not take an adversarial relationship to secular literature but should plunder or convert it, repurposing it and making it subservient to Christian ends. This view, which affirms secular literature—especially of the Platonists—while subordinating it to sacred literature, reflects the polemical context of Augustine's late ancient milieu.

Hugh, however, takes up and tempers the Augustinian position, as recent research on Hugh has shown. The reading of secular literature on the liberal arts, Franklin Harkins argues, has for Hugh some salutary effect in and of itself insofar as it pursues Wisdom. This pursuit of Wisdom is a remedy for what Harkins characterizes as the main dilemma of Hugh's theology: the disordering of the image of God in the soul.[21] Boyd Taylor Coolman has pointed to a related image for the soul's dilemma in Hugh's corpus: the deformation of the soul.[22] For both readers of Hugh, reading—including secular literature—plays a pivotal role in resolving the soul's dilemma by restoring or reforming it. For this reason, Harkins casts Hugh's position on secular literature as preparatory or commencing the process of restoration.[23] The salutary effects of secular reading are "the real beginning of the process whereby the human person is restored to the image of God," even if one

---

20   Augustine, *De doctrina christiana*, II.144–45, trans. R. P. H. Green, 64–65.
21   Franklin T. Harkins, *Reading and the Work of Restoration: History and Scripture in the Theology of Hugh of St. Victor* (Toronto: Pontifical Institute of Medieval Studies, 2009), 60–61, 100–112.
22   Boyd Taylor Coolman, *The Theology of Hugh of St. Victor: An Interpretation* (Cambridge: Cambridge University Press, 2009), 60–78.
23   Harkins, *Reading and Restoration*, 112–36.

needs to fulfill or complete the learning begun in them through the reading of sacred literature.[24] That is, secular reading provides the foundation for sacred reading by ordering one's understanding of creation and history, the outpourings of God's Wisdom or "deeds done in time." Insofar as secular writings treat the natural world or human history, they reflect God's Wisdom, and those who read them begin to restore their souls.

Harkins's description of the preparatory effect of secular literature in Hugh is welcome, especially his identification of the liberal arts' "nascent restorative efficacy."[25] As Hugh emphasizes that the soul is in need of restoration or reformation, reading secular literature plays a critical role in these processes. Harkins's position is even further supported by attention to yet a third way Hugh casts the dilemma faced by the soul—self-ignorance.[26] Not only is the soul disordered in affection or deformed but it has also forgotten itself. That is, Hugh not only casts the major problem reading remedies as the disorder or deformation of the soul but he at times also claims that the soul has simply forgotten its own nature: "For the mind, numbed by bodily passions and seduced outside of itself by sensible forms, has forgotten what it is, and because it has not remembered that it is anything different, it thinks that it is nothing beyond what is seen."[27] Secular literature, then, by facilitating the mind's retrieval of an innate wisdom, reminding the soul of what it already is, and restoring the memory to its pre-fall state, is not only preparatory for the work done by sacred reading but truly has a "nascent restorative efficacy."

Not only does reading secular literature begin to restore and reform the soul by introducing it to Wisdom but it also prepares the reader to read sacred literature. As we will see below, reading sacred writings required that the Victorine reader first attend to the letter of the sacred writing. Only once one understood how the letter made meaning (or "signified") could one seek

---

24   Harkins, *Reading and Restoration*, 11.
25   Franklin T. Harkins, "Introduction," in Hugh, *Didascalicon*, 67.
26   Harkins, *Reading and Restoration*, 106–8.
27   Hugh, *Didascalicon*, I.6, trans. Harkins, 84: *"Animus enim, corporeis passionibus consopitus et per sensibiles formas extra semetipsum abductus, oblitus est quid fuerit, et, quia nil aliud fuisse se meminit, nil preter quod uidetur esse credit."*

deeper spiritual understanding. Having a knowledge of the arts, then, prepared the Victorine to read the difficult writings of Scripture by, for instance, giving them the ability to understand the measurements of Noah's ark or the unfamiliar flora and fauna of the ancient Near East. Equipped with this "literal" understanding, the Victorine could find spiritual significance in the length of Noah's ark in Genesis or the spiky, aromatic plant called *nard* mentioned in the Song of Songs. In this way, reading secular literature not only acquainted one with God's Wisdom since it is the source of all temporal and local things—Noah's ark and nard are examples of God's deeds done in time—but it also prepared one to understand the letter of Scripture itself.

Notice how expansive and integrated was Hugh's understanding of the letter. Reading the letter meant reading everything, even as the purpose or goal of reading everything was to read Scripture and strive for the spiritual understanding available in it. Reading the letter, both secular and sacred writings, was a practice for restoring the soul. By reacquainting the soul with God's Wisdom, the letter re-formed the memory and reminded the reader of who they were. Hugh's emphasis on the role of both secular and sacred literature in the process of restoring the soul suggests his concern with the order of reading: one studied the secular arts in order to read sacred writings. If the Victorine reader was to read everything, in what order and how should they read?

The Order of Reading

At St. Victor, the restoration or reformation of the soul, like every part of monastic life, occurred through orderly, disciplined practice.[28] Reading in Hugh's *Didascalicon* is simply an extension of the monastic discipline practiced by the Victorine canon. Just as the regular canon should eat or drink in moderation, so should they temper their reading. Just as the day was marked by the ritual prayer of the regular divine hours, reading should be frequent,

---

28   See Coolman's description of "Practices of Re-formation," in *Theology of Hugh*, 139–224. Coolman draws on the now classic study by Mary Carruthers, *The Book of Memory: A Study of Medieval Culture* (Cambridge: Cambridge University Press, 1990). In the Prologue to the first book of *On the Sacraments*, Hugh warns of the dangers of disordered reading, "lest [the mind] be carried away by various volumes of writings and a diversity of readings without order or direction." Hugh, *De sacramentis*, PL 176:183, trans. Roy Deferrari, 3.

regular, and orderly. Reading should proceed in an order whether at the level of the disciplines, the books themselves, the narratives, or the exposition of the text.[29] Throughout their commentaries on sacred writings, the Victorines refer to the letter's "order" (*ordo*), "course/flow" (*cursus*), or "sequence" (*series*). We have already seen that for Hugh, reading secular literature is preparatory for reading sacred literature, but what about the order, course, or sequence of reading for sacred literature itself?

The order of reading relied on a division of the sacred writings. Hugh's primary division of sacred literature is between the Old and New Testaments, which themselves are broken down into three sections. While Hugh dedicates a fair amount of space to dividing up and describing the two Testaments, two aspects are of note. First, Hugh retrieves a division of the works traditionally ascribed to Solomon, around since at least Origen of Alexandria in the third century, according to how each advances beyond the other:

> *In Proverbs Solomon teaches a young boy and instructs him by means of aphorisms concerning his duties. . . . In Ecclesiastes, by contrast, Solomon instructs a mature man not to imagine that anything in this world is lasting, but rather to understand that everything we see is perishable and transient. Finally, in the Song of Songs he joins to the Spouse by nuptial embraces an already perfect man who demonstrated his preparation by trampling this present age under foot.*[30]

That is, Solomon himself had written with the intention of laying out a pedagogy of sorts, the culmination of which was his masterpiece, the Song of Songs, an erotic love poem that Christians had long interpreted as a spiritual allegory for the soul and God. That is, the Song is not only the culmination of the Solomonic literature but it was also a text that was appropriate for those who through ordered reading had attained contemplation by looking beyond the present age. While Hugh affirms that the Song is for "the perfect," it should also be noted that for the Victorines, perfection was an

---

29   Hugh, *Didascalicon*, III.58, trans. Harkins, 124–25.
30   Hugh, *Didascalicon*, IV.81, trans. Harkins, 141.

elusive goal for those on the journey of this life (*in via*).[31] The Song, therefore, as multiple commentaries of Thomas Gallus attest, was a sacred writing whose meaning could never be exhausted in this life. As we will see in the commentaries of the last great Victorine, because it depicts the soul's union with the Word, it should be returned to again and again by the one seeking contemplation and Christian perfection.

The second revealing aspect of Hugh's division and ordering of all of sacred literature is the prominent place he gives to extrabiblical texts. That Hugh should encourage his Victorine readers, whose own rule was written by Augustine, to read the Apostolic and Church Fathers is not surprising. However, Hugh curiously places this literature within the boundaries of the New Testament itself, which "can be called the Gospel even though specifically those four books that set forth the words and deeds of the Savior—namely, Matthew, Mark, Luke, and John—deserve to be called the Gospel."[32] A short division of the whole of the Scripture, original to Hugh, shows that he saw this literature as continuous with the canonical New Testament: "All of Sacred Scripture is contained in two Testaments, namely in the Old and the New. Each Testament is divided into three collections. The Old Testament contains the Law, the Prophets, and the Writings. The New Testament contains the Gospels, the Apostles, and the Fathers."[33]

Hugh's commitment to the idea is confirmed when he later expands on it. The Gospels are those of the four evangelists, while "the second collection" is made up of four more "volumes": the Acts of the apostles, Paul's letters, the "canonical epistles," and Revelation. "The Fathers" is made up of the decretals and rules but especially of "the Doctors of the Church: Jerome, Augustine, Gregory, Ambrose, Isidore, Origen, Bede, and many other orthodox writers whose works are so vast that they cannot be counted."[34] Surely included among those "other orthodox writers" was Dionysius the

---

31   A traditional goal of monastic life, perfection (*perfectio*) was an idea informed by both the philosophical concept of a fulfillment or completion of the human person and the Gospel injunction to "be perfect, therefore, as your heavenly Father is perfect" (Matt 5:48).

32   Hugh, *Didascalicon*, IV.83, trans. Harkins, 143.

33   Hugh, *Didascalicon*, IV.71, trans. Harkins, 134.

34   Hugh, *Didascalicon*, IV.72, trans. Harkins, 135.

Areopagite, who was thought by the Victorines to be the Greek convert of the apostle Paul mentioned in the book of Acts and whose works were commented on by Hugh and retranslated by the Victorine John Saracen after Hugh's passing. Though not listed here by Hugh among "the Fathers," Dionysius would certainly have been included among this group, if not among the apostles themselves, thanks to his proximity to Paul, "the Apostle." Hugh laments that it is impossible to read all the Fathers, again hinting that the practice of sacred reading cannot be completed or perfected in this life.

Readers of Hugh have seldom taken seriously this description of the Fathers as contained within the "New Testament." Surely Hugh does not mean that these texts, which he admits are more numerous than he can read, are within the canon of Scripture? While elsewhere Hugh carefully distinguishes between canonical and apocryphal texts, his expansive view of the New Testament and the Gospel had an effect on the school of St. Victor. Once again, Hugh's vision for reading was an orderly one. Just as secular and sacred writings were included and integrated within the letter, so were the Fathers included and integrated within the sacred writings. Not only does this suggests how the letter was divided, ordered, and pedagogically organized, but it also suggests how the letter was a central theological concept that could never be defined finally or exhaustively at the school. Hugh's treatment of the order of reading makes reading an ongoing and never-completed religious practice of engagement with the letter. The fact that reading "flowed" or followed a "course" (*cursus*) through secular and sacred literature made the letter the path along which the Victorine reader traveled as they pursued Christian perfection.

As this treatment suggests, this course was not an easy one. Hugh's division of secular and sacred literature suggests that the Victorine reader encountered an integrated and complex system of texts, each a signpost along the spiritual journey. When it comes to reading the letter itself, it becomes clear that the Victorine was to navigate this system of signs influenced by Augustine's theory of signification.

How to Read

Because the Victorine reader encountered the letter as expansive and orderly, they needed to learn methods for reading. Hugh's explanation of how to read rests primarily on a theory of signification that he drew from Augustine. In a passage that begins his discussion of the matter, Hugh describes signification through the Augustinian distinction between words (*verba*) and things (*res*):

> *It must also be known that in the divine writings not only do words* (verba) *signify, but so too do things* (res). *This mode of signifying is not ordinarily found to such a degree in other writings. The philosopher recognizes only the significance of words, but the significance of things is much more excellent than that of words because custom or common usage has determined the latter, whereas nature established the former. The latter is a human expression* (hominum vox), *whereas the former is the very voice of God* (vox Dei) *speaking to humans. The latter, having been uttered, passes away; the former, having been brought into being, subsists.*[35]

In this passage, Hugh indicates there is a distinction between the signification through words (*verba* or *voces*) and through things (*res*). In a general way recognized even by the pagan philosopher, words are signs that point the hearer to particular things. Hugh says the connection between sign and thing is established by common custom, an implicit agreement between the speaker and hearer. That is, human beings agree that particular words (like *lion*) point to particular things (the large predator cat with a mane). In this case, meaning is established by social convention, and human beings communicate by using expressions or words agreed on as signs to point to things.

Yet Hugh insists, again following Augustine, that in the case of scriptural signification, when the very voice of God speaks, not only words (*verba*) but also the things (*res*) themselves signify. Another passage helps to make clear what Hugh means by this. Hugh calls to mind the "profound" signification in sacred literature, describing how "the reader comes through the word (*vocem*) to a basic concept (*intellectum*), through the concept to a thing (*rem*), through the thing to an idea (*ratio*), and through the idea to the truth (*veritas*)."[36] That is, while in general, signification occurs through the first three steps—the word (*vox*) guiding the hearer to an understanding of the thing (*res*) itself—in scriptural signification, oftentimes the thing (*res*)

---

35   Hugh, *Didascalicon*, V.96, trans. Harkins, 151.
36   Hugh, *Didascalicon*, V.97, trans. Harkins, 152.

itself guides the reader to a further truth (*veritas*). How is this so? Returning to the passage above, Hugh explains that the things (*res*) referred to in Scripture—which consists largely of narratives of God's "deeds done in time" (*res in tempore gestae*)—are established by nature itself. That is, Scripture points to creation and history themselves, which are like the spatial and temporal signs economically arranged by the eternal Word. These things—nature, creation, and history—are expressions of the Word or simply are the voice of God (*vox Dei*). In this way, these things themselves signify, directing one to the eternal truth (*veritas*) from which they come.

This theory of scriptural signification underlies Hugh's more detailed examination of the methods by which Scripture should be read and interpreted. Because Scripture uses both forms of signification—meaning produced by the use of words (*voces*) to refer to things (*res*) *and* meaning produced by the use of the things (*res*) themselves to refer to truths (*veritates*) beyond them—methods should be established to distinguish and interpret each. Indeed, Hugh lays out carefully the distinction between the "disciplines" of, on the one hand, a historical-literal form of scriptural interpretation and, on the other hand, spiritual forms of scriptural interpretation, emphasizing that interpretation of sacred literature in terms of the history of God's deeds done in time should precede any attempts at spiritual interpretation.

Historical methods for interpretation allow the reader to understand the things to which the letter of Scripture points. Though not all sacred writings are primarily historical, Hugh says they all can be read historically: "History is not only the narrative of the things having been done (*res gestae*) but also the first meaning of any narrative that signifies according to the proper nature of words."[37] That is, historical reading is the kind of reading that is done anytime a reader follows the signification of a word pointing to a thing. The historical reading of a sacred writing, therefore, produces basically a literal meaning, in the sense of a literary meaning. It asks what meaning arises when one examines solely the letter of the text itself or "the letter alone." This bifold definition of history (*historia*) allows for some ambiguity on Hugh's part. At times, he seems to say that the historical meaning is important for giving the reader access to the actions performed by the Word

---

37   Hugh, *Didascalicon*, VI.115, trans. Harkins, 166.

in causing "deeds done in time." Historical reading is thus a way to "read" the Word as a creative principle of nature and history. At other times, historical reading is simply the literal (or literary) meaning of a text, which serves as a foundation of a higher or further spiritual interpretation. As we will see much later in this book, the thirteenth-century Victorine Thomas Gallus uses this second understanding of *historia* when he reads the Song of Songs. Gallus's examination of the letter of the Song allows the reader to appreciate the grammar, the basic meaning of foreign terms, and the literary style, all of which facilitate the examination of deeper spiritual meanings or truths.

While the interpretation of history in Scripture gives one knowledge of the creative and restorative actions of the Word—or at least a literal or literary basis for further interpretation—it is with the knowledge of these things (*res*) that one can begin to understand the deeper truths they convey. Two modes of spiritual interpretation—allegorical and tropological—build on the foundation laid by historical or literal understanding. With an understanding of the thing (*res*) firmly in place, one can go on to seek subtler or deeper meanings, which Hugh typically refers to as "mysteries" or—from his treatment of signification—simply "the truth" (*veritas*). To return to our earlier example, the word (*vox*) *lion* signifies the animal itself (the thing, *res*), but this literal understanding is the foundation for a deeper understanding in which the thing (the lion) is itself a sign pointing to the devil.[38] Or the word *ark* in the story of Noah signifies the historical ark itself, which in turn signifies the Church. Notice that Noah's ark, one of God's "deeds done in time," is a thing (*res*) established by God's Wisdom and therefore potentially revealing of a deeper spiritual truth. As Hugh depicts it in the *Didascalicon*, spiritual reading culminates the order of reading and should be practiced only by advanced readers, but it is a task that will never be completed as the sacred letter is arranged with more mysteries or truths than one could fully comprehend. As we will see, the many commentaries from St. Victor draw deeply from Hugh's vision of how to read, searching the letter for a spiritual understanding that exceeded it.[39]

---

38   Hugh, *Didascalicon*, V.97, trans. Harkins, 152.

39   Even in the case of Andrew of St. Victor, whose commentaries are rightly described as historical-literal rather than spiritual, there is evidence of the canon's commitment to Hugh's integrated vision for interpreting Scripture. For example, in his commentary on the

What have we noticed about Hugh's Augustinian approach to the letter? In *Didascalicon*, Hugh moves beyond the warnings about "the letter alone" to a more integrated vision of the role of the letter for those who seek spiritual understanding. The initial Pauline distinction between letter and spirit becomes a roadmap for reading, with Augustinian theories marking out the signposts along the way. Thanks to Augustine's generally positive estimation of the letter—both sacred and secular—and his theory of signs, in Hugh's *Didascalicon,* the letter is a complex and expansive system of signs. The Spirit animates or vivifies the letter, allowing Hugh to state that the reader could be "rooted" in the Spirit while traversing the letter and avoiding any "stumbles" on the letter alone. More frequent than the metaphor of the path with its dangers, however, Hugh developed rich images of the harmonious relation between the letter and the spirit. The letter was the field from which the reader unearthed a spiritual harvest.[40] It was the shadow that led the reader to its true form.[41] It was a honeycomb containing sweet honey.[42] It was the hollow, wooden base of the zither, from which the strings of spiritual understanding resonated their melodious tunes.[43] The flourishing of these metaphors in Hugh's writings suggests how the letter would become a central theological concept at the school of St. Victor, orchestrating religious life, especially practices of reading for the restoration or reformation of the soul. The Victorine reader sought the Spirit through and beyond the letter, making the letter the center of religious life.

---

story of Noah's ark, Andrew comments on the text's mention of a window that Noah built into the ark: "The Jews hand down that this window was crystalline so that it would not allow in water but would administer the light." *Expositio super heptateuchum*, ed. C. Lohr and R. Berndt, Corpus Christianorum Continuatio Mediaevalis 53 (Turnhout, Belgium: Brepols, 1986), 53:1430 (my translation). On the surface, this is a literal or historical comment on the text telling the reader about the window (the thing to which the word points). However, it is likely that the Victorine reader would extrapolate spiritual meanings as the ark was a spiritual symbol of the Church, a refuge from evils, and an administrator of God's light. Though Andrew studiously sticks to the letter and avoids spiritual interpretation as he claims he will, this is the kind of foundational reading on which a spiritual meaning would be built.

40   Hugh, *Didascalicon*, VI.116, trans. Harkins, 166.
41   Hugh, *Didascalicon*, VI.116, trans. Harkins, 166.
42   Hugh, *Didascalicon*, IV.70, V.96, trans. Harkins, 134, 151.
43   Hugh, *Didascalicon*, V.95, trans. Harkins, 150–51.

The Spiritual Practice of Reading

A final note should be made about Hugh's treatment of how to read. The strongest material evidence we have that Hugh's methods for reading Scripture were worked out in practice at St. Victor is the manifold volumes of commentaries produced by Andrew, Richard, Thomas Gallus, and other Victorines, including Hugh himself. These commentaries should be seen both as participating in Hugh's pedagogical efforts—preparing readers of sacred literature for contemplation—and as the practical effects of the Victorines' own practices of reading. That is, each commentary produced by the Victorines is itself a product of a reading of sacred literature, along the lines of the interpretive "disciplines" Hugh lays out. Although the school produced a variety of commentaries, and each Victorine had their own proclivities for how to read—Andrew reading with a historical-literal method, Richard and Thomas Gallus with spiritual methods—this coherent body of literature remarkably fulfills the vision laid out by the school's premier pedagogue in the *Didascalicon*.

Despite this fact, Hugh had reservations about the idea of "commentary" itself. He treats the term among a series of etymologies (drawn from Isidore of Seville) on terms related to reading. Isidore had described two possible origins of the term *commentaria*. It came either from *cum mente* ("with the mind") or *comminiscor* ("to devise by careful thought"). These both suggest, Isidore writes, how *commentaria* are interpretations of sacred literature. Hugh responds, "Some say that the word 'comments' or 'commentary' (*commenta*) should be applied only to the books of the pagans, whereas 'expositions' (*expositiones*) should be reserved for divine writings."[44] That is, while Hugh was comfortable with the project of writing commentaries, he preferred to give them a name that denoted less forcefully the idea that the commentator "devised" something in interpreting the text. Indeed, the Victorines referred to their commentaries as expositions (*expositiones*) and explanations (*explanationes*).

Despite Hugh's reservation in this regard, he also affirmed that writing expository works on sacred literature was a never-ending practice requiring ongoing readerly effort. In the same section where he describes how reading

---

44   Hugh, *Didascalicon*, IV.94, trans. Harkins, 149.

(*lectio*) is a necessary step toward meditation, prayer, operation, and finally contemplation (*contemplatio*), he describes the goal of this process in the following way:

> *You see, then, how perfection* (perfectio) *runs up to meet those who advance upward through these stages, so that the person who remains below cannot be perfect. Our objective, therefore, should always be to ascend, but because the instability of our present life is so great that we cannot remain in one place, we are often compelled to look back at stages that we have completed, and, so that we might not fall from the stage we currently occupy, we from time to time repeat the stages through which we have already advanced. . . . He who has insufficient confidence in his own judgment consults his reading material. And so it happens that, although it is always our desire to ascend, nevertheless we sometimes need to descend.*[45]

This passage depicts the situation in which Hugh imagines the processes of reading, interpreting, and commenting on sacred literature. It should now be clear that for Hugh, reading and writing commentary on the letter were means to contemplation and Christian perfection. Christian perfection or the restoration of the soul, however, is an elusive goal, which requires that the reader turn back again and again ("to descend") to the letter. The task of reading and writing commentary is never complete in this life as one can never have confidence that one has spiritually understood the mysteries of the Word in its entirety. As we will see, this instinct to descend from contemplation in order to further perfect one's reading of the Word will be emphasized again and again in the commentarial writings of the Victorines.

A Theology of the Letter

This chapter has traced a strand of Christian theology related to letter and spirit in the foundational writings of Hugh of St. Victor. We might call this strand of theology a *theology of the letter*. It should be no surprise that Hugh developed this theology by reading the writings of Paul and Augustine.

---

45 Hugh, *Didascalicon*, VI.110, trans. Harkins, 162.

Hugh himself thought the reading of such sacred literature slowly reformed or restored the soul to its divine image. As our opening anecdote from fellow Augustinian canon James of Vitry reminds us, Hugh's theology was attractive to many. But based on our reading of his works *Didascalicon on the Study of Reading* and *On the Sacraments,* what can we conclude about how Victorine readers encountered the letter? What role did Hugh's theology of the letter play at St. Victor?

Under Hugh's influence, the spirit stood at a distance from the letter. The Victorine reader, following the Pauline warning, should strive for the spirit beyond the letter. Yet at the same time, the pursuit of spiritual understanding involved the reader intimately in the letter, and Hugh's theology made the letter an expansive, a complex, and a coherent system of signs. As a result, the Victorine reader should read everything—secular and sacred—as they navigate a long-winding path and a difficult journey toward Wisdom and spiritual understanding. They should strive for the truths of the sacred writing, navigating the letter, convinced of its coherence and proceeding along its path while aware that the journey was not yet fully known to them.

Therefore, at St. Victor, the letter became the key to the reformation or restoration of the human being, the avenue toward the contemplation of God and Christian perfection. And yet it is not quite possible to speak of Hugh's theology as embracing the *mystified* letter that is the subject of this book. While Paul's letter-spirit distinction and Augustine's sign theory made the letter into an expansive, a complex, and a coherent program of spiritual understanding and a central theological concept at St. Victor, it was the introduction of a new set of writings at the school—or, rather, a new translation of some rather old writings—that would complete the transformation of the reading culture into one centered on the *mystified* letter. It is to this other strand of Christian theology—mystical theology—that we now turn.

3

MYSTICAL THEOLOGY: THE LETTER AS GOD'S VEIL

And we have been taught these things in a way appropriate to us, through holy veils, with the divine beneficence of the scriptures and hierarchical traditions covering over intelligible things with sensible things, and transcendent things with existing things, and placing forms and figures over those things which are without form or figure.

—Dionysius, *Divine Names*, 1.4

A New Translation at St. Victor

Building on the scholarly agenda of their "venerable teacher and master" Hugh, the Victorines read, commented on, and translated the letter. Consider the scholarly work of John Saracen, a Victorine translator a generation after Hugh about whom little is known. *Johannes Sarracenus*, as he appears in Latin, bears a surname resembling the term Latin Christians had commonly used for one who was religiously Muslim or ethnically Arab: *Saracen*. John's Victorine brothers benefited from his ability to translate from Greek to Latin as knowledge of Greek was uncommon in Paris, even at St. Victor. While we cannot discern much more about John, his translations, with brief prologues, show that this Victorine brother—like Hugh, Andrew, Richard, and Thomas Gallus—was devoted to the letter. Around 1167, he made a new translation of the sacred writings of Dionysius. This *nova translatio,* as it was referred to by the Victorines and other medieval theologians like Thomas Aquinas, was instrumental in mystifying the letter at St. Victor.

John's new translation reintroduced the writings of an enigmatic figure to St. Victor. Dionysius the Areopagite was thought by the Victorines to be a first-century Athenian convert of the apostle Paul mentioned in the book of Acts (17:34), so his writings had a near-apostolic status. Though today scholars recognize the corpus's dependence on late ancient Neoplatonic philosophers, and so date "Pseudo"-Dionysius (or "false" Dionysius) in the late fifth or early sixth century, in the late twelfth and early thirteenth centuries at St. Victor, Dionysius was the "treasury of the Apostle."[1] That is, Paul's convert was a philosophically minded Christian who had imbibed his teachings. Since we've already seen that at St. Victor "the Fathers" were included under Hugh's designation of the New Testament, it's no great leap to say the writings of Dionysius were counted among the sacred writings. Translated into Latin multiple times before the twelfth century—Hugh himself wrote a commentary on an older translation of a Dionysian treatise on the *Celestial Hierarchy*—it seems that nevertheless John's new translation of the entire corpus made it more accessible to its Latinate readers at St. Victor and beyond.[2] Dionysian themes worked their way into the writings of the Victorines, in particular the last great Victorine, Thomas Gallus.

The Victorines were drawn to the writings of Dionysius not only because of his near-apostolic authority but also because of his mystical theology. It must have seemed that Paul's Athenian convert had *both* the advantages of pagan philosophical wisdom *and* what Thomas Gallus calls the special "wisdom of Christians." What was Dionysius's mystical theology? At its center was the mysterious God beyond being. Building on a fundamental commitment to God's mystery, Dionysius explained its implications for letter and liturgy. He unpacked both the theological language of Scripture in treatises like *Divine Names* and *Mystical Theology* and the Church's liturgical symbols and rituals in *Ecclesiastical Hierarchy* as he showed how the entire Christian way of life was directed toward union with and assimilation to the God hidden beyond being. The Victorines were primed for this theology by their devotion to God, letter, and liturgy, and Dionysius provided them an entire theological apparatus that made sense of the letter and fostered their

---

1   Thomas Gallus, *Explanatio super primam epistolam ad Gaium*, in *Explanatio in libros Dionysii*, ed. Declan Anthony Lawell, Corpus Christianorum Continuatio Mediaevalis 223 (Turnhout, Belgium: Brepolls, 2011), 717.

2   For a more extended treatment of John's translation, see my "Mystical Theology and/in Translation: Re-veiling the Latin *Corpus Dionysiacum*," *Medieval Mystical Theology* 29, no. 1 (Summer 2020): 41–53.

practices of reading, commenting on, and translating it. In short, Dionysius's theology mystified letter and liturgy, explaining how they provided symbolic paths toward the God of mystery.

This chapter and the next delve into the mystical theology developed in the texts of Dionysius and their translation and elaboration at St. Victor. This chapter focuses on Dionysius's theology of God. It shows how Dionysius mystified God by establishing God's "beyond-being-ness" and its corollaries, divine unintelligibility and ineffability. Dionysian theology of God, however, is not simply a series of statements on God's inaccessible transcendence. Rather, it is a tentative attempt to speak of the *presence* of the mysterious God beyond being to creation. This chapter, thus, starts with God, but it points ahead to the next chapter's concern with the Word and the letter, which equip the soul to experience the presence of God's mystery. The Victorines found the beginnings of a theory of the mystified letter in the Dionysian theological concept of the God beyond being, who is present to creation. At St. Victor, Dionysian theology mystified first God and then the letter by stylizing the letter as a symbolic veil covering the hidden divinity, both obscuring and revealing at the same time. This chapter focuses on this hidden divinity, the next on the veil of the letter that covers it. Together they show how the introduction of Dionysian theology mystified the letter at St. Victor.

The Mysterious Providence of the God "beyond Being"

What does Dionysius teach about God? Two features of Dionysius's writings suggest his primary concern is to teach that God is "beyond being" (ὑπερούσιος). First, in the work that most explicitly treats Dionysius's doctrine of God, the *Divine Names*, Dionysius invokes the "beyond-being-ness" (ὑπερουσιότης) of God at critical junctures in the text. *Divine Names*' central problematic is how we are to understand and put to use the various names of God handed down in Scripture, given that God is beyond being and ineffable. Dionysius begins with the most excellent divine names like *Good* and *Love;* continues to divine names like *Being*, *Life*, and *Wisdom;* and culminates the treatise with the divine name *One*. At the end of the final chapter, Dionysius has "unfolded" (ἀναπτύσσω) the various names of God given by Scripture. Now attending at last to the scriptural claim that God is both a Unity and a Trinity, he concludes that, in response to this mysterious affirmation, "we name the Deity, which is inexpressible to things that be, the Beyond-Being (τὴν ὑπερούσιον)."[3] Although Dionysius claims that the "theologians" (as he calls the Scripture writers) give more prestige to negative statements than affirmative statements about God, the fact that the "unfolding" of the affirmative divine names culminates with a final naming of God as "beyond being" suggests what a central teaching it is.[4] This term is one derived from the exegesis of divine names in Scripture.

While the noun *beyond-being-ness* shows up at a few critical junctures in the *Divine Names*, the description of God as "beyond being" is ubiquitous. Based on word count, the Dionysian corpus is more concerned with this point than any other. The writings use the terms *beyond being* and *beyond-being-ness* more frequently than better-known Dionysian terms like *good* (ἀγαθότης), *light* (φῶς), *hierarchy* (ἱεραρχία), *unsaying* (ἀπόφασις), *knowledge* (γνῶσις), *participate* (μετέχω), *intellect/mind* (νοῦς), *order* (τάξις), *hymn/celebrate* (ὑμνέω), and *principle* (ἀρχή). Only the terms *God* (θεός) and *power* (δύναμις) appear more often.[5] In addition, the corpus is littered with the prefix *hyper-* (ὑπερ-) and the preposition *hyper* (ὑπέρ) so that it consistently directs its reader's attention "beyond" as they read. Given this lexical frequency, these terms deserve careful consideration. As we will see, how one understands these *hyper* terms will influence their reading of the entire corpus.[6] What does

---

3   Pseudo-Dionysius, *Divine Names*, 13.3, in *Corpus Dionysiacum I*, ed. Beata Regina Suchla (Berlin: De Gruyter, 1990). Translations of the Dionysian corpus are adapted from John Parker's translation, *The Complete Works of Dionysius the Areopagite* (London: James Parker and Co., 1897–1899; reprint Merrick, NY: Richwood Publishing, 1976).

4   Paul Rorem suggests this final enjoining of negation gestures toward the treatise *Mystical Theology*: "The *Divine Names* now gives way to the *Mystical Theology*. . . . Although that terse essay both summarizes and climaxes the corpus, it would be difficult if not impossible to interpret it without the preparatory fuller exposition of the *Divine Names* and the other treatises." *Pseudo-Dionysius: A Commentary on the Texts and an Introduction to Their Influence* (New York: Oxford University Press, 1993), 166.

5   As will become clear, an important distinction in Dionysius's doctrine of God (θεός) is between God's beyond-being-ness and God's providential power (προνοητικὴ δύναμις).

6   This issue has been recently considered by Timothy D. Knepper, *Negating Negation: Against the Apophatic Abandonment of the Dionysian Corpus* (Eugene, OR: Wipf and Stock, 2014), 47–55, who helpfully explains the ambiguity inherent in the Greek prefix *hyper-*. It was

it mean for God to be beyond being? And why does Dionysius repeat this claim so often throughout his writings? Before we can consider the implications of God's beyond-being-ness for mystifying the letter at St. Victor, we should first consider what the central teaching means.

The claim that God is beyond being in the writings of Dionysius does not mean exactly what modern theologians often mean by God's "transcendence." God's "beyond-being-ness" (ὑπερουσιότης) does describe God's difference from creation, but it also describes the condition for God's creating and sustaining presence—the activity of God's providence (πρόνοια). In addition, in the writings, depictions of the commerce between the God beyond being and creatures abound. There are biblical models of creatures who plunge beyond being like Moses, Paul, and hosts of angels. There are the "powers" (δυνάμεις) and providential "energies" (ἐνεργείαι) that proceed to being from the Source of all being. Most importantly, there is the "God-manifestation" (θεοφάνεια) of the "beyond being" in Jesus, the Light and Love of God, who paradoxically remains unmanifest (ἀφανής). Finally, the Scriptures, written by the "theologians" (θεολόγοι), themselves illuminated by the divine Light Jesus, are the "handing down" (παράδοσις) of divine teaching to human beings. Yet despite all these depictions of God's intercourse with being, Dionysius emphatically and consistently insists that God remains beyond being. By attending to the conceptual ambiguities that appear in Dionysius's most extended treatment of the doctrine of God, the *Divine Names*, it becomes clear that the doctrine of "beyond-being-ness" affirms that God is the ineffable but praiseworthy Cause of all existing things. Dionysius affirms God's "beyond-being-ness" alongside God's providential or causal presence—a dialectic driven by Divine Love.

Beyond-being-ness (ὑπερουσιότης)
On the one hand, Dionysius teaches that God is beyond being and therefore unintelligible and ineffable, a teaching with considerable implications for

---

also noticed by Harry A. Wolfson, who says that *hyper-* terms may "acquire the logical significance of negation, in the sense of exclusion from a universe of discourse." "Negative Attributes in the Church Fathers and the Gnostic Basilides," in *Studies in the History and Philosophy of Religion*, ed. Isadore Twersky and George H. Williams, vol. 1 (Cambridge, MA: Harvard University Press, 1977), 138. See my rehearsal of Knepper's analysis below in ch. 4, 93–97.

the letter. While Dionysius coins the term *beyond-being-ness*, the concept has its roots in Neoplatonism, a prominent school of philosophy in the late ancient world.[7] The Neoplatonist philosophers most influential on Dionysius drew on a short passage from Plato's *Republic* to articulate their view that the First Principle—the Good, or the One—was "beyond being." There Plato writes, "Objects of knowledge not only receive their being known from the presence of the Good, but their very existence and being (τὸ εἶναί τε καὶ τὴν οὐσίαν) is derived from it, though the Good itself is not being but still is above (ὑπερέχοντος), beyond being (ἐπέκεινα τῆς οὐσίας) in dignity and power."[8]

On Plato's authority, then, Neoplatonists like Plotinus and Proclus claim that all things receive their being from the presence of the Good, and what knowledge we have of them likewise comes from the Good. More importantly, here Plato seems to affirm the distinction between the Good and being—the Good, as the cause or source of being, is "beyond being" (ἐπέκεινα τῆς οὐσίας). Plotinus would elaborate that because the One—as he calls the First Principle—is this Cause beyond being, it is also unintelligible:

> *That [One] is the productive power (δύναμις) of all things, and its product is already all things. But if this product is all things, that Principle is beyond all things (ἐπέκεινα τῶν πάντων): therefore "beyond being" (ἐπέκεινα ἄρα οὐσίας); and if the product is all things but the One is before all things and not equal to all things, in this way too it must be "beyond being" (ἐπέκεινα τῆς οὐσίας). That is, also beyond Intellect; there is, then, something beyond Intellect (ἐπέκεινα ἄρα τι νοῦ). For being is not a dead thing, nor is it not life or not thinking; Intellect and being are one and the same thing.*[9]

---

7 The modern designation *Neo*-Platonist is used for late ancient philosophers like Plotinus, Proclus, and Iamblichus, who thought of themselves simply as followers of Plato.

8 Plato, *Republic*, 509B, in *The Collected Dialogues of Plato*, ed. Edith Hamilton and Huntington Cairns (Princeton University Press, 1969). Translation adapted from that of Paul Shorey.

9 Plotinus, *Ennead*, ed. Jeffrey Henderson, trans. A. H. Armstrong (Cambridge, MA: Harvard University Press, 1989), V.4.2.38–44 (translation adapted).

Notice that Plotinus echoes Plato's reasoning, tying the One's causality to its being beyond being. Yet he goes further to stress that because the One is beyond being, it is also beyond understanding or intellection.[10] Since the First Principle, the Good, or the One is beyond being, it is not the kind of object that can be known by an act of intellect.

Another Neoplatonist source for Dionysius, Proclus, both thoroughly embraces the "beyond being" reasoning and rhetoric and tries to resolve the problem of knowledge by elaborating on the realm beyond being. Proclus is the first to both use the adjective *beyond-being* (ὑπερούσιος) that is ubiquitous in Dionysius and also ascribe a "beyond being" mode to the gods with an adverb (ὑπερουσίως). By distinguishing between the gods (henads) and the One (monad), Proclus creates two separate possible objects of knowledge—one the gods who are the more proximate causes of things and therefore more intelligible, the other the One, which is entirely unintelligible.[11] This resolution echoes also the earlier thinking of the Jewish Platonist Philo of Alexandria (another source for Dionysius), who, although he did not posit the existence of "gods," did distinguish between God in Godself and God's active powers. For Philo, when Scripture says that Abraham "sees" the Lord, he has an intellectual vision; however, "we must think of it as the manifestation of one of the Powers (δυνάμεων) which attend [the Lord]."[12] Since God is "ineffable," "inconceivable," and "incomprehensible," Philo concludes that intellectual vision, or knowledge, must be of God's powers. What Dionysius discerned in the writings of Philo and Proclus was that the "beyond-beingness" of God created a problem of knowledge and speech partially resolved by connecting our speech about God to what God does rather than what God is. As we will see, the Victorines would in turn theorize the letter in relation to God's Wisdom or Word, the more proximate causes of God's deeds.

---

10   Cf. Eric D. Perl, *Theophany: The Neoplatonic Philosophy of Dionysius the Areopagite* (Albany, NY: SUNY Press, 2007), 5: "The foundational doctrine of Neoplatonic thought is the doctrine that to be is to be intelligible."

11   Proclus, *Proclus: The Elements of Theology*, ed. and trans. E. R. Dodds (Oxford: Clarendon Press, 1963).

12   Philo, *On the Change of Names*, III.15, in *Philo: On Flight and Finding. On the Change of Names, On Dreams*, ed. and trans. F. H. Colson and G. H. Whitaker (Cambridge, MA: Harvard University Press, 1934).

These philosophical sources are apparent to modern editors of the Dionysian corpus, but the corpus itself casts its claims about God's beyond-beingness, unintelligibility, and ineffability as coming from the "theologians," that is, from Christian Scripture. Consider the use of negative terms for God—especially those that indicate invisibility—in the writings attributed to Paul.[13] For instance, from 1 Timothy, a pair of passages: "To the King of the ages, immortal, invisible (ἀοράτῳ), the only God (μόνῳ θεῷ), be honor and glory forever and ever. Amen" (1:17); "It is he alone who has immortality (ὁ μόνος ἔχων ἀθανασίαν) and dwells in unapproachable (ἀπρόσιτον) light, whom no one has ever seen or can see" (6:16). Elsewhere, Paul uses the terms *invisible* (ἀόρατος), *unsearchable* (ἀνεξερεύνητος), and *inscrutable* (ἀνεξιχνίαστος).[14] On its own, this may not be significant evidence that Dionysius discerned a Pauline teaching of a definite break between God and being or intelligibility, but in the book of Acts, a Neoplatonist reader would encounter Paul making an important claim about the unknowability or incomprehensibility of God—this in the same passage where we find Paul converting Dionysius.[15] Paul, pausing on his journey in Athens, is enjoined by the Athenians to teach them, their interest piqued by the novelty of his message. Paul agrees and begins by claiming he knows they are very religious, for he had come upon an altar there with an inscription, "To an unknown god (Ἀγνώστῳ θεῷ)." Paul teaches that the God who made the world does not live in dwellings made by human beings because God is the one who gives them "life and breath and everything."[16] He claims to preach this very "unknown god," and his reasoning here, in retrospect, looks similar to the Platonic reasoning held later by Plotinus. It is because God is the Creator of all things that God must *not* dwell in those things but must be somewhere beyond those things. Indeed, it is only once Paul begins preaching the resurrection of the dead that some Athenians

---

13 Charles Stang, *Apophasis and Pseudonymity in Dionysius the Areopagite: "No Longer I"* (Oxford: Oxford University Press, 2012), 121–23.

14 Rom 1:20; Col 1:15–16, 1 Tim 1:17; Rom 11:33; Eph 3:8. These are cited in Stang, *Apophasis and Pseudonymity*, 122n16–18. See Dionysius's most extended but still brief treatment of Paul as knowing God "being above all intellection and knowledge (ὑπὲρ πᾶσαν ὄντα νόησιν καὶ γνῶσιν)," in Epistle 5 in *Corpus Dionysiacum II*, ed. Guenter Heil and Adolf Martin Ritter (Berlin: De Gruyter, 1991).

15 Acts 17.

16 Acts 17:22–25.

begin to mock him—not Dionysius, though, who converts.[17] In sum, the Acts passage suggests that Paul taught that God is unknown and unknowable because God is a Creator not able to be seen. Looking at Dionysius's sources comprehensively, it appears the Platonic doctrine of divine "beyond-being-ness" provides the foundation for his reserve about divine intelligibility (or his embrace of divine mystery), even as that doctrine is affirmed by the scriptural witness of God's invisibility, ineffability, and unintelligibility.

At the very beginning of the *Divine Names,* we see the logic of divine unintelligibility at work. Not only, however, is this divine unintelligibility taught by Scripture itself but it is also the reason a scriptural rule is needed for speech about God. God is ineffable and unknown:

> *This is why we must not dare to speak or to think (ἐννοῆσαί) anything concerning the hidden divinity beyond being (τῆς ὑπερουσίου καὶ κρυφίας θεότητος), apart from what the sacred Oracles have divinely revealed. Since unknowing (ἀγνωσία) is of its beyond-being-ness (ὑπερουσιότητος), beyond speech, intellect, and being (ὑπὲρ λόγον καὶ νοῦν καὶ οὐσίαν), let us ascribe to it a technical understanding beyond being (τὴν ὑπερούσιον ἐπιστήμην) . . . [the divinity] is and is as no other being is. It is cause of all existence, and therefore itself not a being because it is beyond all being (πάσης οὐσίας ἐπέκεινα), and it alone could give an authoritative account of what it really is.*[18]

Much of this language and reasoning is Neoplatonic. Because God is the Cause of being, God must be "beyond being" (οὐσίας ἐπέκεινα —a phrase, as we have seen, traceable to Plato's *Republic*). Given that to be is to be intelligible, and that God is beyond being, God must also be beyond speech and intellect (νοῦς). Dionysius mixes the Platonic and Plotinian language with the newer Proclean adjective ὑπερούσιος. Yet he also coins his own term to describe the state or character in which divinity remains—*beyond-being-ness* (ὑπερουσιότης). God's "beyond-being-ness" is unintelligible and ineffable. If one could have any understanding of it, it must be an understanding that, as it were, leaves being behind—that is, nothing but an "unknowing"

---

17   Acts 17:32–34.
18   Pseudo-Dionysius, *Divine Names,* 1.1.

(ἀγνωσία): "For, if all kinds of knowledge (αἱ γνώσεις πᾶσαι) are of things existing, and are limited to things existing, that which is beyond all being (ἡ πάσης οὐσίας ἐπέκεινα), is also elevated above all knowledge (γνώσεώς)."[19] Thus, in this passage, God's "beyond-being-ness" implies something even stronger than God's unintelligibility—it implies there is not even any particular kind of knowledge (*gnosis*) possible of the God beyond being. As we will see, this final claim is one that gives way to a restylization of knowledge elsewhere in the corpus.[20] For now, notice that at the beginning of *Divine Names*, a work that "unfolds" the descriptions of God in Scripture, Dionysius insists that the God beyond being is ineffable, unintelligible, and unknowable.

While the consistent reminder that God is "beyond being" pops up throughout the *Divine Names*, the teaching is most prominent in two other places—at the transition to treating the divine name *Being* and at the end of the treatise. After Dionysius explains the scriptural names related to God as the self-diffusive Good and Love (to which I will return), he treats the name Being. Dionysius reminds his reader of the principle of beyond-being-ness:

> *Let us now pass to the name "Being"—given in the Oracles as truly that of Him, Who truly is. But let us call to mind this much, that the purpose of our treatment is not to reveal the beyond-being being (τὴν ὑπερούσιον οὐσίαν), as it is beyond-being (ἣ ὑπερούσιος)—for this is ineffable (ἄρρητον), and unknowable (ἄγνωστόν), and altogether unrevealed, and surpassing union itself—but to hymn the procession (πρόοδον) of the supremely divine Source of Being, which gives being to all existing things.*[21]

Again, Dionysius insists, one cannot make manifest the beyond-being-ness of God ("the beyond-being being *as* beyond being") because it is ineffable, unintelligible, and unknowable. All one can do is rely on the words of the

---

19 Pseudo-Dionysius, *Divine Names*, 1.4.
20 The distinction between knowledge (*gnosis*) and intellection (*noesis*) is a difficult one to understand, but it is suggested by how Dionysius describes the knowledge (γνῶσις) of God beyond being as both "unknowing" (ἀγνωσία) and as "knowing beyond intellect" (γινώσκειν ὑπὲρ νοῦν).
21 Pseudo-Dionysius, *Divine Names*, 5.1.

Scriptures, which themselves do not even refer to God *as God is* beyond being but instead celebrate or "hymn" God's providential procession.[22]

We have already seen the final mention of God's beyond-being-ness forcefully proclaimed at the end of the treatise. In this last chapter, Dionysius is finishing up a discussion of the name One, which he says is not in opposition to the Christian mystery that God is both Unity and Trinity. In sum, he says, "We name the Deity, which is inexpressible to things that exist, the Beyond-Being."[23] That is, before Dionysius concludes the treatise by noting that the authors of Scripture teach negative statements about God as preferable to affirmative ones, he makes one final qualifying statement about God—God is "beyond being." This teaching is not a rehearsal of a scriptural name for God but the outcome of the "unfolding" of Scripture's conceptual names for God—the end of the *Divine Names*. That is, "beyond-being-ness" is exegetically wrought. Based on our unpacking of the theologians' hymns about God, Dionysius says, we claim that God, the "One," is "beyond being." But notice here that "beyond being" is also a stand-in for the Christian claim that God is Unity and Trinity. Alexander Golitzin has shown that Dionysius's reserve about divine intelligibility is foreshadowed, not only in Neoplatonic doctrine but also in earlier patristic writings on the Trinity.[24] In fact, Dionysius nearly always includes the adjective "beyond-being" (ὑπερούσιος) when invoking the Trinity. It is God as Trinity Itself that is ineffable, unintelligible, and unknown.[25]

---

22 For Proclus, *gnosis* beyond intellect was possible through initiation to the mysteries by rituals known as *theurgy* or "god-work," but this was knowledge of the henads/gods. For Dionysius, *agnosia* (unknowing), also known as *gnosis hyper noun* (knowing beyond intellect), was possible through Christian ritual, most importantly here, scriptural exegesis ("unfolding"). This is because Proclean *gnosis* is exclusively of the gods/henads, not the God/monad (who remains "unknown"), while Dionysian *agnosia/gnosis hyper noun* is of God. That is, Dionysian mysticism produces a "knowledge" of the Trinity always simplified or unified, never divided (following Nicaean orthodoxy), while Proclean mysticism strives to "know" a hierarchized divinity, where *gnosis* beyond intellect is of the henads/gods, and unknowing is of the monad/God. On "unknowing" and "knowing beyond mind," see ch. 5.
23 Pseudo-Dionysius, *Divine Names*, 13.3.
24 Alexander Golitzin, *Mystagogy: A Monastic Reading of Dionysius Areopagita* (Collegeville, MN: Cistercian, 2013), 59.
25 Here it is most clear that for Dionysius, beyond-being-ness cannot be a state devoid of meaning, as some readings of Plotinus's philosophy as a speculative enterprise

Thus, Dionysius forcefully depicts the distinction between God and being. The Trinity beyond being is hidden by a cloud of unknowing, removed from being and unintelligible.[26] A couple of lines of Dionysius's first Epistle are confirmation of the *Divine Names*' most frequent claim: "His pre-eminent (ὑπερκείμενον) darkness . . . is hidden from every knowledge (γνῶσιν)." And yet notice how the next line, which seems to drive home the point, ends in a curious way: "He himself, highly established above intellect and above being (ὑπὲρ νοῦν καὶ οὐσίαν), by the very fact of His being wholly unknown, and not being, both is in a way beyond being (ὑπερουσίως), and is known beyond intellect (ὑπὲρ νοῦν γινώσκεται)."[27] That is, Dionysius's doctrine of beyond-being-ness may be a negative doctrine, but it is not a privative one—it does not simply claim that God is "not being" and therefore cannot be known or experienced. The adverb "beyond-being-ly" (ὑπερουσίως) affirms that God exists or operates *in a way beyond being* and that God can therefore be known or experienced only beyond-being-ly or beyond intellect. That is, God is mystery in God's very mode of existence.

Providence (πρόνοια)

On the other hand, Dionysius's reservation about speech and knowledge moderates when it comes to God's providential activity. The constant reminders about beyond-being-ness qualify the ample descriptions of God's providential procession, the more proximate source, as it were, of divine names. As the following passage from the beginning of *Divine Names* shows, the divine names derive from God's providential activity. It appears to suggest the divine names do not actually hymn the God beyond being as beyond being: "To none, indeed, who are lovers of the Truth beyond all Truth, is it permitted to hymn the supremely-Divine Beyond-being-ness (ὑπερουσιότητα), whatever it is. . . . But since, as sustaining source of goodness, by the very fact of Its being, It is the cause of all things that exist (τῶν

---

make it, because Dionysius affirms the meaningful abundance of Trinitarian life, even if he remains largely (and tellingly) silent about it. How God's beyond-being-ness is meaningful, though, is harder to say.

26   Pseudo-Dionysius, *Mystical Theology*, 1.3, in *Corpus Dionysiacum II*, ed. Guenter Heil and Adolf Martin Ritter (Berlin: De Gruyter, 1991).
27   Pseudo-Dionysius, Epistle 1.

ὄντων αἰτία), from all created things we must hymn the benevolent Providence (πρόνοιαν) of the Godhead."[28]

Here again is the familiar claim that beyond-being-ness is ineffable. In contrast to God's beyond-being-ness (ὑπερουσιότης), however, is God's providence (πρόνοια). Scholars sometimes refer to this distinction as an "essence-energies" distinction, a claim that associates beyond-being-ness with the ineffable and unintelligible transcendent Trinitarian essence and providence with its speakable and intelligible energies, powers, or activities.[29] Is Dionysius saying that God's essence is ineffable, while God's energies can be spoken of? Would this not imply a distinction between God and some realm of knowable realities akin to the Neoplatonist Proclus's distinction between monad and henads?

It appears Dionysius thinks not. Dionysius writes that not only does the name *Good* uniquely apply to the whole divinity but also the divine names, while each derived from particular providences, nonetheless "are hymned (ὑμνεῖσθαι) upon (ἐπί) the whole and entire and complete and full Divinity," not only on individual intelligible realities.[30] *Divine Names* only treats those scriptural names derived from God's providence, ending with the name "Beyond-Being," though Dionysius ensures that beyond-being-ness is a constant complement to the reader's encounter with all the scriptural designations of God. Yet all divine names are hymns to God entirely, not just the divine energies (ἐνεργείαι) or powers (δυνάμεις) that appear throughout the writings. These powers *are* God. In the same passage, Dionysius writes, "If anyone should say that this is not spoken concerning the whole Deity, he blasphemes, and dares, without right, to cleave asunder the super-unified Unity."[31]

---

28   Pseudo-Dionysius, *Divine Names*, 1.5.
29   The essence-energies distinction is used primarily by Orthodox readers of Dionysius, who appeal to the Cappadocians as interpreted by Gregory Palamas (1296–1359). See the treatment of the work of John D. Jones below in ch. 4, 93–97.
30   Pseudo-Dionysius, *Divine Names*, 2.1. He goes on to note "that all of them are referred impartitively, absolutely, unreservedly, entirely, to all the Entirety of the entirely complete and every Deity."
     It is also worth noting how the construction (ἐπί + genitive) suggests that divine names are figuratively placed on or before God. As we will see, veils are the primary Dionysian metaphor for scriptural language.
31   Pseudo-Dionysius, *Divine Names*, 2.1.

One might be forgiven for thinking Dionysian theology manifests a divine intelligible world akin to Plotinus or even divine henads like Proclus. Providence "bubbles forth from the Deity beyond being (ὑπερουσίου), Cause of all things."[32] God "is present to all by the irresistible embrace of all, and by His providential progressions (προνοητικαῖς προόδοις) and energies (ἐνεργείαις) to all existing things."[33] Elsewhere, Dionysius lauds "the all holy and most honored Powers (δυνάμεις) truly being, and established, as it were, in the vestibule of the Triad beyond being."[34] This vestibule appears fairly crowded, where we find "those First Beings, who are established after the Godhead, who gave [the angels their] Being, and who are marshalled, as it were in Its very vestibule, who surpass every unseen and seen created power."[35] It is worth noting that although Dionysius uses multiple terms to describe God's intercourse with being—chief among them *energy*, *power*, and *providence*—he fairly consistently uses these in the singular to refer to their unity with the Godhead and the in plural to refer to their diffusion throughout being. As we will see, while these energies, powers, and providential progressions are hymned with divine names, because they are unified with the Godhead, they are not known. That is, they remain beyond being and unintelligible—even God's providential power is mysterious. A final passage drives home this point: "The supremely Divine Power (δύναμις) in visiting all, advances and penetrates all irresistibly, and yet is invisible (ἀφανὴς) to all, not only as being elevated above all in a way beyond being (ὑπερουσίως), but as secretly transmitting its providential energies (τὰς προνοητικὰς αὐτῆς ἐνεργείας) to all."[36]

This power "is everywhere and nowhere present."[37] If God's beyond-being-ness describes God as alone and isolated and removed from being, God's providence describes God's creating and sustaining power. Yet even providential activities, insists Dionysius, do not finally reveal the God beyond

---

32   Pseudo-Dionysius, *Celestial Hierarchy*, 4.1, in *Corpus Dionysiacum II*, ed. Guenter Heil and Adolf Martin Ritter (Berlin: De Gruyter, 1991).
33   Pseudo-Dionysius, *Divine Names*, 9.9.
34   Pseudo-Dionysius, *Divine Names*, 5.8.
35   Pseudo-Dionysius, *Celestial Hierarchy*, 7.2.
36   Pseudo-Dionysius, *Celestial Hierarchy*, 13.3.
37   Pseudo-Dionysius, *Divine Names*, 2.1.

being.[38] How can such a providential progression of the God beyond being remain unknown? Is it not an affirmation of divine intimacy, presence, and intelligibility? That is, what are we to make of the seeming paradox that being is shot through, as it were, with the presence of the God beyond being? How can God be *both* beyond being and providentially or causally present?

Good (ἀγαθος) and Love (ἔρως)

For Dionysius, Scripture (θεολογία) celebrates the God beyond being who is also present to being; it hymns the mysterious providence of God. The names Dionysius "unfolds" toward the beginning of the *Divine Names*—Good, Light, Beauty, Love, Ecstasy, and Jealousy—are the preeminent names of the "beyond-divine Deity."[39] Among these, Good and Love get the most attention. These divine names are those that hymn more comprehensively the procession of providential power from the beyond-being Source than other divine names, which seem to refer more narrowly to the providential powers themselves. This is a fine distinction but one that marks the difference between the preeminent divine names in the beginning of the treatise and those that start with Being in the middle. Thus, they are the names that get closest to properly significant affirmative speech about the God beyond being as they describe how such a God could become providentially present to being. What do they tell us about the basic relation of creation to God's beyond-being-ness?

---

38   Here I depart from Perl, *Theophany*, who claims that although *theophany* is not frequently employed by Dionysius—it appears more often in John Scotus Eriugena's interpretations of the Dionysian corpus—it is nonetheless the key to understanding the Neoplatonist Dionysius (see 32n25). Yet, for Dionysius, providence does not "reveal" the God beyond being. That God cannot be seen or grasped intellectually, even in God's causal presence. Perl claims that theophany is the logical consequence of the Neoplatonic principle that to be is to be intelligible. Everything that gets its being from the First Principle is thus revelatory of that First Principle. Yet, for Dionysius, to claim that God is providentially present in creation is to reveal nothing definitive about who God is, neither anything discursively representable nor anything intellectually graspable, because God remains beyond being, unmanifest (ἀφάνης). Dionysius dialectically presents divine presence alongside divine unintelligibility, so every *theophany* is therefore also an *aphany*; every unveiling is itself a veiling. Perl admits a simultaneous concealment with every revelation (see 17–34), but this gives me pause about *theophany* as an interpretive key to the corpus.

39   Pseudo-Dionysius, *Divine Names*, 4.1.

It is worth pausing here to highlight a related question. Why does Dionysius avoid the consistent negation of these preeminent names when he so systematically negates the other divine names throughout? That is, names from the middle of the treatise like Being, Intellect, and Life are often attached with a negative (α-) or *hyperochic* (ὑπερ-) prefix.[40] Yet God is never called "not-good." Although God is sparingly called "beyond good," God is never called "not-love" nor "beyond love." This question suggests implicitly what Dionysius says explicitly—that the first divine names in the treatise are in some way the preeminent or most excellent. In what way are they so? If the theologians use all sorts of divine names for God—names that ought not, Dionysius insists, be applied to only part of God—how do these names differ?[41] All this suggests that the language of love and goodness is uniquely suited to hymn the God beyond being, who is providentially present to being.

Dionysius, following the practice of the scripture-writing "theologians," does not shy from putting the preeminent divine names to work: "Let then the self-existent Goodness (αὐτοαγαθότης) be sung from the Oracles as defining and manifesting (ἐκφαίνουσα) the whole supremely-Divine Reality, whatever it is (ὅ τι ποτέ ἐστιν)."[42] Again, "let us examine the all-perfect

---

40 For example, Pseudo-Dionysius, *Divine Names*, 4.3: "But if the Good is beyond all things being, as indeed it is, and gives form to the formless, even in Itself alone (ἐν αὐτῷ μόνῳ), both the Non-Being is a *hyperbole* of being (τὸ ἀνούσιον οὐσίας ὑπερβολή), and the Non-Living *hyper*-has life (τὸ ἄζωον ὑπερέχουσα ζωή), and the Non-Intellect is a *hyper*-possessing wisdom (τὸ ἄνουν ὑπεραίρουσα σοφία)."

41 Again the comparison to a Neoplatonic predecessor is illuminating. Plotinus himself calls the One "lovable and love and love of himself, in that he is beautiful only from himself and in himself" without his typical "apophatic marker," *hoion*, anywhere in the passage. *Ennead*, VI.8.15.1–2. Plotinus's habit is to use an apophatic marker, which works something like Dionysius's consistent positing of "beyond-being-ness," as a reminder of the inadequacy of language for God. For the concept of apophatic marker, see Sells, *Mystical Languages of Unsaying*, 16–17. This habit is so consistent in Plotinus that John M. Rist, even in highlighting the place of Love in the Dionysian corpus by noting Neoplatonic precedent, mistakenly claims that Plotinus uses the apophatic marker when calling the One "Love" in VI.8.15. "Love, Knowing and Incarnation in Pseudo-Dionysius," in *Traditions of Platonism: Essays in Honour of John Dillon*, ed. John J. Cleary (Aldershot: Ashgate, 1999), 376. Dionysius, like Plotinus, shows nothing of his typical reserve when it comes to using the language of love for God.

42 Pseudo-Dionysius, *Divine Names*, 2.1.

Name of Goodness, which is revealing of the whole progressions (προόδων) of Almighty God, having invoked the supremely good, and beyond-good Triad—the Name revealing Its whole best Providences (προνοιῶν)."[43] That is, Good is the divine name that evokes the progression of the Trinity in providential energies that create and sustain existing things. It directs one to all of God's providential activities in creating and sustaining all that participates in being and even describes providence as it includes things not existing. That is, in relation to other names, *Good* is the preeminent term, one that celebrates God as more than the divine name *Being* expresses.

In addition, the name Good does not only apply to God as creating and sustaining cause of being, and therefore exceeding the bounds of being. It also applies to God as the end of all being: "Goodness turns all things to Itself . . . and it is the Good, as the Oracles say, from Which all things subsisted, and are being brought into being by an all-perfect Cause; and in Which all things consisted, as guarded and governed in an all-controlling route; and to Which all things are turned, as to their own proper end; and to Which all aspire."[44] That is, when the theologians call God *Good*, they affirm that God creates and sustains all things by his providence "bubbling forth" and directs all things back to that Source.

Though contemporary scholars recognize a resonance here with the Proclean dynamic of procession, remaining, and return, Dionysius draws on scriptural language to describe how the Good beyond being both produces being and calls being back to itself.[45] Notice how the end of this passage calls the Good that "to Which all aspire." Dionysius describes the movement of divine goodness with the most unreservedly and consistently cataphatic language in the corpus. Love—a further designation of the Good—is the key to the procession of the God beyond being, which nevertheless remains in itself and which draws all being back to itself in its return.

---

43   Pseudo-Dionysius, *Divine Names*, 3.1.
44   Pseudo-Dionysius, *Divine Names*, 4.4.
45   McGinn, *Foundations of Mysticism*, 162; Perl, *Theophany*, 35–52. Both McGinn and Perl emphasize the Proclean dynamic while also discussing divine Goodness and Love, but neither identifies a connection between the two. Dionysius is clearly influenced by Proclus, using the logic of procession, remaining, and return, but he casts this as characteristic of divine loving goodness.

The theologians use the divine name *Love* (*Eros*, ἔρως) to hymn God. Yet Dionysius is aware this may seem surprising to the reader. Is it not unfitting or dishonorable to attribute erotic love to God? Surely the more frequent scriptural designation of God as *Agape*—love that is characterized by selfless giving—is more fitting since it is a term that does not connote desire akin to that of carnal relations. Yet, Dionysius insists, the theologians seem to have treated the names *Agape* and *Eros* as equivalent.[46] Therefore, Dionysius refuses to distinguish between the two terms. This elision of divine *Agape* and divine *Eros* explains how Dionysius can proclaim the apparently Proclus-inspired movement of the God beyond being as procession, remaining, and return. How is this so? Consider what Dionysius perceives to be the nature of both goodness and agapic-erotic love. They are both productive and attractive. He writes:

> *Further, it may be boldly said with truth, that even the very Cause of all things, by reason of overflowing Goodness (δι' ἀγαθότητος ὑπερβολὴν), loves (ἐρᾷ) all, makes all, perfects all, sustains all, attracts all; and even the Divine Love (ἔρως) is Good from Good through the Good. For Love itself, the force working good for existing things, pre-existing overflowingly in the Good, did not permit itself to remain unproductive in itself, but moved itself to creation, as befits the overflow which is generative of all.*[47]

In addition, this productivity is self-diffusive, allowing itself to be drawn: "The very Cause of all things, by the beautiful and good love of everything, through an overflow (ὑπερβολὴν) of his loving goodness, becomes out of Himself, by His providences (προνοίαις) for all existing things, and is, as it were, cozened by goodness and affection (ἀγαπήσει) and love, and is led down from the Eminence above all, and surpassing all, to being in all, as befits an ecstatic power beyond being centered in Itself."[48]

That is, creation, its sustaining, and its return to God are all understood to be activities of Divine Love. Love leads the Good to create and

---

46 Pseudo-Dionysius, *Divine Names*, 4.12.
47 Pseudo-Dionysius, *Divine Names*, 4.10.
48 Pseudo-Dionysius, *Divine Names*, 4.13.

sustain creation, continually pouring out its providential energies with agapic abandon.[49] This is the result of God's abounding goodness, but it is also an ecstatic drawing of God *beyond* or *out of* Godself, so to speak. God abounds with goodness and so overflows, *and* God is pulled out of Godself by desire for creation. That is, God both grants being its creation and sustenance by pouring Godself out and is drawn to be present to being by desire for it, reflecting the elision of the agapic and the erotic. Good is by nature overflowing, self-diffusive. Love is by nature creative and ecstasy-inducing: "Divine Love is ecstatic, not permitting any to be lovers of themselves, but of those beloved."[50] Thus, the force of Love accounts for the continued presence of the God beyond being. In fact, the last of the preeminent divine names praises God as *Jealous* for creation.[51]

In sum, the Good beyond being relates to being as Love. The name Love, affirmed by the theologians, is a way of unfolding or interpreting the divine name Goodness, which, as for Plato in the *Republic*, must, by nature as Cause, be beyond being. Ultimately, Dionysius never addresses the dialectical tension inherent in the repeated claim that the God beyond being is present to being through Providence. This is a mystery experienced by the theologians, and Dionysius does not refer to the divine name Love as resolving this tension. Rather, it heightens or highlights it. Good and Love describe the mode of God's beyond-being-ness, how the beyond-being is present to being. In hymning the mystery of Divine Love and unfolding its name, Dionysius begins to engage his reader in a process of coming to "know" the God of mystery. The Victorines would find in Dionysius's writings on divine names a set of theoretical tools for the relationship between the God of Love and the letter.

---

49   Also, to those who "reproach" and "depart from Him," he "clings lovingly (ἐρωτικῶς ἔχεται)" and "further promises to serve them, and runs towards and meets [them] . . . and when His entire self has embraced their entire selves, He kisses them." Pseudo-Dionysius, Epistle 8.1.
50   Pseudo-Dionysius, *Divine Names*, 4.13. As the longer quote above makes clear, the "any" here includes both God and the creature. Divine Love does not allow God to love Godself alone, and it pulls the creature out of itself.
51   Pseudo-Dionysius, *Divine Names*, 4.13.

The Mystery of God at St. Victor

How did the Dionysian theology of God's mystery translate at St. Victor? What did Victorines like John Saracen and Thomas Gallus see in this theology of God? As we have seen, Dionysius's teaching about divine beyond-being-ness followed centuries of Neoplatonic developments and was supported by what he took to be compatible scriptural witness. To a surprising degree, given their unfamiliarity with the Neoplatonic sources, the Victorines rehearsed the philosophical reasoning and embraced the reading of Scripture that emphasized God's beyond-being-ness, goodness, and love. John Saracen's new translation made possible the encounter with God's beyond-being-ness (ὑπερουσιότης), though now through a set of Latin terms. Prime among them are vocabulary clusters describing God's super-essentiality (*superessentialitas*) and super-substantiality (*supersubstantialitas*), the terms John uses to translate beyond-being-ness (ὑπερουσιότης).[52] Thomas Gallus largely accepted Dionysius's take on divine beyond-being-ness, unintelligibility, and ineffability, situating it in the context of Augustinian sign theory and highlighting Trinitarian plenitude or abundance. Thomas Gallus's theology of God, then, does not innovate greatly on Dionysian mystical theology but shows how adaptable it was to the Victorine milieu. The God of mystery, as we will see, fits well within a reading culture already devoted to the letter.

Superessentialitas and Supersubstantialitas

John Saracen's translation and Thomas Gallus's commentaries embrace Dionysian beyond-being-ness at St. Victor, surprising given that scholars of medieval Latin theology have often assumed that alternatives to ontotheology (or the theology of being) in Latin cultures were few.[53] In fact, the embrace of Dionysius at St. Victor suggests there was a lot more room for God's mysterious beyond-being-ness in Latin theology than has been

---

52   Gallus used John Saracen's "new" translation in conjunction with Eriugena's "old" or "other" translation, and both texts laid out a language of beyond-being-ness that mimicked Dionysius's Greek closely. See Tichelkamp, "Mystical Theology and/in Translation," 41–42, 48–51.

53   Declan Lawell notes this in "Affective Excess: Ontology and Knowledge in the Thought of Thomas Gallus," *Dionysius* 26 (2008): 139–74.

previously recognized. Gallus proves his robust understanding of the Dionysian concept. For instance, when Dionysius states that God "dwells above (*supra*) all things," Gallus writes this "means beyond one and oneness, being and being-ness (*super unum et unitatem et ens et entitatem*)."[54] Where Dionysius invokes "the super-substantial Trinity," Gallus adds "incomparably super-exceeding all substance (*substantiam*) and all being (*ens*)."[55] In a more extended discussion, Gallus works out Dionysian beyond-being-ness: "**God is set apart from substance** through an incomparable and infinite departure (*excessum*); **and** nevertheless is **simply super-substantial** . . . because the deity subsists eternally without any accidental or substantial mode of existence, but not without goodness (*bonitate*)."[56]

In these glosses are many of the hallmarks of Dionysian beyond-being-ness that we have seen. God is separated from the regular order of all things existing, including substance and being-ness itself. Just as the prefix *hyper-* (ὑπερ-) and preposition *hyper* (ὑπέρ) pervaded the Greek corpus, the Latin prefix *super-* and preposition *super* litter John's translation of the text,

---

54   Thomas Gallus, *Explanatio super Mystica Theologia* 1, in *Explanatio in Libros Dionysii*, ed. Declan Anthony Lawell, Corpus Christianorum Continuatio Mediaevalis 223 (Turnhout, Belgium: Brepols, 2011), 26.

55   Gallus, *Explanatio super Mystica Theologia* 1, 8. Gallus often lumps together technical terms related to being, having heard from a Greek speaker that the Greek τὸ ὄν is often incorrectly translated *ens* (as noted by Coolman, *Eternally Spiraling into God*, 40n44). As Jones has shown in "*The Divine Names* in John Sarracen's Translation: Misconstruing Dionysius' Language about God," *American Catholic Philosophical Quarterly* 82, no.4 (2008): 661–82, John Saracen often used different Latin terms than Eriugena when it came to the philosophical rhetoric of being and beyond-being-ness. Because Gallus consulted both translations, he does not seem to carefully distinguish between terms like *substantia*, *ens*, *entitas*, and *esse*, and it is safe to understand these terms as variously translating Greek terms like οὐσία and τὸ ὄν. For instance, for *beyond-being-ness* (ὑπερουσιότης), Eriugena used *superessentialitas*, while John Saracen used *supersubstantialitas*. I have not been able to work out any meaningful distinctions between these terms in Gallus's commentaries. He apparently uses them largely interchangeably when glossing the rhetoric of being and beyond-being-ness.

56   Thomas Gallus, *Explanatio de Divinis Nominibus* 4, in *Explanatio in Libros Dionysii*, ed. Declan Anthony Lawell, Corpus Christianorum Continuatio Mediaevalis 223 (Turnhout, Belgium: Brepols, 2011), 270: "**Et Deus segregatur a substantia** *per incomparabilem et infinitum excessum;* **et** *tamen est* **supersubstantialis simpliciter** . . . *quia ad minus deitas sine omni habitu accidentali et substantiali eternaliter subsistit, sed non sine bonitate.*"

ensuring his rendering of God's beyond-being-ness was just as thorough. Finally, God's beyond-being-ness or super-substantiality is closely related to God's goodness, which is predicated of God without reservation.[57]

Gallus expounds on God's beyond-being-ness (*superessentialitas*) while considering the divine name Being (*esse*), which is the first divine name after the preeminent names of Good and Love. Gallus is unaware of the Neoplatonic provenance of beyond-being-ness and claims it is a special insight of those advanced in Christian wisdom. The uninitiated, Dionysius says in *Mystical Theology*, think "nothing exists super-substantially beyond existing things (*super existentia*)." Gallus adds that these "philosophers of the world" think being (*ens*) is all that exists and is the proper subject of metaphysics (*subjectum metaphysice*).[58] Exhibiting a characteristic appreciation for secular philosophy's potential, however circumscribed, Gallus argues there is, in fact, some scriptural witness for their position exalting being to such a privileged place. He asks, "What is 'He who is' if not being?"[59] That is, Exodus 3:14—"He who is sent me to you"—seemed to provide scriptural warrant for pagan philosophy's exaltation of Being. God may be called Being, as Dionysius also taught in the *Divine Names*. Nevertheless, Gallus continues in the same gloss, God is ineffable (*ineffabilis*) and unnamable (*innominabilis*), beyond being and understanding (*super ens et intellectum*).[60] While God has given himself the name "He who is," the divine name of Being, one ought not think that God is any kind of speakable or thinkable being or substance. Despite the scriptural justification for

---

57   On which, see below, 78–81. Despite the difference with Thomas Aquinas, Gallus is not the only medieval investigator of Platonism who makes much of the distinction between the Good and Being, indicating that for at least some medieval Latin Platonists, the Good is beyond Being not only conceptually but really. Berthold of Moosburg, a Dominican like Aquinas, between 1327 and 1361, makes this claim. Jan A. Aertsen, "Platonism," in *Cambridge History of Medieval Philosophy*, ed. Robert Pasnau (Cambridge: Cambridge University Press, 2010), 1:76–85. Berthold had the advantage of knowing Proclus's writings, but Gallus seems to have made the same conclusion that the Good was beyond Being from the order of divine names in Dionysius's treatise as well as his frequent invocation of *beyond-being-ness*.
58   Gallus, *Explanatio super Mystica Theologia* 1, 19.
59   Gallus, *Explanatio super Mystica Theologia* 1, 20: "*Quid est enim 'Qui est' nisi ens?*"
60   Gallus, *Explanatio super Mystica Theologia* 1, 20.

using the name Being of God, the philosophers of the world who exalt Being lack the wisdom of Christians who understand the ambiguous use of such a name given God's beyond-being-ness. If Gallus embraces the Dionysian divine name Being for the God beyond being, we must ask: how does he think about its use?

Let's look at the major passages on beyond-being-ness in the *Divine Names* that we treated earlier. There we noted that God's beyond-being-ness (ὑπερουσιότης), a term coined by Dionysius himself, was invoked at key junctures in the text—most notably in the first chapter, at the beginning of the fifth chapter (at the transition from preeminent names to the name Being), and at the end of the treatise. In the first chapter, Dionysius ties "unknowing (*ignorantia*)" to "beyond-being-ness (*supersubstantialitas*)" since God is beyond reason, intellect, and being (*super rationem et intellectum et ipsam substantiam*). Gallus glosses the terms. *Supersubstantialitas* is "the divinity which is unknown and excels beyond all being (*enti*)."[61] For God to be

---

61 Gallus, *Explanatio de Divinis Nominibus* 1, 59: "**Ignorantie supersubstantialitatis**, *id est divinitatis que ignoratur et omni enti supereminet.*" Notice that beyond-being-ness, for Gallus, does not refer to the way God "possesses" being preeminently. In this, he contrasts with a more well-known reader of the Dionysian corpus, Thomas Aquinas. Aquinas concluded that these *super-* terms indicate God possesses the attributes preeminently. Dionysius is not clear on the matter, as we saw above. Thus, on this issue, I disagree with the characterization of Dionysius by Knepper, *Negating Negation*, and the characterization of Gallus by Coolman, *Eternally Spiraling into God*. Both put forth an interpretation of Dionysian theology on this issue that is closer to Aquinas. As we will see, although Coolman is on firmer ground with Gallus thanks to Gallus's rhetoric of divine plenitude and abundance, I will argue that even this should not be taken to indicate a preeminent possession. That God is Being is only said because God is the cause of being and is beyond being.

Neither, however, do I hold that Gallus reads Dionysius as a thoroughgoing speculative Plotinian, advancing a kind of negative purity of the One where any affirmation of God must be entirely removed. He wasn't aware of the influence of Neoplatonic philosophical reasoning. Rather, Gallus's concern is to keep the attention on God's Word, which issues from God's good beyond-being-ness but, in creating and restoring the world, gives one the language that allows for hymning the God beyond being. Both concepts—God's "preeminent possession" and the One's "negative purity"—belie Gallus's concern with depicting theological language as working equivocally but potently to transform the intellect and the affect of the reader or hearer. They both risk resolving God's mystery, something Gallus never does.

beyond *substantia* is to be beyond "the very being (*ens*) which is first and highest in understanding, and beyond which intellectual and worldly philosophy seeks or investigates nothing."[62] Here it appears Gallus firmly grasps both the concept of beyond-being-ness and the Neoplatonic principle that ties intelligibility to being. God is beyond being and therefore unintelligible.

At the beginning of his fifth chapter, Dionysius reminds his reader of God's beyond-being-ness, just as he has finished his treatment of the divine names Good and Love and is transitioning to the divine name Being. Gallus's gloss of the passage echoes the Neoplatonic logic: "**The intention of our discourse**, that is, we intend in this treatise **not to manifest**, that is, to lead to intellectual cognition, **the super-substantial substance, according to how it is super-substantial**, that is, the divinity according to how it is in itself above all substance and cognition . . . **for this is unknown and perfectly not manifested** to all understanding."[63]

Gallus is aware that even the name Being, which is about to be treated, does not give one an intellectual understanding or knowledge of God as beyond being, which can only be unknown. Intellectual cognition is only possible of *substantia*, which God is far beyond (*super*). The language of super-substantiality or beyond-being-ness is connected closely to what the divinity is "in itself (*in se*)," which can be distinguished from what the divinity is "outside itself (*extra se*)."[64] The divine name Being, like all divine names after it, either refers to God as the cause of Being or refers super-essentially to God as not Being. That is, Being describes God *extra se* but not *in se*.

Dionysius's final invocation of beyond-being-ness at the end of *Divine Names* gave Gallus a chance to consider the relation between God's beyond-being-ness and ineffability.

---

62 Gallus, *Explanatio de Divinis Nominibus* 1, 59: "*Ipsum ens quod primum est in intellectu et summum et extra quod nihil querit aut investigat philosophia intellectualis et mundane.*"

63 Gallus, *Explanatio de Divinis Nominibus* 5, 326: "**Intentio est sermoni** *nostro, id est intendimus in hoc tractatu,* **non manifestare**, *id est ad cognitionem intellectualem deducere,* **substantiam supersubstantialem secundum quod est supersubstantialis**, *id est divinitatem secundum quod in se est super omnem substantiam et cognitionem, sicut dicitur MT 1b.* **Hoc enim ignotum est et perfecte non manifestum** *omni intelligentie.*"

64 See Coolman, *Eternally Spiraling into God*, 56ff.

> **But in order that truly** *in a universal way* **we may praise** *in some way according to our capacity* **the super-union,** *that is, the unity exceeding all things,* **of it** *divinity,* **and the generation of God,** *that is, the generation of the Word of God, in which is understood also the breath of the Holy Spirit proceeding from the Father and the Son. Therefore* **we name the super-nameable,** *that is, God exceeding every name and every act of naming,* **with the naming of God the Trinity and Unity,** *by saying that God is one in essence and three in persons,* **and by existing things,** *that is, we praise God with names of things existing* **as the "super-essential."**[65]

Here again is a rehearsal of familiar reasoning. God the Trinity and Unity, Dionysius suggested, is best named as *beyond being* or *super-essential*. God's ineffability or unnameability, like God's unintelligibility, is closely tied to God's beyond-being-ness.

Besides the close association of beyond-being-ness or super-substantiality with unintelligibility and ineffability, Gallus also recognized the causal logic that leads one to affirm beyond-being-ness in the first place. God, Gallus affirms, is the first cause or principle of being (*esse*). Being (*esse*) is "not properly attributed to the first cause," but instead "to be" (*esse*) is simply "to flow from the first cause, because it naturally goes forth."[66] Here is the Platonic insight that being itself must have a greater cause than itself. This first cause naturally issues in being and so must be beyond being. Gallus, not

---

65   Gallus, *Explanatio de Divinis Nominibus* 13, 465: "**Sed ut vere** *catholice* **laudemus** *aliquatenus secundum nostrum possibilitatem* **superunitum,** *id est unitatem omnia excedentem,* **ipsius** *divinitatis,* **et Dei genitum,** *id est generationem Verbi Dei, in qua intelligitur et spiratio Spiritus Sancti a Patre et Filio procedentis. Ideo* **nominamus supernominabilem,** *id est Deum excedentem omne nomen et omnem nominationem,* **Dei nominatione Trinitatis et unitatis,** *dicendo Deum esse unum in essentia et trinum in personis,* **et existentibus,** *id est nominibus existentium laudamus Deum* **superessentialem.**"

66   Thomas Gallus, *Explanatio super Angelica Ierarchia* 1, in *Explanatio in Libros Dionysii*, ed. Declan Anthony Lawell, Corpus Christianorum Continuatio Mediaevalis 223 (Turnhout, Belgium: Brepols, 2011), 485–86: "*Verumtamen esse improprie attribuitur prime cause, nec enim vere bonum usque ad esse descendit, nec vere malum, scilicet peccati deformitas, peruenit usque ad esse. Esse siquidem est a prima causa fluere, quod naturaliter precedit et agere et pati.*"

knowing of this Platonic provenance, thought this was an insight of Christians, who knew that being was not all there was and who experienced God beyond what metaphysical speculation could produce. This God, Dionysius affirmed, was beyond being, or super-essential. However, just as Gallus thoroughly embraces the Dionysian Neoplatonic concept and logic of beyond-being-ness, he also has a firm grasp on Dionysian divine presence. Before turning to God's causal presence, however, two of Gallus's qualifications of Dionysian beyond-being-ness should be noted.

First, one typically Victorine way that Gallus qualifies Dionysius's depiction of God's beyond-being-ness, ineffability, and unintelligibility is in situating these concepts within the Augustinian concern with signification (*significatio*).[67] God's beyond-being-ness makes proper signification impossible. When Dionysius writes that "we do not know its super-substantial, incomprehensible, and ineffable infinity," Gallus responds there is a breakdown in the process of signification: "It is necessary that the one who signifies and the one to whom it is signified understand the signification of the word or letter to some extent."[68] That is, a central premise of Augustinian signification theory is that language can effectively communicate only when the speaker and hearer agree on a system of reference in which they both have a common understanding of the thing (*res*) referred to and agree that a particular word or sign (*signum*) customarily points to that thing. God is not something that can be understood or signified in the way existing things can. In turn, Gallus thoroughly embraces the Dionysian preference for negations as a naturally superior form of speaking about God. A negative term, using the *super-* prefix, "suggests to us the knowledge of God (whatever sort it is) less improperly, less defectively, and somehow more effectively."[69] Put in terms of Augustinian signification theory, negative terms are more capable

---

67   See ch. 2, 17–21.
68   Gallus, *Explanatio super Angelica Ierarchia* 2, 513: "**Ignoramus infinitatem ipsius supersubstantialem et incomprehensibilem et ineffabilem**. *Quod autem penitus ignoramus nec possumus aliis significare nec potest nobis ab aliis significari. Necesse est enim et significantem et cui significatur aliquatenus intelligere vocis vel littere significationem.*"
69   Gallus, *Explanatio super Angelica Ierarchia* 2, 513: "*Minus improprie, minus defective et quodammodo efficacius nobis insinuat qualemcumque Dei notitiam.*"

of signifying the God beyond being because more certain agreement and understanding can be had of what God is not.[70]

Second, Gallus's treatment of divine beyond-being-ness is even more thoroughly Trinitarian than Dionysius.[71] When beyond-being-ness appears in the texts, Gallus tends to associate it with the inner life or dynamic of the Trinity turned in on itself (*in se*), in contrast to the outpouring of Trinitarian activity in being (*esse*).[72] God is called "beyond-being-ness (*superessentialitas*) because of the fact that he is in his nature beyond every cognition, and he is being turned back to itself, not proceeding to things."[73] Here, God's beyond-being-ness is turned toward itself. That is, Gallus casts beyond-being-ness as Trinitarian self-referentiality, that which is beyond any human cognition since it belongs only to God. Not only is beyond-being-ness about separation or transcendence, but it is also the mode of existence belonging only to God as Trinity, knowable by the human being only by union and assimilation to God: "For in itself it [God's *superessentialitas*] is not known by intellect but by union."[74] Just as God had told Moses to provide the people a name for him ("He who is"), God provided the name "I am who I am" to Moses alone, whom Gallus thinks attained a "knowing" beyond being.[75] Gallus's concern with signification and his Trinitarianism do not mark a great departure from

---

70   Although other strategies of signifying in a purposefully ambiguous way can also work. Compare Gallus's gloss of the Song of Songs' construction "Whom my soul loves," which he took to be an attempt to signify the Word experienced and therefore "known" by the bride. Those who have experienced can in a way signify to others with the same experience. Ch. 5, 171–72.

71   Though, for one reading of Dionysius that insists on the centrality of earlier Trinitarian thought to his treatment of divine unintelligibility and ineffability, see Golitzin, *Mystagogy*.

72   For an extended discussion of Gallus's Trinitarianism, especially a useful distinction between *ecstasis* and *enstasis* as modes of Trinitarian activity, see Coolman, *Eternally Spiraling into God*, 31–74.

73   Gallus, *Explanatio de Divinis Nominibus* 4, 290: "*Dicitur enim vera entitas vel superessentialitas secundum quod est in natura sua super omnem cognitionem, et est esse in se reflexum, non ad res procedens.*"

74   Gallus, *Explanatio de Divinis Nominibus* 4, 290: "*Secundum se enim non cognoscitur intellective sed unitive.*"

75   Gallus, *Explanatio de Divinis Nominibus* 4, 290. Exodus 3:14: "*Ego sum qui sum.*"

the Dionysian doctrine of beyond-being-ness but suggest how the Victorines adapted the Dionysian theology of God.

Causality and Presence: Plenitudo, Habundantia, Bonitas, Amor

Just as Gallus embraced God's beyond-being-ness (and unintelligibility and ineffability), he also rehearsed and explained its Dionysian counterpoint, God's causal presence. As we saw above, the Dionysian affirmation of divine causality and presence was not antithetical to the affirmation of divine beyond-being-ness but intimately related to it. Because a cause must be greater than its effect, the Neoplatonic reasoning held, each existing thing, including being itself, must have a cause better than itself that is not itself. Consequently, Plato referred to the First Cause as the *Good beyond being*. As it was expressed by Dionysius and embraced by Thomas Gallus, beyond-being-ness (*supersubstantialitas*) became a shorthand for this insight as to be beyond being was to be the good source or cause of being. As we have seen, Dionysius's treatment of the divine name Being consistently drew on this philosophical logic. God was called 'Being' only insofar as God was the beyond-being cause of being.

John Saracen's new translation of the Dionysian corpus conveyed the central elements of this reasoning. It affirmed, for instance, that "the divinity which is beyond being (*super esse*) is the being (*esse*) of all things."[76] Or, as Gallus points out, the "old" translation put it this way: "The being (*esse*) of all things is the super-substantial (*supersubstantialis*) divinity." The alternate translations did not trip Gallus up. He proves he understands the Dionysian logic: the God beyond being is being "in a causal and super-essential manner (*causaliter et superessentialiter*)."[77] That is, Being is attributed to God only in the sense that God is the cause of being and therefore beyond being. In fact, Gallus affirms, it is God's "plenitude of super-substantiality itself from which being (*ens*) itself or being (*esse*) in general emanates causally."[78]

---

76   Pseudo-Dionysius, *Celestial Hierarchy*, 4.1: "τὸ γὰρ εἶναι πάντων ἐστὶν ἡ ὑπὲρ τὸ εἶναι θεότης"; John Saracen: "*Etenim esse omnium est que super esse est deitas*"; John Scotus Eriugena: "*Esse enim omnium est supersubstantialis divinitatis.*"
77   Gallus, *Explanatio super Angelica Ierarchia* 4, 556.
78   Gallus, *Explanatio de Divinis Nominibus* 5, 334: "*Plenitudo superessentialitatis, a qua ipsum ens vel esse in generali causaliter emanat.*"

Super-substantiality or beyond-being-ness describes the transcendent Trinitarian condition for God's causality—an insight Gallus associates not with Neoplatonism or even Plato himself but with the Christian wisdom of Dionysius, the "Treasury of the Apostle."[79] Dionysius conveyed the teaching that God is the beyond-being cause of being.

Gallus's glossing of Dionysian super-essential causality as a matter of plenitude (*plenitudo*) is his most significant elaboration or innovation on the Neoplatonic logic. At first glance, the rhetoric of plenitude appears at odds with the affirmation of beyond-being-ness or transcendence. Is God beyond being or full of being? For Gallus, the terms *plenitude* and *abundance* (*habundantia*) point to the causal efficacy of the God beyond being. While God the cause of being should be affirmed to be beyond being, it is this very beyond-being-ness that is greater and better than being, as the cause of being. Gallus uses the rhetoric of plenitude to evoke how the Neoplatonist Dionysius's affirmation of beyond-being-ness is a function of or intimately related to divine causality. Even though he was unaware of its Neoplatonic provenance, Gallus echoed an aspect of the Neoplatonic logic often overlooked. God's beyond-being-ness could not be abstracted from God's causality. What was caused flowed, as it were, from the Good, which itself could not be known intellectually. As the very condition of divine causality and presence, God's *supersubstantialitas* simply was the ultimate principle or first cause of all being—*ens, esse, substantia*. This is what makes the term *beyond-being-ness* differ from the modern term *transcendence*. Beyond-being-ness is not characteristic of a capricious and removed God choosing to act from a distance but the very condition of the cosmos's ordered dependence on its divine source—the "fullness" from which providence progresses. It was the mysterious Cause of all things, which are in turn imbued with divine mystery, so to speak.[80]

---

79   Gallus, *Explanatio super primam epistolam ad Gaium*, 717.
80   This does not mean we can say about God's *supersubstantialitas* that it "possesses" anything in a "preeminent" manner. The most we can say is that it is the mysterious source, origin, or principle from which all forms of God's causal presence come. God's "fullness" or "abundance" does not capture God's mystery, only our experience of its graciousness and beneficence. Thus, my account of plenitude in Thomas Gallus differs from the "preeminent possession" position of Coolman in *Eternally Spiraling into God*, 38–43.

Just as we saw above, in Dionysian theology, God's superabundant beyond-being-ness is most closely approximated by the divine names Good and Love. Gallus found the break between the *Divine Names*' fourth chapter on Good and the fifth on Being significant. He writes that "after [Dionysius] treated in the fourth chapter about the Good than which nothing higher or better can be thought among the spectacles (*theoriae*) of eternal Wisdom, he continues down to existence (*existentiam*), which is the first emanation from goodness, as it were."[81] Gallus recognized that Good is more properly attributed to the pre-causality, as it were, of the God beyond being or the Trinity *in se*. The transition from the Trinity *in se* to the Trinity *extra se*, or from God's pre-causality to causality, was a central concern of Gallus, even if these were perhaps more conceptually than really distinct. We will see that his preferred metaphor for describing this transition is that of communication. Even the language of procession—so awkward for Neoplatonist Christians, whose accounts of creation tended to avoid the emanationist logic of their pagan predecessors—shows up in Gallus's glosses: "God, existing super-essentially and eternally, fixedly and immobile in his own goodness (*bonitate*), processes out through the communication of his own goodness."[82] God, or "the Good," is that which pours forth in creating out of its plenitude and as a function of its goodness.

By this point, it should be no surprise that Gallus also appropriates the Dionysian logic of Divine Love, which was meant to describe this dynamic: "Love is so great in power that not only does it draw the human being out of himself toward God, but, if it is permissible to say, it draws God out of himself toward the human being, as it were, so that it may unite those things that are distant to the infinite."[83] That is, the Dionysian elision of agapic and

---

81 Gallus, *Explanatio de Divinis Nominibus* 5, 325: "*Postquam enim in quarto capitulo tractauit de bono, quo nihil anterius aut superius cogitabile est in eterne sapientie theoriis, descendit ad existentiam que est quasi prima emanatio a bonitate.*"

82 Gallus, *Explanatio de Divinis Nominibus* 4, 247: "*Deus in sua bonitate superessentialiter et eternaliter existens fixe et immobiliter, sine ulla sui mutatione ad existentia per sue bonitatis communicationem procedit.*"

83 Gallus, *Explanatio super Mystica Theologia* 1, 6: "*Tante autem virtutis est dilectio ut non tantum hominem extra se ad Deum sed, si fas est dicere, quasi Deum extra se trahit ad hominem ut in infinitum distantes uniat.*"

erotic love made possible a cumulative vision of divine activity in terms of the dynamic of love. Whether articulated as creation, procession, or communication, the movement from beyond being to being, the presence of God to being, was best accounted for with the divine name Love. We saw above how important Love (*Eros*) is to the Dionysian theology of God, and it is not shocking that Gallus found in the Song of Songs a model of its effects.

Yet for all this causal activity—the plenitude and abundance, goodness and love—Gallus echoes Dionysius in his constant reminder of the unintelligibility of God, even as cause: "It is necessary to attribute to him (as if the cause of all things) every form, figure, essence, and creature altogether, but to attribute nothing to him as if he were subjected, but rather to rightly and truly remove all things from him."[84] Though God is the Cause, God is so only super-essentially or super-substantially. Even the "presence of God (*presentia Dei*)," Gallus insists, "exceeds every understanding, coming down upon those first essences and manifest to the rest through them."[85] We again return to the Dionysian theology of God: the presence of God does not reveal God. Rather, as we will see in the following chapter, Gallus elaborates on Dionysian creation, manifestation, and presence primarily through situating them in an Augustinian theology of the Word communicated by God.

Conclusion: Letter as Mystical Veil

This chapter has begun explaining a second strand of theology to arrive at St. Victor—Dionysian mystical theology. Under the influence of Dionysius, the Victorines embraced the beyond-being-ness of God. Mystical theology did not just proclaim God's unintelligibility and ineffability, though. Rather,

---

84 Gallus, *Explanatio super Mystica Theologia* 1, 22: "*Oportet omnem formam vel figuram vel essentiam et omnem omnino creaturam ipsi attribuere tamquam omnium cause, nihil autem ei attribuere tamquam subiecto, sed potius ab eo omnia proprie et ueraciter remouere.*"
85 Gallus, *Explanatio super Mystica Theologia* 1, 27: "*Et Dei presentia, que omnem superat intellectum, superueniens illis primis essentiis per eas manifestatur aliis.*" Moderating Dionysius's Neoplatonic view of presence, for Gallus, presence is a matter of causal efficacy and is manifested through the eternal reasons. This is the reason for his extensive elaboration of the soul's hierarchy and the Word's *theoriae*. Knowing or experiencing God's presence requires the Word's mediating activity. On the mental hierarchy and the Word's *theoriae*, see ch. 5.

it articulated the intimate relation between the God beyond being and creation, tying God's mystery to God's creating and sustaining powers, in effect, mystifying the God who is present to all creation. In mystical theology, creation was shot through, as it were, with the mystery of God. In turn, as we will see, the letter must be a vehicle for conveying God's mysterious presence. What happened when Dionysian mystical theology came into contact with the Victorine theology of the letter? What effects did mystical theology have on the Victorines' reading culture, already centered on the letter? While this chapter focused on the Dionysian theology of God's mystery, the next will begin to show how the two strands of theology—the theology of the letter and mystical theology—wove themselves together, slowly imbuing the letter with a sense of divine mystery.

The theology of God's hidden mystery led Dionysius to a favorite metaphor for the letter: the veil. Dionysius claims that when it comes to the God beyond being, who is present to creation, human beings need appropriate or fitting guidance, which comes through "the divine beneficence of the scriptures and hierarchical traditions." That is, letter and liturgy are "holy veils (*sancta velamina*)" that cover over divine things by "placing forms and figures over those things which are without form or figure."[86] While the primary Augustinian metaphor for the letter at St. Victor was the sign, Dionysian mystical theology stressed that the letter did not point to or refer to the God of mystery (how could it?) but nevertheless makes accessible this hidden God, just as a veil makes accessible that which is covered or hidden. Having looked at God in mystical theology, let's now turn to the mystified letter.

---

86   Pseudo-Dionysius, *Divine Names*, 1.4.

4

MYSTICAL THEOLOGY: THE LETTER AND THE WORD OF GOD

Thomas Gallus: The Commentary Writer

The Victorines wrote commentaries as a spiritual practice. Thomas Gallus's voluminous commentaries showcase the role reading played among the Victorines. A telling image for reading among the Victorines appears in the prologue to his third commentary on the Song of Songs. Gallus describes how by commenting on the Song anew he "follow[s] the courses of the *theoriae*" or "wanders" among the "spectacles" of the eternal Word. Though he does not have his earlier commentaries on the Song at hand, he is confident that, being caught up in the Word, he will not contradict them.[1] The image suggests the reason a Victorine like Gallus engaged in commentary writing was not just as a pedagogical practicality but because commentary writing engaged the mind of the commentator in experiencing the Word itself.

While John Saracen's new translation of the Dionysian corpus brought mystical theology to St. Victor around 1167, Gallus was the great interpreter of Dionysius. Over the course of his career, he read and commented on the Dionysian corpus and the Song of Songs repeatedly, alternating from text to text. In just the final decade of his life, Gallus wrote his second commentary on the Song (1237); his *Extractio*, a paraphrase of the Dionysian corpus (1238); his *Explanatio* commentaries on the Dionysian treatises *Mystical Theology* (1241) and *Divine Names* (1242); a third commentary on the Song (1243); and his *Explanatio* commentary on the *Letters* (1243), the *Celestial Hierarchy* (1243), and the *Ecclesiastical Hierarchy* (1244). Having written commentaries for many years, he exclaims that he worked on the Dionysian corpus "with such vigilance! with such labor!"[2] Just his final commentarial

---

1   Thomas Gallus, *Song Commentary III*, in *Thomas Gallus: Commentaires du Cantique des Cantiques*, ed. Jeanne Barbet (Paris: Vrin, 1967), Prlg.P, 109.
2   Quoted in Rorem, *Pseudo-Dionysius*, 218.

project, the *Explanatio* on the entire Dionysian corpus, comes in at over one thousand pages in its modern edition.

This chapter continues unpacking the influence of the mystical theology of Dionysius on the reading culture of St. Victor, especially the school's approach to scriptural language or the letter. Because the authors of Scripture ("the theologians" in Dionysian parlance) are attuned to the mysterious providence of the God beyond being, when they use language for God, they "hymn" God with special techniques to inculcate a sense of the presence of divine mystery. When Dionysius's theology of scriptural language came to St. Victor, Thomas Gallus reasoned through the mystical use of language. When it came to the letter, there was a "figurative," "causal," or ultimately "estimative" relation between it and God Godself, a mysterious connection established by God's mystery. That is, the letter was a medium for manifesting God but only insofar as it also hid God. Because of the letter's "estimative" relation to the God it "covered over" or "veiled," it became fully mystified.

Theological Language: Hymning the God beyond Being

If Dionysius never resolves the tension between God's beyond-being-ness and providential presence, it should be clear that, although all of being serves as a potential site for *theophany* (θεοφάνεια) or God revelation, God also remains *aphanous* (ἀφανής) or ever unrevealed.[3] Because God is providentially present to all existing things, to a "clear-sighted mind," everything can manifest God.[4] Yet because God remains beyond being (invisible and unintelligible), God remains always unmanifest.[5] Thus, perfection (τελείωσις) for

---

3   Again, a lexical examination confirms what is stated explicitly. The terms *theophany* (θεοφάνεια) and *aphanous* (ἀφανής) each appear a total of twelve times in the *writings of Dionysius*. Corpus Dionysiacum II, "Griesches Register," 276, 284.
4   Cf. Pseudo-Dionysius, *Celestial Hierarchy* 15.5. For Dionysius's appeal to the Pauline idea that invisible things are known through the visible, see Pseudo-Dionysius, Epistle 9.2.
5   Perhaps most telling is Dionysius's claim that even Jesus does not finally reveal or unveil the beyond-being-ness of God: "The Word of God (θεολογίαν) suggests even this, that the Beyond-being (τὸν ὑπερούσιον) proceeded forth out of the hidden, into the manifestation (ἐμφάνειαν) amongst us, by having taken substance as man. But, He is hidden, even after the manifestation, or to speak more divinely, has been kept hidden, and the mystery with respect

Dionysius does not entail intellectual vision of the divine nature, which may never be available for intellectual cognition.[6] What should the reader of the Dionysian corpus make of this dilemma? If everything has the potential for revealing God but consistently frustrates the revelation of God, what can overcome this problem? How does Dionysius describe the manifestation of the unmanifest?

Just from perusing the titles of Dionysius's treatises, we can posit that his primary approach to this problem is a Christian way of life, wherein letter and liturgy are administered hierarchically. On the way, as it were, to the God beyond being, the human mind uses the "material guidance suitable to itself (τῇ κατ' αὐτὸν ὑλαίᾳ χειραγωγίᾳ)" in order to move from visible things to invisible things.[7] This material guidance comes from the liturgical rites interpreted in the *Ecclesiastical Hierarchy*, but it also includes the linguistic or cognitive practices described and performed, for example, in the treatises on the *Divine Names*, the *Mystical Theology*, and the first few chapters of the *Celestial Hierarchy*. That is, there is remarkable consonance in the Dionysian corpus between hermeneutic and liturgical practice, between letter and sacrament, both involving forms of "material guidance" toward the God of mystery, which Dionysius famously associates with the use of symbols (σύμβολα).[8] Yet, as we will see, Dionysius's treatment of these symbols is just as ambiguous as his teaching about God. I will show that for Dionysius, Scripture uses "symbols" or "veils" to hymn God as both beyond being and providentially present, with the result that hymning ought to be interpreted both causally and *hyperochically* (or "beyond-having-ly"). While the meaning of *hyperoche* is fundamentally ambiguous, suggesting both the adequacy and inadequacy of any symbol for God, recent treatments of the issue have

---

to Him has been reached by no word or intellect (οὐδενὶ λόγῳ οὔτε νῷ), but even when spoken, remains unsaid, and when conceived unknown (ἄγνωστον)." Pseudo-Dionysius, Epistle 3.

6   Although we will see that Dionysius allows for revelatory experience, especially among the "theologians" (authors of Scripture), this is never an intellectual grasp of an object of vision. See below, 87–90.

7   Pseudo-Dionysius, *Celestial Hierarchy* 1.3.

8   As Golitzin says, Dionysius applies that "pattern" of divine worship "to both the Christian assembly at worship, *and* to the Christian soul, and he does so in order to keep both anchored in each other." *Mystagogy*, 54.

attempted to resolve or downplay this ambiguity. After a brief look at two of those treatments, I highlight another conceptual tension in the Dionysian corpus—the letter veils God in its very unveiling of God.

Theology (θεολογία): Hymns (ὕμνοι), Symbols (σύμβολα), and Veils (παραπέτασμα)

If liturgy and scriptural interpretation are the "material guidance" necessary for Christian perfection—for the right mode of relation to the unmanifest manifest in creation—how do they work? More specifically, how can theological language, the letter of Scripture, "guide" one when one's goal is the ineffable God beyond being?

Dionysius acknowledges that this problem will confront the reader of Scripture. In *Divine Names*, he asks, "If It is superior to every expression (λόγου) and every knowledge (γνώσεως), and is altogether placed beyond mind (ὑπὲρ νοῦν) and essence (οὐσίαν), . . . in what way will our treatise thoroughly investigate the meaning of the Divine Names, when the beyond-being Deity is shown to be without Name, and beyond Name?"[9] That is, how does Scripture use divine names if God's beyond-being-ness means that God is unintelligible and ineffable?

The immediate answer that Dionysius gives to this question has led contemporary readers to too quickly resolve this tension in his corpus. As we have seen, he answers that the theologians (the writers of Scripture) do not use divine names to hymn the beyond-being-ness (ὑπερουσιότης) of God but to hymn God's providence (πρόνοια).[10] Therefore, the divine names refer to God's providential activity but not to God's beyond-being-ness.[11]

Yet there are two reasons the distinction between God's beyond-being-ness and providence cannot be the final word on theological language. First, as we have already traced in chapter 3, the distinction is only presented with a consistent qualifier of God's simplicity.[12] God's beyond-being-ness and God's providential presence are unified in the work of divine love in the Dionysian corpus. It is the very God beyond being that is providentially

---

9   Pseudo-Dionysius, *Divine Names*, 1.5.
10   Pseudo-Dionysius, *Divine Names*, 1.5.
11   Jones, "The *Divine Names* in John Sarracen's Translation."
12   See discussion and quotations on divine unity, ch. 3, 63.

present to all. The theological language will thus continue to conceal God, even as it attempts to reveal God by hymning God's providential powers.

Second, in a passage just below the claim that the theologians attribute the divine names to the work of providence, Dionysius states that the theologians in addition derive the divine names from "certain occasional divine appearances (θείων φασμάτων)" of "the beyond-bright and beyond-name Goodness (τὴν ὑπερφαῆ καὶ ὑπερώνυμον ἀγαθότητα)."[13] That is, the theological language (hymning) of the prophets and the apostles comes from some integration of general participation in providentially arranged being, with special encounter with the Good beyond being. Dionysius prays that he and his reader, too, will become initiated into these God-revealing contemplations.[14] This is why Scripture and liturgy, "handed down" (παράδοσις) from the "theologians," are the central tools for perfection.[15] Scripture and liturgy

---

13   Pseudo-Dionysius, *Divine Names*, 1.8. It is important to note that Dionysius describes these as *distinct* from the "universal or particular Providences" mentioned above.
14   Pseudo-Dionysius, *Divine Names*, 1.8.
15   What Dionysius describes here as the special appearances to the theologians, which are likewise the goal of Dionysius and Timothy, and presumably the reader of the corpus, need not be understood as extralinguistic and extraliturgical. They take place in "temples" among the "initiated." That is, divine appearances (φάσματα) are wrought through or given in the performance of symbolic ritual *and* go on to engender the positing of certain symbols for God. But it is possible to overemphasize the liturgical, symbolic frame of the Dionysian corpus so that one does not recognize the excessive experience at its foundation, which in turn is the basis of prophetic and apostolic authority and the aspiration of adherents. I have reservations about recent attempts to downplay the role of the treatise *Mystical Theology* and mysticism in the corpus in favor of liturgy and hierarchy (cf. Denys Turner, "How to Read Pseudo-Denys Today?" *International Journal of Systematic Theology* 7, no. 4 [2005]: 428–40; and Golitzin, *Mystagogy*). Perhaps it is best to risk the formulation favored by Henri De Lubac, a close reader of Dionysius, that in these experiences "grace perfects nature," neither leaving it behind nor reducible to it. *The Mystery of the Supernatural,* trans. Rosemary Sheed (New York: Crossroad Publishing, 1998). That is, theological and liturgical symbols, like those used in the *Ecclesiastical Hierarchy*, are integral to the very divine act that suddenly draws one super-intellectually "beyond" them. But, according to Dionysius, special experiences of the theologians are the basis of the Christian liturgico-symbolic system, what he calls *hymning*. They provide the authority for that system, an authority to which the author of the Dionysian corpus appeals by adopting the pseudonym.

The confluence of special experiences, religious rituals, and philosophical reflection is a hallmark of late ancient *theurgy*. The Neoplatonic theurgist Iamblichus had likewise

teach one how to proceed given that the God beyond being is unintelligibly present to being. And the especially reliable character of the symbols used in this theological hymning comes from the theologians' encounter with the God beyond being.[16] What should be clear from these two considerations is that any quick identification of divine effability with divine providence (and divine ineffability with divine beyond-being-ness) is misguided. Theological hymning comes somehow from the experiential discernment of or encounter with the God beyond being providentially present to being.

If the theologians' "hymning" does not reveal or represent God by referring directly and comprehensively to God's providential powers or energies, what does it do? A couple of passages help disabuse us of our modern

---

distinguished the variety of welcome divine appearances (φάσματα) from lowly visions (φαντάσματα), the former being "true icons of [the gods] themselves (τὰς ἀληθινὰς ἑαυτῶν εἰκόνας)," the latter cheap and false offerings of magicians (*De Mysteriis*, 111). Thus, an icon is a material or linguistic tool, as it were, that works on the viewer, allowing them to participate in divine work (*theurgy*) and transforming the soul. But not just anything is an icon. Golitzin's reading of the Dionysian corpus likewise stresses the *iconic* character of Dionysian mystical "uplifting" (*Mystagogy*). Something of this iconic mechanism at play here is alluded to by Iamblichus: "But if the soul weaves together its intellectual and its divine part with higher powers, then its own visions (φαντάσματα) will be purer" (*De Mysteriis*, 127). Both Iamblichus and Dionysius make the iconic a prime tool for accessing the divine—participation in rituals of iconic worship lead to more divine visions (φαντάσματα).

Gregory Shaw has pointed to one distinction between the two in "Neoplatonic Theurgy and Dionysius the Areopagite," *Journal of Early Christian Studies* 7, no. 4 (1999): 573–99. Iamblichean theory encapsulated multiple culture-specific theurgic systems, while Dionysian theory restricted theurgic symbols to those of the Christian Church. Yet, while Iamblichus's theory is more pluralistic, as we might say today, it is worth noting that both systems relied on the accounts of and aspirations for authoritative experiences of illuminated individuals. That is, Iamblichean theurgy has been rightly credited as being formative for Christian sacramentalism, and both systems draw on special experience.

16 In this passage on divine apparition, Dionysius is explicitly referring to the prophets and those "initiated" presumably into what he calls "the hierarchy of the Law." Dionysius does not spend much time treating Christology, but by calling Jesus the *manifestation of the unmanifest* and the "Hierarch," it suggests the significance of the apostolic encounter with Jesus Christ, who manifests the unmanifest. Further evidence for the centrality of divine encounter with Jesus is found in Epistle 4: "He who sees divinely (ὁ θείως ὁρῶν), will know beyond intellect even the things affirmed respecting the love towards man of Jesus—things which possess a force of *hyperochic* negation."

associations of language with reference and representation. Given that God is beyond being, theological language does not refer to God, as Dionysius's consistent use of *hymning* to describe theological writings suggests. Instead, "we are led by [the Scriptures] to the supremely Divine Hymns (τοὺς θεαρχικοὺς ὕμνους), by which we are supermundanely enlightened and moulded to the sacred hymn-singings (τὰς ἱερὰς ὑμνολογίας), so as both to see the supremely Divine illuminations given to us by them, according to our capacities, and to hymn the good-giving Source."[17] That is, scriptural language guides, illumines, and transforms from beyond.[18] It conducts one

---

[17] *Divine Names*, 1.3. It is perhaps worth noting that here language appears to give way to even more perfect language, which may point vaguely to Dionysius's Christology since this more perfect language may be something like participation in the Word itself, indistinguishable from theology and hymnology. Given the centrality of veil imagery we will see below, we might think of successive folding back and putting on of various hymns. Notice, though, that theological language neither refers to nor represents its object but transforms and illumines the speaker.

Here, Dionysius seems especially indebted to Iamblichus. On theurgic "invocations (κλήσεις)," Iamblichus writes:

> For the illumination that comes about as a result of invocations is self-manifesting (αὐτοφανὴς) and self-willed, and is far removed from being drawn down by force, but rather proceeds to manifestation (εἰς τὸ ἐμφανές) by reason of its own divine energy and perfection, and is as far superior to (human) voluntary motion as the divine will of the Good is to the life of ordinary deliberation and choice. . . . It is plain, indeed, from the rites themselves, that what we are speaking of just now is a method of salvation for the soul; for in the contemplation of the blessed visions the soul exchanges one life for another and exerts a different activity (ἑτέραν ἐνέργειαν ἐνεργεῖ), and considers itself then to be no longer human—and quite rightly so: for often, having abandoned its own life, it has gained in exchange the most blessed activity of the gods (τῶν θεῶν ἐνέργειαν). (*De Mysteriis*, 51, 53)

This passage suggests that Iamblichean theurgic prayer and Dionysian hymning use ritual or scriptural language to exchange one's energy for divine energy—in the case of Dionysius, energy already acquired by the theologians. Invocations or hymns are perhaps the conditions for deifying "self-manifesting illumination." What they certainly do not do is signify or refer one to an intelligible object, as in the case of Augustinian signification.

[18] Thus, unlike the angels, human beings are "led to the Divine by the varied texture of holy and representational contemplation (τῆς ἱερογραφικῆς θεωρίας)." In contrast, angels are "filled with all kinds of immaterial knowledge of higher light, and satiated, as permissible, with the beautifying and original beauty of superessential and thrice manifested

toward angelic "hymning" and makes one an imitator of the theologians, able to see and sing, as it were, as they did: "But now, to the best of our ability, we use symbols (συμβόλοις) appropriate to things Divine, and from these again we elevate ourselves, according to our degree, to the simple and unified truth of the intellectual contemplations (τῶν νοητῶν θεαμάτων)."[19]

Again, the use of theological language is akin to the use of symbols or icons (εἰκόνες) in the liturgy.[20] Even more tellingly, Dionysius calls theological language "sacred veils (παραπετασμάτων) of the love toward humanity (φιλανθρωπίας), made known in the Oracles and hierarchical traditions." These veils "envelope things intellectual in things sensible, and things beyond being in things that are."[21] However, here Dionysius reveals little about how symbolic veils, or hymning, works. How does hymning conduct one toward or unify or assimilate one to the God beyond being? More specifically, what relation is there between the God beyond being and the divine names hymned in Scripture? What happens when God is hymned as "Good," "Being," or "Life"? "Beyond being" or "Unliving"? As we will see, the answer to this question is tellingly unclear since Dionysius prefers a mystical approach to theological language.

How Do Divine Names Work?

When the theologians "hymn" God, how are they using language?[22] Dionysius is perhaps most famous for the use of both affirmative statements

---

contemplation (ὑπερουσίου καὶ τριφανοῦς θεωρίας)." Pseudo-Dionysius, *Celestial Hierarchy*, 7.2. That is, Scripture and liturgy provide the mechanism of perfection necessary for human beings, who need "sensible and intellectual symbols," unlike the angels, who contemplate the beyond-being Trinity according to their own capacity.

19   Pseudo-Dionysius, *Divine Names*, 1.4.
20   And hermeneutic practice is akin to liturgical practice: "The many discredit the expressions concerning the Divine Mysteries. For, we contemplate them only through the sensible symbols that have grown upon them. We must then strip them, and view them by themselves in their naked purity. For, thus contemplating them, we should reverence a fountain of Life flowing into Itself.... We thought it necessary then ... that we should, as far as possible, unfold (ἀναπτυχθῆναι) the varied forms of the Divine symbolic representations (συμβολικῆς ἱεροπλαστίας) of God." Pseudo-Dionysius, Epistle 9.1.
21   Pseudo-Dionysius, *Divine Names*, 1.4.
22   Plenty of readers of the Dionysian corpus, especially *Divine Names*, have thought they found in it a theory for the predication of divine attributes. In a series of articles from

(*cataphasis*) and negative statements (*apophasis*) about God. Though the end of the *Divine Names* claims that negative statements are the more preferred locutions since God is beyond being and intellect,[23] Dionysius consistently presents affirmations and negations as complementary or even dialectical. How, then, ought they be interpreted? We will see that one ought to interpret theological statements (or, rather, "hymning") causally and *hyperochically* ("beyond-having-ly").[24] However, by expositing the theology of hymning in the corpus, we will also see that contemporary readers have gone too far in resolving the fundamental mystery in causal and *hyperochic* hymning. To interpret a statement about God *hyperochically* is to interpret it in a negative, though non-privative, way.[25] This negative but non-privative theology

the 1950s, Harry Wolfson lays out some of the options. Wolfson describes five major approaches to predication of divine attributes from Plotinus to Thomas Aquinas: negation, causality, eminence (*hyperoche*), equivocation/univocation, and analogy. As we will see, Wolfson is right when he claims that Dionysian predication is both causal and *hyperochic*. Briefly, causal predication uses language to refer to God as the source or origin of human attributes (God is wise = God is the cause of wisdom). *Hyperochic* (literally, "beyond-having") predication is more complicated. It suggests that the predication of a divine attribute both inculcates the sense that God has the attribute in question and that the way God has this quality is so excessive that it cannot be understood or even should be denied (God is wise = God is so wise as to create an aporia when we try to understand). See below.

23   "Wherefore, even [the theologians] have given the preference to the ascent through negations (διὰ τῶν ἀποφάσεων), as lifting the soul out of things kindred to itself, and conducting it through all the Divine conceptions, above which towers that which is above every name, and every expression and knowledge, and at the furthest extremity attaching it to Him, as far indeed as is possible for us to be attached to that Being." Pseudo-Dionysius, *Divine Names*, 13.3.

24   At times, Dionysius seems to propose that hyperochic predication is the way to understand negative statements, while causal predication is the way to understand affirmative statements. Yet the dialectical and hymnic presentation of the divine names suggests that the positing of an affirmative name like Life (ζωή) for God also *implies* the positing of its negative, "Unliving" (ἄζωος). Thus, we can talk about hyperochic and causal predication as two sides of the same coin—or, rather, like musical counterpoint. When Scripture (θεολογία) sings these two terms together, it affects one's capacity to discern the God beyond being in some way.

25   "Varied knowledge conceals the Unknowing (τὴν ἀγνωσίαν ἀφανίζουσι αἱ γνώσεις). Take this in a *hyperochic* (ὑπεροχικῶς), but not in a privative sense (μὴ κατὰ στέρησιν), and reply in a way beyond truth, that the unknowing, respecting God, escapes those who possess existing light, and knowledge of things being." Pseudo-Dionysius, Epistle 1. Timothy Knepper, *Negating Negation*, has most recently called attention to this important and misunderstood aspect of the Dionysian corpus.

of hymning is a second conceptual tension in the Dionysian corpus since hymned theological symbols repeatedly unveil and veil the God beyond being who is present to being. Let's first consider some passages on hymning as both causally and *hyperochically* understood. Then we will consider how two recent interpreters of Dionysius have made sense of his *hyperochic* predication of divine attributes. Keeping in mind Dionysius's consistent use of the language of "hymning" and properly understanding *hyperoche* as ambiguous will help to avoid the temptation to resolve the mystery inherent in speaking about God.

One lexical curiosity in the Dionysian corpus is the consistent use not only of divine names but of *alpha-* (ἀ-) and *hyper-* (ὑπερ-) prefixes appended to those same names. That is, Dionysius posits that God is both "Good" (ἄγαθος) and "Beyond-Good" (ὑπεράγαθος), "Life" (ζωή) and "Unliving" (ἄζωος). The theologians use affirmative and negative terms like these to hymn God. These names for the Deity can denote either "whatever belongs to *hyperochic* removal (ὅσα τῆς ὑπεροχικῆς ἐστιν ἀφαιρέσεως)" or "the Cause (αἰτία) of all good things."[26] That is, theological hymning negates God *hyperochically* (or "beyond-having-ly") and affirms God as the Cause of all. This should look familiar. Dionysius is claiming that scriptural hymning takes into account *both* God's beyond-being-ness *and* God's providential presence. Another passage suggests the same: "For, to those who hymn worthily of God, all these [divine names] signify (σημαίνει) Him by every conception (ἐπίνοιαν) as Beyond-being Being (ὑπερουσίως εἶναι), and Cause in every way of things existing."[27] Theological hymning is a form of language that takes account of God both as beyond being and as the Cause of all, as is appropriate to the God beyond being, who is causally present.

One final passage makes clear that theological hymning ought to be understood as a mode of dialectical expression of God as cause of being *and* beyond being:

> *No doubt, the mystical traditions of the revealing Oracles sometimes hymn the august Blessedness of the beyond being Godhead (ὑπερουσίου θεαρχίας), as Word, and Intellect, and Being, manifesting its God-becoming expression and wisdom, both as*

---

26   Pseudo-Dionysius, *Divine Names*, 2.3.
27   Pseudo-Dionysius, *Divine Names*, 5.8.

really being Origin, and true Cause of the origin of things in being, and they describe it as Light, and call it Life . . . [even though these] in reality fall short of the supremely Divine similitude. For it is above every being (ὑπὲρ πᾶσαν οὐσίαν) and life.[28]

By using positive affirmations and negative terms (prefixed with ἀ- or ὑπερ-) together, the theologians are able to effectively hymn the mysterious God beyond being, whom they have encountered as the providentially present Cause of all. As we will see, contemporary readers of Dionysius have been particularly interested in the negative terms, but they have also tended to hastily resolve the basic ambiguity in *hyperochic* negation. What does it mean to say something about God *hyperochically* or "beyond-having-ly"?[29]

Two Accounts of Hyperochic Negation

In John D. Jones's assessment, Western readers of Dionysius misunderstand his frequently used alpha-privatives, which negate some attribute of God. Dionysius refers to God as *inaccessible* (ἄβατος), *unknown* (ἄγνωστος), *unliving* (ἄζωος), *unmovable* (ἀκίνητος), *inimitable* (ἀμίμητος), *unintellectual* (ἄνοος), *invisible* (ἀόρατος), *infinite* (ἄπειρος), *incomprehensible* (ἀπερίληπτος), and *ineffable* (ἄρρητος).[30] Jones claims Orthodox readers most often recognize a twofold sense of Dionysian negativity. On the one hand, these alpha-privatives do not simply *deny* these characteristics of God—they do so preeminently.[31] That is, because God is beyond being and intellection, saying God is "not such-and-such" means that God exceeds any human understanding of what "such-and-such" could mean for God. If God is "unliving" (ἄζωος), this does not mean that God lacks life but that God so exceeds or surpasses life preeminently that God must be said to be *not living*. On the other hand, Jones states

---

28 Pseudo-Dionysius, *Celestial Hierarchy*, 2.3.
29 We might likewise ask what it means to predicate something "causally," though this has not raised as much attention among scholars as *hyperochic* predication.
30 Gathered from *Corpus Dionysiacum* II, "Griechisches Register," 269–76. Jones's characterization of the Western position relies on Albert Magnus and Thomas Aquinas. Was Western reception of these terms in the Dionysian corpus so unified?
31 Jones, "The *Divine Names* in John Sarracen's Translation." By fortunate coincidence, or judicious editing, Jones's and Knepper's articles that address this same issue appear side by side in *American Catholic Philosophical Quarterly*.

that while alpha-privatives perform this "preeminent denial" (God does not *lack*), this should take nothing away from what has been called Dionysius's radical apophaticism, or the "silencing" effected by Dionysian negation. For Jones, *ἀ-* does not refer to a lack in God's essence, but he stresses that neither does it in turn refer to some*thing* else. God *in Godself* cannot properly be said to have life, even in a preeminent way. God has no preeminent possession of life. God in Godself is beyond life and therefore not "living."

For Jones, this all turns on a "paradoxical/antinomical way" of talking about God among Dionysius's Orthodox readers that we have already seen hinted at in our treatment of his doctrine of God. The Greek tradition eventually distinguishes between the "essence" (οὐσία) and "energies" or "activities" (ἐνέργειαι) of God—both terms, as we have seen, that appear in the corpus. For Dionysius and his Orthodox readers, says Jones, the "essence" (οὐσία) of God can only be spoken of with the semantic qualifiers of "hyper-essential" (ὑπερούσιος) or the phrase "whatever it is" (ὅ τι ποτέ ἐστιν) because God in Godself is unknowable.[32] On the other hand, divine "energies," as the causal principles of the world, *are* amenable to signification. This distinction between essence and energies is what makes possible the use of language for the "ineffable," but, Jones stresses, the essence of God in itself remains "unknown and incomprehensible to any created being," who knows and participates in divine energies, not in the divine *beyond-being being* (ὑπερούσιον οὐσίαν).[33] That is, all language spoken of God must refer only to God's activities in relation to creation—what we have summed up under the Dionysian term *providence*. There can never be a "seeing" or "knowing" God in Godself because God's essence is beyond being and therefore beyond intellection.

As we have already seen, Jones's essence-energies distinction cannot hold for Dionysius, who presents the distinction alongside consistent claims to the unified nature of the Godhead, both present to creation and beyond being. The God beyond being remains unintelligible and hidden, even in God's providential presence. Yet Jones is correct to claim that Dionysian

---

32 Cf. Michael Sells's description of the Plotinian "apophatic marker" *hoion* (οἷον) that reminds the reader to remove the semantic content from any affirmative statement about the One. *Mystical Languages of Unsaying*, 16–17.
33 Jones, "The *Divine Names* in John Sarracen's Translation," 665.

negation is neither privative nor does it denote preeminent possession. That is, predicating alpha-terms or negating positive terms of God ought not to be interpreted to mean there is some *lack* of the predicated quality in God. Yet to Jones, no language will be adequate to the divine essence, which is "beyond having." In his telling, the end of Dionysian mysticism, if it is to reach, as it were, to the divine essence, must be radically apophatic, negating all terms of the God beyond being.

For Timothy Knepper, this construal is just the kind of misleading story that is often told about Dionysian negation, which he characterizes as a tendency toward "apophatic abandonment." Too often it is assumed that Dionysius negates predicates of God, as when he uses alpha-privatives, "in order to state their literal falsity of God and thereby to show the inapplicability of predication in general with respect to God."[34] Knepper, like Jones, claims that a different "logic" of negation is at work in the Dionysian corpus and that attention to Dionysius's other favorite prefix, *hyper-* (ὑπερ-), helps to bear it out.

If negation does not deny the possibility of predication or signification of God, what does it do? Knepper claims that Dionysius consistently qualifies negation (his persistent *a-* prefixes) with a reminder that "denial" or "removal" (ἀφαίρεσις) of a predicate from God ought to be interpreted "excessively," or *hyperochically* (ὑπεροχικῶς).[35] *Hyperoche* ("hyper-having") describes the way in which attributes that are negated ought to be thought to belong properly to God. God *has* those qualities, but God has them "excessively." Alpha-privatives, which seem to deny some attribute of God, actually affirm that attribute in an excessive way. So when Dionysius says that God is "unliving" (ἄζωος), he means God is living excessively or preeminently. Alpha-privatives, and Dionysian negation more generally, must be thought of with this excessive logic. Knepper proffers a formula for this logic: *not-p* signifies *more-p-than-most-p*.[36] This seemingly counterintuitive formula is Knepper's key to the Dionysian corpus, and he suggests that it fits logically within Dionysius's participatory metaphysics.

---

34 Timothy D. Knepper, "Not Not: The Method and Logic of Dionysian Negation," *American Catholic Philosophical Quarterly* 82, no. 4 (2008): 619.

35 See Knepper's treatment of the logic of negation, including *aphairesis* and *apophasis*, in *Negating Negation*, 35–68.

36 Knepper, "Not Not: The Method and Logic of Dionysian Negation," 620.

Knepper admits that *hyperoche* (and the prefix *hyper-*), like the English translations *excess* or *preeminence*, can cover two semantic domains. The Greek prefix can refer either to an "exceeding beyond" something or to having something in "an excessive measure."[37] That is, *hyperoche* in the first sense marks a transcendent break with that which is predicated of God—*hyper-* is best translated as "beyond," *hyperoche* as "beyond-having."[38] In the second sense, it suggests a continuation or abundance of that which is predicated—*hyper-* is best translated as "hyper," *hyperoche* as "hyper-having."[39] So when Dionysius speaks of what we have called God's "beyond-being-ness" (ὑπερουσιότης), it is actually unclear whether he refers to God's "other-than-being-ness" (a break with being) or God's "hyper-being-ness" (more-being-than-most-being). Though Knepper helpfully lays out this ambiguity and admits it could be a productive tension for Dionysius, he tends to emphasize this second interpretation in order to avoid the danger of "apophatic abandonment" that he sees in the work of Jones and others. Jones's radical unknowing is an appropriate mystical goal for a God whose essence (*ousia*) is "beyond being," but, Knepper worries, to interpret in this way is "to risk making God functionally equivalent to absolutely nothing at all."[40] God's relationship to being must be understood in terms of participation, not transcendence.[41] In fact, Knepper provides important conceptual

---

37   Knepper, *Negating Negation*, 48–49.
38   This, he would claim, is the primary way that Jones understands the prefix—as a preeminent *denial*.
39   Knepper, *Negating Negation*, 48.
40   Knepper, "Not Not: The Method and Logic of Dionysian Negation," 637.
41   The following chart shows the interpretive tendency toward Dionysian negation of the two treatments we have seen. Both prefixes have a possible double meaning—both scholars agree that, according to Dionysius, *hyperoche* is the correct way to interpret alpha-privatives, but they differ on how to interpret *hyperoche*:

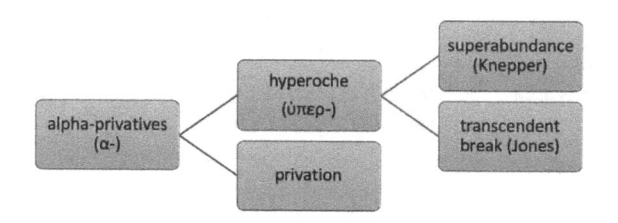

tools for avoiding the distinction, but his polemical purpose—to show that negation must itself be negated to avoid radical apophaticism—at times gets in the way of his helpful clarification of *hyperoche*.

What this brief treatment of two contemporary takes on *hyperochic* hymning shows is that the resolution of Dionysius's dialectical presentation is tempting, particularly when one loses sight of the language and imagery of "veils" and "symbols." Does the letter basically obscure the divine, suggesting that theological statements about God always occur with the understanding that there is a sharper "dis-analogy" at work? That is, does the veil of the letter *hide* who or what God is? Or does the letter reveal or make possible the discernment of the God beyond being, at least as providentially present? A telling passage from *Divine Names* first offers a litany of names "received from the holy Oracles" for both "the Divine Causes" and "the beyond-being Hiddenness" (names like "God, or Life, or Being, or Light, or Word") and then makes the following succinct statement: "But how these things are, it is neither possible to say, nor to conceive (ἐννοῆσαι)."[42] Here is the second conceptual tension in the Dionysian corpus that mystifies the letter. Its theology of hymning affirms that the symbols the theologians use, the very letter itself, are like veils, both hiding God *and* making God accessible. Even Dionysian negation is understood *hyperochically*, as suggesting an "excess" or "otherness" in God that both makes intellectual awareness impossible *and* that makes some apprehension or encounter possible. Put more simply, theology hymns the radical otherness of God alongside God's intimacy with being.[43] The letter reveals and conceals God, the mystery present to all things.

Word and Letter at St. Victor

While Victorines like Thomas Gallus embraced the Dionysian doctrine of God, their take on Dionysius's theology of language or hymning was the real

---

42   Pseudo-Dionysius, *Divine Names*, 2.7.
43   Charles Stang uses the language of "alterity" and "intimacy" rather than "transcendence" and "immanence" in more recent work, which I think better reflects the Platonic distinction between "beyond-being-ness" and "presence." See "Negative Theology from Gregory of Nyssa to Dionysius the Areopagite" in *The Wiley-Blackwell Companion to Christian Mysticism* (Hoboken, NJ: Wiley-Blackwell, 2013), 161–76.

innovation for the letter. By making theological language a kind of hymning that refers to God causally and "beyond-having-ly," Dionysius mystified the letter. While influenced by Dionysius, the Victorines—Augustinian canons—often drew on an Augustinian theology of the Word, a major piece of which was a presumed analogy between divine and human speech. For Thomas Gallus, for instance, Dionysian divine causality or presence was best expressed in terms of the divine communication (*communicatio*) of the Word, which arises, as we have seen, from the super-abundance of God's beyond-being-ness. Given that, as we will see in chapter 5, Gallus conceives of Dionysian union as primarily a matter of the soul's intimacy with this Word, it should be no surprise that the Word pervades Gallus's commentaries on the Dionysian corpus as well. Gallus's theology of the Word (*Verbum*) not only provides a coherent account of divine causality and presence; it also underlies his theology of sacred letters (*litterae*).

This section uses the Augustinian analogy between the Word's operation and human speech as a lens through which to examine Gallus's views on Jesus, creation, and sacred letters in the *Explanatio* on the Dionysian corpus. Moving from the Word eternally spoken by the God beyond being to the incarnate Word as source of the letter, it maps a movement akin to the human speaker's progression from an inner concept (*conceptio cordis*) to an inward word (*verbum intrinsecum*) to an exteriorized word (*verbum exterius*). What emerges is an account of Gallus's Word-centric and "cosmic" Christology, which is related to the Dionysian doctrines of God's beyond-being-ness and the theology of scriptural language. Appreciating Gallus's theology of the Word is necessary for understanding his views on sacred language and literature (*sacrae litterae*), which seek to convey that Word as both beyond being and present, eternal and incarnate.

This section makes two moves. First, I show that Gallus articulates a Word-centric, cosmic Christology informed by Augustine and the twelfth-century Victorine masters, harmonizing it with the Dionysian corpus. Moving from the eternal Word to the incarnate Word, it is possible to see how the Word was a prism through which other aspects of Gallus's theology can be understood. Second, Gallus's Word-centric Christology puts sacred literature at the center of Christian practice as it allows one to experience the Word by means of purposefully mystifying theological language.

After treating the eternal and incarnate Word, I move to his theology of the mystical letter, which relates to God in a way beyond understanding.

Eternal Word: Inner Concept and Inward Word

Gallus's theology of the Word assumes an analogy put forth by Augustine between the incarnation of the eternal Word and the human act of communication of a mental concept. While "the Word" (*Λόγος-Verbum*) appears in the Scriptures primarily in the Johannine and Wisdom literature, the notion of the Word as the principle or reason creating and governing the world had a long Hellenistic provenance. The Jewish philosopher Philo of Alexandria wrote of the divine Word, and early Christian apologists likewise took advantage of the notion's cultural cachet in order to articulate a Christology that could defend and make intelligible their faith. Augustine, however, was the most important avenue for ideas about the Word in the medieval period, having fleshed out a theology of the Word by exploring the implicit analogy between the divine Word and the human production of words. Augustine's treatment of the Word was built on his understanding of how human beings produce an exterior, spoken word from an inner, anterior word.[44] This inner word itself begins as a prelinguistic concept before becoming a linguistically formed but prespoken word. That is, on its way to becoming a spoken utterance or vocal expression (*vox*), a word begins first as an inner prelinguistic concept (*conceptio cordis*), then an inwardly pronounced word (*verbum intrinsecum*), until finally manifesting as an exterior word (*verbum exterius* or *vox*).

Each of these steps in the production of a word had its own analogue in the generation and activity of the divine Word. The generation of an inner, prelinguistic concept was like the Father's generation of the Son or the eternal Word of God, which conciliar orthodox Trinitarian theology had described as a distinct hypostasis or person while affirming one deity. How

---

[44] Luisa Valente, "*Verbum mentis—Vox clamantis*: The Notion of the Mental Word in Twelfth-Century Theology," in *The Word in Medieval Logic, Theology and Psychology: Acts of the XIIIth International Colloquium of the Société Internationale pour l'Étude de la Philosophie Médiévale*, ed. T. Shimizu and C. Burnett (Turnhout: Brepols, 2009), 366–69, 388–91. In this and the paragraph that follows, I am indebted to Valente's treatment.

the Word was God was unknowable and ineffable, but it was hinted at in the way an intimate concept, prerational or prelinguistic, is indistinguishable from the speaker because it is not yet formed linguistically. Next, just as a prelinguistic concept manifests an inward linguistically formed word in the mind, the eternal Word contains the providential plans of creation and incarnation, or the eternal reasons (*rationes aeternae*).[45] The inner word (*verbum intrinsecum*) of the human being refers to both the conceptual and the prespoken but linguistically formed moments. In the same way, the eternal Word (*verbum aeternum*) describes the Son as both united to the Father and as the principle or design of creation. Finally, the analogy plays out with the production of the exterior word or voice. In the analogy with the divine Word, this exteriorization of the Word is the incarnation, which Augustine understands to be the Son's taking on human flesh and a rational soul in Christ Jesus, the perfect form of manifestation of the divine Word. Thus, the Word incarnate is the voice (*vox*) of God.

In the analogy with the human production of an exterior word, Augustine mostly focuses on the incarnation of the Word in Jesus Christ, but his use of the craftsman analogy, where an inner project is realized in exterior form, shows that he considered creation itself to be potentially another analogue of the exterior word. The Victorines would take this cosmic christological instinct—the Word is manifested in all creation—and run with it. For them, God's exterior word could be encountered in any visible manifestation of divine invisible providential order.[46] According to the Augustinian analogy, creation contrasted with Jesus Christ in that creation was God's externalized word that was not God. That is, creatures, as true expressions of the Word's design, would be much like the Word incarnate themselves were it not for the obstacles posed by the deformation

---

45 In this aspect, Augustine's treatment looks both like the traditional Platonic understanding of creation as preplanned and precontained by the Demiurge (a kind of divine craftsman) and like the descriptions of the Word of God as creative power in the Wisdom literature of the Old Testament.

46 A Pauline passage from Romans (1:20) was the central justification of this position. The Victorines' embrace of the passage has been treated extensively by Dale Coulter, *Per Visibilia ad Invisibilia: Theological Method in Richard of St. Victor (d. 1173)*, Bibliotecha Victorina XVIII (Turnhout: Brepols, 2006).

of their nature by sin and the need for reformation or deification of the soul.[47] As we saw in chapter 2, the primary means of this reformation or deification for the Victorines is sacred literature. So for the Victorines, the Word is communicated broadly in Jesus, creation, the Scriptures, and, importantly for Gallus, special instances of contemplative experience. Thus, they, more so than Augustine, emphasized identification with the cosmic Christ, who was the principle of creation and the reformation of the soul—especially through the interpretation of Scripture and special experience of the Word.

Besides generally expanding the imagined scope of the Word's incarnation to include creation, Scripture, and this special experience, Hugh of St. Victor made another modification of Augustine's thinking about the Word.[48] The influence of Dionysius may have been the cause of Hugh positing that the inner word remains hidden with God.[49] Following what we saw with Dionysius in chapter 3, this must be so even when exteriorized. That is, the exterior, incarnate Word in Jesus, creation, and Scripture remains hidden as it remains the interior, eternal Word of the God beyond being. For Dionysius, even in the providential presence of the God beyond being, God remains hidden. Most surprisingly, as we saw, this was the case even in the perfect instance of divine manifestation in Jesus.[50] It is worth noting what this subtle theological shift means for the understanding of words and the Word for those like Gallus, who draw from both Augustine and Dionysius. If for Augustine an exteriorized word (*verbum*) or utterance (*vox*) is a sign that *points back to* the original interior word or concept, the Dionysius-influenced Hugh may accept that an exteriorized word also continues to *hide* the inner word or concept since the inner word remains hidden

---

47 Hugh's early work in the *Didascalicon* places forgetfulness alongside deformation as one of his primary descriptors of the consequences of sin and the fall. Thus, in the definitive curricular statement of the Victorines, while divinely instituted pedagogy was a central concern, the effects of the fall do not always seem very severe, and the potential for assimilation to the Word is great. See ch. 2, 38–39.

48 Valente notes this distinction ("*Verbum mentis*," 379) but does not identify the possible influence of Dionysius as its source.

49 Valente, "*Verbum mentis*," 378.

50 See above, 84–85n5.

even when exteriorized. Visible things are the media of return to invisible things but only insofar as those invisible things are able to be apprehended. Hugh's introduction of Dionysius to the curriculum at the Victorine school ensured there was a hearty dose of skepticism as to the extent to which invisible things or the eternal Word could be so apprehended, at least by the intellect. Gallus's account of the soul, treated in the next chapter, can be understood as an attempt to think through the mechanism or practice of apprehension of invisible things and the inner or eternal Word given this dilemma.

In his commentaries, Gallus embraced the analogy, highlighting the eternal Word's aspects. First, the Word simply *is* God in the way an inner concept is indistinguishable from the speaker, and, second, it is the source or storeroom, as it were, of the eternal reasons in the way an inward word is a plan of speech.[51] As for the first aspect, in his *Explanatio* on the *Mystical Theology*, Gallus invokes "the eternal Word, which the Father speaks eternally."[52] That is, the Word is eternally with the Father. To Dionysius's statement that "this Theology (*theologia*) is placed beyond all things supersubstantially and is manifested unveiled and truly only to those who pass through pure and impure things," Gallus adds that "the Word of God (*Verbum Dei*), which truly is theology (*theologia*), incomparably exceeds every created thing and being."[53] That is, the eternal Word of God, the true Theology, is itself beyond being, united to God.

---

51   In the Song commentaries, Gallus remarks on grammatical number of the term *storeroom(s)* in verses 1:3b ("*the king led me into his storerooms*") and 2:4 ("*he led me into the wine storeroom*"), arguing that they refer, respectively, to the Word's "spectacles" (*theoriae*) and "the Word containing all the spectacles (*Verbum continens omnes theorias*)." *Song Commentary III*, 2.C, 147. That is, Gallus articulates how the eternal Word, as the divine source of multiplicity, is both singular and multiple.
52   Gallus, *Explanatio super Mystica Theologia*, 1, 12.
53   Gallus, *Explanatio super Mystica Theologia* 1, 24. Gallus recognized what can be easily overlooked by readers of the Dionysian corpus—*theology* (θεολογία) was simply Dionysius's preferred term for the *Word of God*, which the (supposedly) apostolic author used interchangeably to refer to both Scripture (which itself was written by the "theologians") and the principle of the created order. This aspect of Dionysius fit well with the Victorine tendency to weave creation and Scripture.

Again, these descriptions align with the view that the eternal Word in its first aspect is like an inner concept (*conceptio cordis*) even before it is linguistically formed, intimate to and indistinguishable from the mind in which it exists. Put another way, the Word of God in its first aspect is "simple," indivisible from and one with God. When Dionysius, in a list of "affirmations" about God, says that "the Lights dwelling in the heart of Goodness sprang forth and remained . . . without departing from their coeternal abiding," Gallus glosses that "the Father is called the heart (*cor*) because, just as our word (*verbum*) and breath proceed from our heart, so also do the Son and the Holy Spirit proceed from the Father, and the same Lights have remained in the Son and in the Holy Spirit from eternity and remain into eternity."[54] This gloss, which reminds us of how closely Gallus associates the concepts of goodness and Trinity, also illuminates his thinking on the analogy between the eternal Word and the inner concept. Just as the concept, even when linguistically formed, remains in the mind of the speaker, so also the eternal Word, even when it multiplies with eternal reasons, remains eternally with the Father.[55]

Yet if the eternal Word remains eternally with the Father like an inner concept, it also contains the eternal reasons (*rationes aeternae*): "In that highest, simple Word all things are written eternally, on high, and simply as if in the first workmanship (*arte*)."[56] These things written in the simple Word were the eternal reasons.[57] This is the eternal Word in its second aspect, which, like the idea or plan of the house in the carpenter's mind or a linguistically formed inward word (*verbum intrinsecum*), predetermines what the builder or speaker will produce.

A string of passages from Gallus's final work, the *Explanatio* on the *Ecclesiastical Hierarchy*, speaks of the eternal Word more explicitly, depicting

---

54   Gallus, *Explanatio super Mystica Theologia* 3, 37.
55   For an account of Gallus's Trinitarian theology, including how it fits in his historical context, see Coolman, *Eternally Spiraling into God*, 31–55.
56   Gallus, *Explanatio super Mystica Theologia* 1, 10–11.
57   Although he was unaware of the Neoplatonic provenance of the concept of beyond-being-ness, Gallus recognized the Platonic origin of these ideas or exemplars, which Augustine had Christianized by placing as "archetypes" in the mind of God. Gallus, *Explanatio super Mystica Theologia* 1, 27.

the divine operation in which the simple Word, even prior to its incarnation or externalization, proceeds to a state of predetermining multiplicity: "The Lord speaks this sentence among others *from the whirlwind*, that is, the inscrutable and uncontemplatable profundity of eternal Wisdom."[58] That is, the Word is spoken from the beyond-being-ness, as it were. The eternal reasons come from this deep whirlwind, which is an image for "the plenitude of the eternal Word, in which there exist eternally the ideas of universal things, or the exemplars, archetypes, substance-making reasons, predeterminations, or whatever other name is chosen."[59] The eternal reasons are contained by the eternal Word. As chapter 5 will show, Gallus calls the eternal reasons *theoriae,* or "spectacles," from the perspective of the soul seeking union with the eternal Word. While they are eternal, they are the multiple rational principles for all that exists, or, to extend the Augustinian metaphor, the inward forms of all the ways in which the Word is exteriorized.

One final passage calls to mind the Augustinian metaphor explicitly and makes clear how the eternal Word is simple and multiple in its two aspects.

> *But the mental word* (verbum mentis) *forms the spoken words* (verba oris), *because from the abundance of the heart* (habundantia cordis) *the mouth speaks. Hence when the discourse* (sermo) *of the intellect fails, so also does the discourse of the mouth. But it must be noted that the Gospel is made of short sayings* (brevium dictionum) *because it is grasped by the very highpoint of the intellect; for this reason the Gospel is expansive when treated by the imagination, senses, or even reason, and it is ineffable in the Word of God, as much to humans as to angels, not only having few words, but only one, and that one, ineffable.*[60]

In this passage, Gallus's theology of the Word is explicitly linked to his understanding of sacred letters. The eternal Word, as it is united to God like an

---

58   Thomas Gallus, *Explanatio de Ecclesiastica Hierarchia*, in *Explanatio in Libros Dionysii*, ed. Declan Anthony Lawell, Corpus Christianorum Continuatio Mediaevalis 223 (Turnhout: Brepols, 2011), Pref., 733.
59   Gallus, *Explanatio de Ecclesiastica Hierarchia* Pref., 735.
60   Gallus, *Explanatio super Mystica Theologia* 1, 23.

inner concept, is ineffable and one. It is simply the one Word, eternally spoken and indistinguishable from the God beyond being. Yet when expressed to the human intellect or other lower mental faculties, it is multiplied. The eternal Word is both the single principle of every multiplicity, and it contains the eternal reasons that predetermine the forms of multiple things. Together, these two aspects of the eternal Word are akin to an Augustinian inner concept (*conceptio cordis*) and inward word (*verbum intrinsecum*).

It is worth remembering here that in the Song of Songs commentaries, Gallus interprets the bridegroom as the eternal Word, whose union is elusive but whose *theoriae* continually and progressively draw near and renew the soul. Chapter 5 will argue that to "wander" among the *theoriae*, following the "itineraries of eternity," was an important image of mystical advancement for Gallus. It is only by progressive experience of the *theoriae* of the eternal Word—the aspect of the eternal Word akin to an inward word—that the soul can be transformed. However, even the soul's encounter with the *theoriae* depends initially on the Word's exteriorization or incarnation.

Incarnate Word: Exterior Word
Completing the Augustinian analogy with human communication, the eternal Word becomes exteriorized (*verbum exterius*) or vocalized (*vox*). In Victorine theology, this exteriorization of the Word occurs both narrowly and broadly: narrowly in the special or "dominical incarnation (*dominica incarnatio*)" of the Word in the human being Jesus and broadly in the creative operation of the Word in all history. In fact, although a "cosmic Christology" that saw all of creation and history as an exterior expression of the eternal Word is characteristic of the Victorines, and perhaps even twelfth-century theology in general, Dionysius's descriptions of the Word of God (*Theologia*) and Jesus reinforced in Gallus the Victorine tendency to broaden the dominical incarnation to include the "incarnation" of the Word in creation or history.[61] In Gallus's thought, Jesus Christ the incarnate Word

---

61 Even Gallus's occasional use of the adjective in the formulation *dominica incarnatio* suggests he feels the need to qualify *incarnatio* when speaking of the specific incarnation treated in the Gospels. There may also be a broader or more expansive understanding of *incarnatio*, which nevertheless has Jesus as its principle, as we will see.

is, as we will see, also the principle of creation. As the Augustinian metaphor suggests, both the particular incarnation of the Word in Jesus Christ and the general manifestation of the Word in creation and history are like exteriorizations of the inward word. The resulting elision of the incarnate and the cosmic Word—or the particular and general exteriorizations of the Word—has implications for Gallus's understanding of sacred letters. Sacred letters (*sacrae litterae*) were themselves like "explanations" of the Word, attempts to explain, pass on, or interpret knowledge of both the exterior Word in creation, incarnation, and history and the inward word and inner concept in the eternal Word.

Because Dionysius's christological reflections were occasional and infrequent, Gallus's treatment of the matter is likewise scattered across the *Explanatio*. One important cluster of glosses, however, appears in the *Explanatio* on the *Letters*, the only place Dionysius treats the incarnation in any depth. The incarnation, Dionysius says, involves the Word of God (*Theologia*) suddenly being made manifest from the nonmanifest. Gallus glosses that this is "the work of the dominical incarnation, namely the Lord Jesus himself."[62] This special exteriorization or revelation of what had been hidden was "**a certain new operation** of him **as God and human**, that is, with Christ, God and human, performing untried things."[63] The Word becoming flesh, suddenly and newly, was "Jesus, the mediator of God and human beings (*Ihesum mediatorem Dei et hominum*)."[64]

These statements are standard rehearsals of a common Christian theology of incarnation—God or the Word became flesh in Jesus. What Dionysius adds, it should be no surprise, is a description of the incarnation in terms of beyond-being-ness. Gallus glosses, "**And** he, **truly coming to substance (*substantiam*)**, that is, to being (*esse*), when before he was so beyond being (*esse*) and being (*ens*), or **coming** into the world to receive human substance **was made substance beyond** all **substance**, with a lone virtue

---

62 Gallus, *Explanatio* on the *Epistles*, in *Explanatio in Libros Dionysii*, ed. Declan Anthony Lawell, Corpus Christianorum Continuatio Mediaevalis 223 (Turnhout: Brepols, 2011), 723.

63 Gallus, *Explanatio in Libros Dionysii* 728.

64 Gallus, *Explanatio super Angelica Ierarchia*, 1, 487.

divine and super-substantial, or only in such a way that he was incomparably pre-eminent over every other pure creature."[65]

The incarnation is a special instance of the beyond-being, eternal Word's exteriorization. Though God and the Word spoken eternally are beyond being, when the Word is incarnated, it comes to being. It takes on human substance even as it remains beyond substance.

Jesus: The Word as Hierarch

Indeed, Jesus was for Gallus, as for Dionysius, the principle and end of every hierarchy or divine operation that deifies and unites to God. When Dionysius invokes "Jesus" in his *Ecclesiastical Hierarchy,* Gallus glosses, "the principal and universal hierarch, from whose plenitude all hierarchies receive. . . . But the Lord Jesus is one and the same universal hierarch with the triune deity or the divine Trinity."[66] That is, Jesus, one with the Trinity and the source of all goodness, is the single and simple source of all multiple hierarchies: "**Jesus himself,** who is **the most thearchic mind**, that is, divine and principal wisdom . . . the Lord Jesus himself, as our principal hierarch, **contains**, that is, unites and simplifies . . . **many differences**, that is, various divisions of thoughts and affections."[67] Again, Gallus's Christology stresses the distinction between the eternal Word as simple and united to God (like an inner concept) and the eternal Word as containing and actuating the multiple eternal reasons (like an inward word and exterior word). In Jesus himself, God and human, these aspects come together and serve as the source or model for all hierarchic, deifying operations. Jesus is the Hierarch, the principle of history and creation, as it were—the Christ of the cosmos.

Gallus thus describes a narrow and a broad exteriorization of the Word: the former, dominical and human; the latter, cosmic and understood as the principal outpouring of the Trinity's beyond-being-ness. Gallus invokes "the incarnate Word, in whom alone the fullest universality of beyond-being-ness (*superessentialitas*), of essence, of life, of sensuality, of rationality, of wisdom,

---

65   Gallus, *Explanatio in Libros Dionysii,* 726.
66   Gallus, *Explanatio de Ecclesiastica Hierarchia* 5, 916.
67   Gallus, *Explanatio de Ecclesiastica Hierarchia* 1, 741–42.

and of goodness are united and in agreement."[68] Here is a rather frank statement that the incarnate Word, the Word exteriorized, Jesus himself, cannot be separated from the eternal Word, the inward word, the principle of creation. While the Word is externalized, manifested, and incarnated in the "dominical incarnation" of Jesus, Jesus is himself the eternal Word containing the principles of creation. Elsewhere, Gallus states that the "incarnation of the Word (*Verbi incarnationem*)" is simply the "fulfillment of goodness (*bonitatis plenitudinem*)," which, as we have seen, is for Gallus the prime affirmation of the God beyond being.[69]

Keeping in mind the underlying Augustinian metaphor of communication helps to illuminate Gallus's cosmic Christology. Although Jesus is a special instance of the Word's exteriorization, because the Word is also the creative and guiding principle of history, Gallus follows Dionysius in downplaying the distinction between the two aspects, as it were, of the Word's exteriorization. On the one hand, Gallus affirms that Jesus, the Word incarnate, God made flesh, is a special fulfillment of goodness, the knowledge of which, along with God's beyond-being-ness, makes the wisdom of Christians distinct from and privileged over gentile wisdom. In the following passage from *Divine Names*, Dionysius has invoked the "harmony" that all things receive from the "wise and beautiful" God. Gallus glosses, "The philosophers of the gentiles investigated this harmony in no middling way, and it was fulfilled in the incarnate Word, where the highest, the lowest, and the middle were joined in one person, who is the fullness of every desirable beauty, namely essence, life, wisdom, goodness, blessedness, etc., and this is the testimony of the highest kindness."[70]

Here Gallus depicts the incarnation as the supreme, special, or singular instance of a more general cosmic harmony that could be known even by those who do not know of the incarnation in Jesus. The dominical incarnation (*dominica incarnatio*) is a perfect and perfecting instance of the exteriorization of the eternal Word.

---

68 Gallus, *Explanatio de Divinis Nominibus*, 4, 249.
69 Gallus, *Explanatio de Divinis Nominibus* 4, 283.
70 Gallus, *Explanatio de Divinis Nominibus* 1, 86–87.

Creation: The Word Exteriorized

Though Jesus was the perfect exteriorization of the Word, the Augustinian analogy, with its roots in Platonism, suggested that creation and history in general were also an exteriorization of the Word, the outpouring of the "storeroom" of the eternal reasons. A suggestive formulation in the middle of *Ecclesiastical Hierarchy* ties the two ideas together. Dionysius, in a discussion of the Eucharist, refers to "the creator of signs (*creator signorum*)," whom Gallus glosses as "Christ, who first and principally is the arranger of signs (*ordinator signorum*)."[71] That is, Jesus Christ is not the only sign (*signum*), exterior word (*verbum exterius*), or voice (*vox*) of the eternal Word but the Sign of signs, the one who like an inward word plans out or predetermines the exterior expression. With the assurance that Jesus Christ, the incarnate Word, is the arranger of all signs, Gallus can say that everything created by the Word from the eternal reasons is an exteriorization of the Word: "Existing things [are those things] which come forth from the Word into being (*esse*) through creation; those things are called non-existing which only exist in the super-essential Word, and nevertheless can be contemplated in the Word itself."[72] Gallus goes on to explain that these "non-existing" things are the *theoriae,* or the eternal reasons, but what this passage shows is that the Word is the principle of creation and history, and therefore created things exteriorize, reflect, or convey the Word. If creation and history themselves are also like exteriorizations of the inward Word, like the outpouring of a king's private storeroom, how do they relate to the exteriorization of the Word in Jesus?

Thanks to Dionysius's discussion of sacred signification in *Celestial Hierarchy,* Gallus concludes that created things are themselves capable of signifying celestial and divine things: "Hence the lowest creatures can, by reason of their participation, rightly signify the plenitude and the very excellent participations in the Good of the kind which are in the celestial substances. . . . Moreover, because everything participates in the Good, it shows the authority of the scriptures, because **the truth of the eloquences speaks.**"[73] Two points can be made from this passage. First, created things

---

71 Gallus, *Explanatio de Ecclesiastica Hierarchia* 3, 811. Dionysius: ὁ τῶν συμβόλων δημιουργός.
72 Gallus, *Explanatio super Mystica Theologia* 1, 16.
73 Gallus, *Explanatio super Angelica Ierarchia* 2, 517.

participate in God's Word and can therefore "rightly signify." They are predetermined by the eternal reasons, which reside in the eternal Word; thus, they communicate God's intention or profound inner concept. Everything, in turn, has the potential to be a sign. Second, Gallus concludes that the signs of the created order are rightly harnessed by the theologians who wrote the Scriptures (*eloquia*). Creation and history provide the material guidance for hymning the God beyond being, especially the Word eternally spoken.[74]

In rehearsing Dionysius's arguments in *Celestial Hierarchy* about the use of base or material images for the God beyond being, Gallus reinforces a major principle of the school of St. Victor—invisible things (*invisibilia*) are known through visible things (*visibilia*). Paul's statement in Romans 1:20 that "the invisible things of him, from the creation of the world, are clearly seen, being understood by the things that are made" provided the spiritual justification for much of the school's focus on the liberal arts.[75] Knowing visible things was the prerequisite or foundation for knowing invisible, spiritual things.[76] The Augustinian analogy with human speech supports this Pauline principle. If creation and history—visible things—are the Word exteriorized, one should follow them back to the inward Word and eternal reasons—invisible things—which they represent. Yet while the principle of *visibilia-invisibilia* was foundational for wisdom, even appreciated to some extent by pagan philosophers, it was not sufficient for the special wisdom of Christians. Gallus characterizes the deficiency of pagan philosophers as their

---

[74] Though, as we will see, scriptural signification must be understood to refer to God in particular ways and is ordered by the Word itself, which the theologians experienced. It is not that the authors of Scripture compose their works from a general experience of creation and history—though for Gallus, like Hugh of St. Victor, there can be some wonderful achievements made simply from the effortful collation and composition of things in the world; pagan philosophy and literature were to be admired for the wisdom they achieved in this way. Rather, it is the special experience of the Word itself, when the mind is drawn beyond general experience, that ensured how truthfully the Scriptures spoke.

[75] For a treatment of the theme among the Victorines, see Coulter, *Per visibilia ad invisibilia*.

[76] Cf. ch. 5's account of Gallus's typically Victorine method of spiritual interpretation. Literal interpretation is the foundation of spiritual interpretation, even in the most spiritual of sacred writings. Because it was so critical to understand the letter, which could be drawn from creation or history, Hugh exhorted to "learn everything." Hugh, *Didascalicon*, VI.3.115, trans. Harkins, 166.

incapacity to consider a knowledge beyond this method: "Such the Apostle calls '*animal men*' (I Cor. 2:14), who namely determine that there is no knowledge of the invisible things except that which is gathered from visible things."[77] The theologians knew the Word *in toto* as Jesus, the beyond-being principle of creation and history, who is known beyond the mind by those who attain the wisdom of Christians.

Sacred Letters: Experiencing and Explaining the Word

Gallus's approach to sacred letters depends on this Word-centric, cosmic Christology and its analogy to human speech. As we have seen, Dionysius emphasized (1) the theologians' (the prophets' and apostles') experience of the presence of the God beyond being, (2) the capacity of theological symbols to both veil and unveil God, and (3) the use of theological hymning causally and *hyperochically*. Gallus's theology of the Word helps him to navigate each of these issues. The theologians experienced the eternal Word in mystical union, while the incarnate Word's causal presence in creation and history, including preeminently but not exclusively in Jesus Christ, provided potential signs for the eternal Word. In turn, these signs are harnessed by the theologians to signify figuratively, causally, and super-essentially in an ambiguous way adapted to their experience of the eternal Word.[78] That is, the theologians, by both considering the Word in creation and history and experiencing the Word in mystical union, in turn explained the Word in sacred writings with techniques of mystical language that go beyond properly signifying. Sacred letters conveyed or performed an experience of the Word. Sacred writings could for that reason themselves be called the Word of God and as such needed to be read (*lectio*), experienced (*experientia*), and explained (*explanatio*).

The Word Experienced by the Theologians

Gallus notably innovates on the Dionysian corpus by interjecting the language of experience (*experientia*) into its mystical theology. As with much

---

77   Gallus, *Explanatio de Divinis Nominibus* 1, 117.
78   Again, Gallus's favorite designation of the Word, drawn from the Song, was "Whom my soul loves" because the eternal Word was ineffable and unintelligible but not undesirable. See ch. 5, 171–72. Figural, causal, and super-essential significations are all attempts to put into language the relation between the soul and "Whom my soul loves."

of Gallus's thought, there is some basis for this in the Dionysian corpus, as Dionysius describes the "suffering" or "experience" (πάθος) from which the bishop of Athens Hierotheus gains wisdom.[79] Denys Turner has suggested that the interjection of experience into the Dionysian picture transformed the understanding of Christian mysticism in ways that continue to shape theological and religious studies today.[80] As I argued in chapter 1, experience has been an orienting and much discussed category for the field of religious studies in general and the study of mysticism in particular. Turner identifies a tendency in modern religious studies to equate religious experience and doctrine/symbols as first- and second-order phenomena, respectively. He connects this to the experiential Dionysianism of the late medieval period. By claiming that theological teaching or symbol-making is a secondary response to a primary experience of the divine, late medieval mysticism mistakenly advanced the notion that experience itself may be prelinguistic and can be abstracted from culture and language. Turner argues that the explicitly "experiential" mystical turn inaugurated by Gallus was a fundamental alteration of the Neoplatonic mystical theology of Dionysius. Special affective experience, Turner argues, was not a goal or object of Neoplatonic mystical theology, which sought instead a speculative intuition of the One *through* a preexisting liturgico-symbolic and rational system.[81] To Turner, the medieval Western and subsequent modern focus on the *Mystical Theology* as the key to the Dionysian corpus—rather than the liturgically oriented *Ecclesiastical Hierarchy*—downplayed the significance of the linguistic and ritual condition of religious experience.

However, Turner's argument itself does not account for Dionysius's treatment of the special experience of the theologians, a feature of Dionysian theology Gallus frequently pointed out. The prophets and the apostles who composed the mysteries of the Scriptures themselves experienced the Word of God in apparitions and mystical ascents. The Augustinian analogy to human speech suggests how their experience of the Word was understood as both inward and exteriorized, eternal and incarnate. The theologians experienced

---

79 Pseudo-Dionysius, *Divine Names*, 2.9.
80 Turner, "How to Read Pseudo-Denys Today."
81 Turner, "How to Read Pseudo-Denys Today," 430–31.

the Word's general exteriorization in creation and history, the Word's particular incarnation in Jesus, and special instances of mystical union with the eternal Word.[82] That is, the authors of Scripture come to have and pass down both the "pagan wisdom" gathered from the created order and the "wisdom of Christians" known only to those who experience it. The Scriptures and liturgy are not just the linguistic and ritual *conditions* for Christian experience; they are the outpouring of the theologians' experience of the Word as both incarnate and eternal. They are like commentaries on the theologians' reading of the Word.

Dionysius presented a model of theological experience in Hierotheus, traditionally held to be the first bishop of Athens and so his direct superior. Dionysius even quotes at length from Hierotheus's (otherwise unknown) works, such as his *Hymns of Love*. Gallus glosses Dionysius's account of Hierotheus's experience: Hierotheus **"was taught from a certain more divine inspiration, not only learning divine things**, through an intellectual drinking in, of which our intellect is capable through divine and angelic inflowing, **but also suffering divine things** through the apex of the affection, namely, a union experiencing divine sweetness, softness, and flame through taste, smell, and touch."[83]

Here, Gallus invokes his major teaching on Dionysian mystical union—that it engages both intellect and affect—in explicating the experience that inspires the writing of Hierotheus's hymns. Hierotheus not only received Christian wisdom from the theologians themselves but experienced, intellectually and affectively, a perfecting mystical union. Elsewhere, Gallus calls this Hierotheus's "most profound and experiential knowledge (*profundissime et experientialis cognitionis*)."[84] Hierotheus, the bishop of Athens

---

82   For a brief description of Gallus's expansive use of "experience" to refer to everything from everyday consciousness to special instances of divine union, see ch. 5, 136–37.

83   Gallus, *Explanatio de Divinis Nominibus* 2, 154–55. Dionysius's felicitous rhyme (οὐ μόνον μαθὼν ἀλλὰ καὶ παθών) is somewhat lost in translation (*non solum discens sed et patiens*), but Gallus caught the significance. Experience of divine things enhanced or supplemented learning about them.

84   Gallus, *Explanatio de Divinis Nominibus* 3, 172. Saracen's translation carefully conveyed the following terms in this way: "knowledge" (γνῶσις) as *cognitio*, "intellect" (νοῦς) as *intellectus*, and "understanding" (νόησις) as *intelligentia*.

and Dionysius's teacher after Paul, provided an example of one who receives apostolic wisdom, experiences mystical union and mystical knowing, and hymns in response.

While the next chapter will treat the nature of mystical experience in more detail, it is important to notice here how Gallus attends to the experience of the theologians. He says that apostolic speech (*sermo*) is "not from intellectual teachings, which by the exercise of human skill are compounded and founded in the pre-existing cognition of sensible things, but from the super-intellectual unions and experiences of the holy theologians through the departure of the mind toward the Holy Spirit teaching and admonishing them."[85] That is, the forms of theological communication (hymning, praising, preaching, etc.) are not like the kind of teaching done by those with the wisdom of pagans, which is drawn from common consideration of the created order and history alone, but with the wisdom of Christians, which is drawn, at least in part, from the experience of and union with the Word. "But this union is felt," Gallus insists, "by an experience of the principal affection beyond the intellect,"[86] and it "has a super-intellectual experience both in the journey of this life and in the homeland of the next."[87] That is, the theologians realized the promise of Christian wisdom or mystical theology. Their hymning or writing of the Scriptures was an attempt to convey this experience and thus cooperate and participate in the exteriorization of the Word. If the theologians experienced the Word, how did they explain their experiences?

The Word Explained by the Theologians Figuratively, Causally, and Super-essentially

On the one hand, the theologians' task of writing or passing on an experience of the Word is impossible. "The super-intellectual experience" of the eternal Word is ineffable. On this experience, Gallus writes that "it cannot be stated what sorts of things the mind experiences which no one knows except who receives . . . because it is beyond the mind. For this reason, neither can it be

---

85   Gallus, *Explanatio de Divinis Nominibus* 1, 50.
86   Gallus, *Explanatio de Divinis Nominibus* 1, 85.
87   Gallus, *Explanatio de Divinis Nominibus* 1, 92: "*Habet enim ipsa unitio experientiam superintellectualem et in via et in patria.*"

spoken by any word of the mind, much less a word of the body."[88] Again, "although I may try to express the meaning of these words, nevertheless for certain we hold that the power of the apostolic experience cannot be expressed worthily in writing, in speech, or in thought."[89] To put it frankly, "the word of the mind (*verbum mentis*) is not able to express in writing or in words those super-intellectual experiences."[90] The most Gallus will say is that "those experienced (*experti*) in such matters can instruct and inflame those who are experiencing (*experientes*). . . . But he who has never tasted sweetness cannot teach someone about sweetness with words."[91] How, then, do the experienced, who cannot "worthily express" their experience, instruct and inflame those who seek to experience?

Gallus appreciated that Dionysius's theology of scriptural language drew on the potential of purposeful ambiguity. Dionysius had explained, particularly in the first few chapters of *Celestial Hierarchy*, why theological language posed a problem, given that the God beyond being was ineffable. Gallus, too, inspired by the Song of Songs, held that the best one could say about the eternal Word was to call it "Whom my soul loves" because the experience of mystical union, like the one to Whom the soul is united, is itself ineffable and unintelligible. The theologians must resort to ambiguous or equivocal uses of language in the Scriptures or "the eloquences."[92] Gallus glosses, "**and** the mystical traditions of the eloquences **reform**, that is, they speak by describing **it** the divine blessedness **as light . . . and they call** it **life**."[93] That is, the authors of Scripture engage in an act of literary or rhetorical composition of the divine, which they experienced. This is an act of creative reforming or remaking and is accommodating to their readers: "Theology (*theologia*) **attends to our mind**, has compassion, as it were, for

---

88   Gallus, *Explanatio de Divinis Nominibus* 2, 155. One of Gallus's favorite citations, quoted six times in the third Song commentary alone, was this verse, Revelation 2:17: "No one knows it except the one who receives (*nemo illud scit nisi qui accipit*)."
89   Gallus, *Explanatio de Divinis Nominibus* 4, 240.
90   Gallus, *Explanatio de Divinis Nominibus* 4, 234.
91   Gallus, *Explanatio de Divinis Nominibus* 2, 155.
92   John Saracen translates Dionysius's preferred term for the Scriptures, τὰ λόγια ("oracles, sayings") with *eloquia* ("eloquences, communications").
93   Gallus, *Explanatio super Angelica Ierarchia* 2, 510–11.

our infirmity, thanks to the intention of God and the theologians . . . **and through sensible forms provides it** our mind **an uplifting** for contemplating, investigating, imitating celestial and divine things, **which acquaints** by aligning or joining (*coaptationem*) properties to invisible things."[94]

That is, the theological language of the Scriptures uses the properties of sensible or visible things to instruct and inflame the mind, making it possible for the mind to investigate and contemplate things otherwise inaccessible to it. How does theological language do this?

As we saw earlier in this chapter, Dionysius describes theological language as working both causally and *hyperochically* ("beyond-having-ly"). This is what distinguishes hymning from more common uses of speech or communication that refer to the sensible and visible things of creation. Theological hymning takes into account God both as beyond being and as cause. That is, when a divine name like Being, for instance, is used for God, it may refer to how God is the cause of being, or it may refer to the fact that God is beyond being. Gallus rehearsed both of these modes of theological language, glossing that God was Being "in a causal and a super-essential manner (*causaliter et superessentialiter*)."[95] The following passage also shows Gallus's concern with the use of varied language for God as cause: "Although I think that there is truly only one perfection of perfectible and rational natures, the super-simple deity . . . nevertheless it is designated in many ways because of various and multiple efficacies, just as in Romans 1:20 it is said: *the invisible things of God* . . . , and in *DN* 7h: 'He is all things in all things and nothing in none.'"[96] Again, following Paul and Dionysius, because God is the cause of all "various and multiple efficacies," there are many appropriate uses of language to hymn God as cause. Divine causality in creation and history—the general activity of the Word's exteriorization—is the foundation for the use of various terms.

At the same time, Gallus reckoned with Dionysius's claim that theological language also works hyperochically, or, in the Latin translation, "super-essentially" (*superessentialiter*). We saw earlier in this chapter that even

---

94 Gallus, *Explanatio super Angelica Ierarchia* 2, 505.
95 Gallus, *Explanatio super Angelica Ierarchia* 4, 556.
96 Gallus, *Explanatio super Angelica Ierarchia* 1, 481.

among contemporary readers, there is disagreement about what Dionysius means by this as there is a fundamental ambiguity already built into the prefix *hyper-*. How did Gallus understand language to work super-essentially? Despite his use of plenitude and abundance to describe the super-essentiality of God, Gallus does not characterize theological language as depicting how God possesses some quality in a preeminent fashion.[97] Rather, for theological language to work super-essentially means for it to work negatively or at least ambiguously. For instance, "Moreover, this name 'super-principal' is actually negative. For it removes principality and 'passes over' (*transmittit*) it to a higher thing, as it were, by positing nothing (*nihil ponendo*). It is likewise with similar things, as it is with super-substantial, super-intellectual, super-simple, super-beautiful, super-exalted, super-wise, and all other similar things. For this reason, such words are attributed to God less improperly than others: below 2d: 'negations are truly in divine things, etc.'"[98] Otherwise put, theological language with the *super-* prefix not only refers to God as the Cause of all things but is used to remind the hearer or reader to "pass over" the signifying sign, to ensure obstacles are removed from their mind. The word *principality* is an obstacle to knowing or experiencing union with the Word beyond the word, but it is an obstacle that should be overcome.[99]

While Gallus appreciates how causal and super-essential modes of theological language are used for the God beyond being, he most often comments on a third special use of language: figurative language. Figural representation is drawn from visible things for invisible things. This is thanks to the preponderance of "invisible things" in the Dionysian corpus—not just

---

97 In this, Gallus contrasts with Thomas Aquinas's conclusion that when Dionysius claimed that theological language worked *hyperochically*, he meant it refers to God "pre-eminently." For Aquinas, the predication of divine attributes could be used to refer to God as Cause of that quality, or it could refer to God as having that quality in a superlative way. Put another way, Aquinas consistently sees the *super-* prefix as less negative, or at least less aporetic, than Gallus. See Wolfson, "St. Thomas on Divine Attributes," in Twersky and Williams, *Studies in the History of Philosophy and Religion*, 673–700.

98 Gallus, *Explanatio super Angelica Ierarchia* 1, 490. Notice that Gallus's gloss of the *super-* prefix here emphasizes its transcendent valence rather than its superlative valence.

99 Cf. the practice of "unveiling of the mind (*revelatio mentis*)" described in ch. 5, 159–60, and prescribed by Dionysius.

the God beyond being but also celestial and divine realities like angels and the eternal reasons/*theoriae*. Even this use of theological language, which does not refer directly to God as the beyond being Cause, is employed ambiguously. Figurative language for invisible things, drawn from visible things, takes advantage of what Gallus calls an "inward relation (*intrinseca relatio*)" between the visible and the invisible.[100] The following extended passage from Gallus's early *Glossae* on the *Celestial Hierarchy* suggests the extent to which he emphasizes the ambiguity of theological language and the mysterious relation between the visible and the invisible.

> *This inward relation between visible and invisible things . . . is a difficult question, which rises from the letter (*ex littera*). For I seek with what kind of sameness invisible celestial things, greatly divine, are united to visible things. They are united to them neither in kind, appearance, species, accident, property, nor as a whole. For any divine invisible thing differs more from any visible thing than any visible thing from another, because even contrary things are united in kind. For example, whiteness of body differs more from cleanliness of the mind which it signifies, or the clarity of invisible light which it signifies, than from blackness.*
>
> *Therefore how does that from which it is entirely different signify? Or what similitude or acquaintance of whatever visible things can be found to their signified invisible things? I think not in any general way (*aliquo universali*), which indeed could settle (*caderet*) into the intellect, but only in an inner natural estimation (*intima naturali estimatione*), which is not anticipated nor rightly grasped by the word of the mind (*verbo mentis*) and the intellect. And in this way, clarity in body is estimatively (*estimative*) a cleanliness in mind or light in eternity.*[101]

There are a number of things to notice here about Gallus's understanding of the figurative use of visible things for invisible things. First, visible and

---

100   Gallus, *Explanatio super Angelica Ierarchia* 2, 518.
101   Thomas Gallus, *Glose super Angelica Ierarchia*, ed. Declan Lawell Corpus Christianorum Continuatio Mediaevalis 223A (Turnhout: Brepols, 2011), 2, 20.

invisible things are entirely and categorically different, sharing no common properties or appearances, their relation established mysteriously. In Gallus's later *Explanatio* on the *Celestial Hierarchy*, he drives home the point by saying that "it is not because of a union that the sensible things are spoken" for invisible things.[102] That is, nothing unites the visible signs to their invisible counterparts. For this reason, the intellect cannot gather them together in any concrete way that could be effable or intelligible. Rather, the visible and invisible things have what Gallus calls an "inward relation (*intrinseca relatio*)," which issues in the mind's inner alignment of the two but which is never linguistically formable or intellectually graspable. In the *Explanatio* on the same passage, he calls this "estimation" not only "intimate" but "super-intellectual."[103] For Gallus, theological figuration is not simply metaphor but involves an intellectually ungraspable connection or alignment between the visible signs and the invisible things signified.[104] This relation is ineffable and unintelligible.

Figural representation of invisible things is dependent on super-intellectual knowledge. Though this figurative theological language refers explicitly to celestial and divine things that are not properly God—angels and the eternal reasons of creation—it suggests how ambiguously theological language must work when it refers to the very God beyond being. If *visibilia* have only a super-intellectual "inward relation" to *invisibilia*, theological language for the beyond-being Cause must be even more super-intellectual, as it were. This suggests just how inadequate an interpretation of theological signification as "preeminent" or "superlative" would be for Gallus. Indeed, in his *Glossae* on the *Celestial Hierarchy*, Gallus says that even in signifying the Trinity, there is but an "estimation" between sensible sign and transcendent

---

102   Gallus, *Explanatio super Angelica Ierarchia* 2, 518.
103   Gallus, *Explanatio super Angelica Ierarchia* 2, 518.
104   This is a reminder that the *theoriae* belong to the eternal Word of the God beyond being and are not simply knowable through rational speculation. Perhaps "lower" and "higher" *theoriae* differ in this, given that Gallus also seems to claim at times that even pagan wisdom—which works only from collection, consideration, and intellection—attains to the eternal reasons. But the relation discussed in these remarks is one of the mind's dependence on and ecstasy toward the Word, who alone makes effective the figurative language. For more on the *theoriae*, see ch. 5, 149–52.

signified: "For the divine operations in the Trinity, which are natural and eternal, are not united at all with angelic or human operations, unless by a natural estimation, but . . . they also occur supernaturally and beyond the intellect. This [estimation] is agreeable to the affection and established in advance (*ante radicem*), as it were. For union of predicable things is agreeable to the intellect."[105] Here, Gallus's best-known teaching comes to bear even on theological signification. Just as between visible signs and invisible celestial or divine things there is only a super-intellectual "estimation" that makes possible the process of signification, so also between the Trinity itself and the human operations from which the theologians draw their descriptions there is but a predetermined "estimation" that can be appreciated by the affection beyond the intellect but does not have the kind of union graspable by the intellect. Theological language activates the affect more than the intellect, and this is thanks to the effecting work of the divine Word.[106]

Unlike Thomas Aquinas, who interpreted *hyperoche* predication of divine attributes in terms of God's superlative and preeminent possession,[107] and more in line with Dionysius's original mystical rhetoric, Gallus understands theological language—especially of the God beyond being— to work "estimatively," reliant on a connection established by and continually sustained by the eternal Word itself, whose gracious action alone makes possible the affective knowledge of God, and the letter that arises from it. The theologians write figurally, causally, and super-essentially to explain their experience of the Word, as they knew not only of its communicative work in creation and history but of its fundamental ineffability. Figurative, causal, and super-essential language directs one to the eternal Word's *theoriae*, experiences of the mysterious providence of the God beyond being. In general, however, theological language affects one thanks to the mysterious working of divine grace. For Gallus, reading (*lectio*) the

---

105   Gallus, *Glose super Angelica Ierarchia*, 3, 35. "Predicables" is drawn from Aristotelian logic. They are the classes to which predicates belong: genus, species, difference, property, and accident. Gallus means to say that the similarity between the Trinity and humanity is not predicable or according to any shared class and therefore not graspable by the intellect.
106   On how the Word "effects" the affective experience of the alignment between visible and invisible, see ch. 5, 159–66.
107   See Wolfson, "St. Thomas on Divine Attributes," 506–9.

letter, the theologians' writings, is not only a pedagogical prerequisite of contemplation (*contemplatio*), as "the venerable doctor master Hugh" had described, but was itself a contemplative practice, allowing one to experience the Word.

Reading and Commenting on the Word

The major difference between Dionysius and Gallus on sacred letters, then, was not necessarily in their theoretical framework for understanding theological language. Though Gallus's commentaries reflect Augustinian influences, placing Dionysius's theology of language in the context of sign theory and the analogy between human communication and the divine Word, Gallus largely embraced the Dionysian insights about theological language. The theologians spoke figuratively, causally, or super-essentially of the eternal Word and its eternal reasons or *theoriae*. Rather, the difference between Dionysius and Gallus was a matter of their respective concerns. Dionysius's theology of sacred letters emphasized literary or rhetorical composition—the way the theologians, or the authors of Scripture, took advantage of purposefully ambiguous uses of language to convey divine things. Gallus was, thanks to his training in the Victorine school, much more attuned to the resulting theory of spiritual interpretation and pedagogy—the way readers of sacred literature, moving from letter to spirit, could "follow the courses of the *theoriae*" back to the God beyond being. In other words, Dionysius's was a theology of Scripture writing, while Thomas Gallus's was a theology of Scripture reading. If the theologians wrote figuratively, causally, and super-essentially, how should one understand the way this language works in turn on the soul? What effect does the letter have on the reader? What reading practice does Gallus imagine as a result?

Given Gallus's training at the Victorine school, it should be no surprise that the interpretation of sacred language and literature is at the heart of his moral program for transforming the soul, setting it in the right relation to the Word.[108] His writings reflect long-established Victorine sensibilities about sacred literature and spiritual formation: namely, that sacred literature had been divinely arranged so that those with proper training in spiritual

---

108   See ch. 2's account of the Victorine theology of the letter.

interpretation could follow an ordered path from reading (*lectio*) to contemplation (*contemplatio*):[109] "Invisible mysteries are taught to us through sensible forms in the sacred scriptures or in the ecclesiastical operations and sacraments";[110] "Therefore spiritual understandings are handed down under signs and figures, in order that they may be concealed from the unworthy and revealed to the faithful, who are zealous for celestial wisdom."[111] Spiritual interpretation of Scripture was the culminating activity of the school's pedagogy established by Hugh of St. Victor. Thomas Gallus sounds much like Hugh when he writes that only those "erring, who cleave firmly to the letter, do not know spiritual understanding."[112]

While it is a mistake to cling to the letter when one may know the simple, eternal Word, Gallus exhibits a characteristic Victorine esteem for the letter as well, describing its salutary pedagogical and preparatory benefits and reflecting once again the relation between the visible and the invisible: "For the multitude, it is necessary to teach by using certain figures or figurative kinds of speech in which, as it were, the purity of the meaning is restrained and tempered. This is the fact that the dough is hidden in the vestment (Ex. 12e), that is, the pure truth from which the souls of the faithful are nourished (Dt. 8b; Matt. 4a; Wis. 16g) in the exterior letter (*in littera exteriori*)."[113]

The truth is hidden within the exterior letter. While the letter was for the untrained, the spiritually advanced knew the unfigured spirit beyond it. Gallus, in a characteristic intertextual reference, associates the vestment from Exodus mentioned in the above passage with the veil of the Song of

---

109   Gallus appeals directly to Hugh's language from the *Didascalicon* when he writes how Dionysius's readers "cooperate with the divine light so that they may participate in the true wisdom of Christians. Hence in this text he indicates to us a threefold way of stretching toward that wisdom, namely, contemplative prayer, reading, and meditation with the suspension of the soul." Gallus, *Explanatio super Mystica Theologia* 1, 14.
Cf. Hugh: "The life of a just person is trained in four things, which serve as certain stages through which he is raised to future perfection: namely, reading (*lectio*), meditation, prayer, and action. Then follows a fifth, contemplation (*contemplatio*)." *Didascalicon*, 161.
110   Gallus, *Explanatio de Ecclesiastica Hierarchia* 1, 749.
111   Gallus, *Explanatio de Ecclesiastica Hierarchia* 1, 761.
112   Gallus, *Explanatio super Angelica Ierarchia* 2, 503.
113   Gallus, *Explanatio super Mystica Theologia* 1, 11.

Songs 5:7b ("the keepers of the walls took away my veil from me"). Gallus writes, "The keepers removed it by expounding the scriptures."[114] That is, spiritual interpretation of Scripture is like the removal of a veil, an image reinforced by Dionysius's own consistent use of the language of "unfolding" or "unwrapping" (*ἀνάπτυξις, reseratio*) of divine names.

The expounding, unfolding, or opening of Scripture through spiritual interpretation did not involve the use of discursive reason in a way that would allow one to collate, compare, and make propositional deductions from the letter. Rather, the Christian wisdom treated by Dionysius and Solomon was a super-intellectual knowledge (*cognitio*). Gallus invokes and glosses a couple of passages from the *Divine Names* and *Ecclesiastical Hierarchy* to explain: "*DN* 2q: 'All divine things are known by participations alone,' and for this reason this knowledge (*cognitio*), incommunicable through words and writings, comes to be, and he does not know it *except who receives* (Rev. 2f). Nevertheless, he can be kindled by words or writings in possessing it: *EH* 7x: 'I trust that I will kindle sparks of divine fire restored in you through the things spoken.'"[115]

Notice that Gallus, after dismissing the idea that super-intellectual knowledge could be communicated through words, nevertheless characterizes theological language as able to kindle the mind of the reader. Gallus embraced the Dionysian metaphor of uplifting, or "anagogy," to describe the way the soul is "inflamed" toward God in the practice of spiritual interpretation. The practice of mental movements from visible sign to invisible thing could be understood as "alignments (*transumptiones*) of the terms of sensible things in order to uplifting-ly (*anagogice*) designate divine invisible things."[116] Theological language could not express super-intellectual experience, but it could serve as the medium for the mind's uplifting or excess, which involves a kind of affective knowledge that is "effected" by the Word.

As we will see in chapter 5, much of the activity of experiential union occurs due to the Word's gracious "effecting" of the mind's mental exercise. Gallus's theology of language thus ensures it is the Word that does

---

114   Gallus, *Explanatio super Mystica Theologia* 1, 11.
115   Gallus, *Explanatio super Angelica Ierarchia* 1, 483.
116   Gallus, *Explanatio super Mystica Theologia* 3, 38.

most of the work, establishing the mysterious relation between visible and invisible, translating the mind from the visible to the invisible through a mental ecstasy. But it is nevertheless possible to participate in the Word's effective communication, being assimilated to the Word, and so both the apostolic theologian and the modern school master use theological language to instruct their readers. The following passage suggests how common it was for Gallus and his brothers to engage in the practice of scriptural interpretation and commentary writing, and it reminds us that this practice is geared toward the cognition of the Word: "Figurative teaching can be expounded in many ways, whether morally or mystically, as we experience daily, turned sometimes to one meaning, sometimes to another, and even to an opposite meaning. But the truth is simple just as it is. It exists eternally and invariably, and the sacred teaching of Scripture, which in words and writings is variable . . . is invariable in itself."[117]

A loving knowledge of or experiential union with the eternal Word, simple and invariable, is the goal of spiritual interpretation. Gallus reasons that the theologians write figuratively, causally, and super-essentially in order to meet this goal. In the next chapter, we will return to Gallus's own practice of explaining and glossing the sacred letter of the Song as an example of this mode of mystical reading.

Conclusion

So far, I've explained how two strands of Christian theology came together at St. Victor to mystify the letter. From Paul and Augustine, the Victorines learned to see the letter as a *sign* pointing to the Spirit beyond it. The letter mimicked creation in its capacity to exteriorize the eternal Word of God. Reading the letter, then, was the way back to its internal living Spirit, the thing toward which the letter, as a glorious system of signs, ultimately pointed. Thus, the Victorine reader engaging with the letter is on a path or a journey to God's eternal Word.

Dionysian theology fostered a sense of God's mystery at St. Victor. The Victorines learned to see the letter less as a sign than as a *veil* that revealed and concealed the God beyond being. Gallus reasoned that the relation between

---

117   Gallus, *Explanatio super Mystica Theologia* 1, 12.

the letter and the Spirit, between the veil and God, was a mysterious one, established ultimately by the God of mystery. There was no intelligible or speakable connection between the letter and its mystical counterpart, only an "estimative" one. By mystifying the letter, shifting it from sign to veil, Gallus preserved the mystery of its object. The letter did not refer, or point to, God. How could it? How could anything point beyond being?

However, the mysterious relation between letter and spirit, veil and God, was not a limitation to the Victorines but a marvelous accommodation. With the letter mystified, reading became a mystical practice, capable of transforming the soul of the reader, uplifting it and leading it beyond itself. Following Dionysius, Gallus used metaphors of ecstatic uplifting and uniting assimilation to describe the effects of the mystified letter on the reader. Reading takes us out of ourselves and unites us to the creative and sustaining mystery from which the letter draws. Following the signs to their unknown and unknowable mystery, the practice of reading exercises the mind, slowly assimilating it and uniting it to the Word. While the last two chapters provided the theology that theorizes the mystified letter, the next chapter presents an example of the practice of mystical reading, focusing on how the mystified letter transforms and transports its readers.

5

THE LETTER AND EXPERIENCE

The Practice of Christian Wisdom

Thomas Gallus, the last great Victorine, composed most of his works not at the Paris school but far away in Vercelli, where he moved to lead a community of Augustinian canons. His commentaries suggest how he spread the Victorine reading culture to his new locale. We saw in chapter 4 that Gallus was a commentator through and through. However, unlike some medieval commentators whose commentaries were occasional, addressing Scriptures and other texts to meet the needs of a religious community, Gallus's were the result of a carefully planned agenda to systematically expound the greatest works of Christian wisdom—the writings of "blessed Dionysius the Areopagite" and Solomon's Song of Songs.

Gallus himself offers a brief account of this scholarly project, his examination of "the wisdom of Christians," in the prologue to his third Song commentary. There he explains there are two forms of knowledge of God (*cognitio Dei*). The first is "intellectual (*intellectualis*) and based on the consideration of created things." The second is beyond intellectual (*superintellectualis*), a special experiential knowledge of God. About this second form of knowledge of God, which comes directly from God, Gallus adds: "From the teaching of the Apostle, the great Dionysius the Areopagite wrote the theoretical part (*theoricam*) of this superintellectual wisdom, to the extent it can be written, in his little book on *Mystical Theology*, which I expounded carefully ten years ago. But in this present book, Solomon hands down the practical part (*practicam*) of the same mystical theology, as is clear throughout the sequence of the entire book."[1] This distinction between the "theoretical" work of Dionysius and the "practical" treatment of Solomon says

---

[1] Gallus, *Song Commentary III*, Prologue, 107. Gallus repeats the idea at 1.F, 128, where he calls the wisdom of Christians "the portion of Mary," who was traditionally understood to represent the contemplative life, superior to her active sister Martha.

explicitly what is at evidence across Gallus's commentaries on both works: the intertextual relationship between the Song and the Dionysian corpus is indispensable for understanding and appropriating, both intellectually and affectively, the program for Christian wisdom, that which Dionysius calls "mystical theology."

Having looked at how Dionysian mystical theology mystified the letter at St. Victor, we can now turn to the practice of reading the mystified letter. For Gallus, reading the Song of Songs could lead to the soul's affective union with the Word, as the reader engages with literal and spiritual interpretation. In Gallus's Song commentaries, we get the most vivid depiction of the interplay of reading and mystical progress. We see how the experience of the mystified letter transforms and transports the soul, uniting it to the Word and making it effective in mystical practice.

Mystical Union

As we saw in chapter 3, Dionysius ambiguously depicts union (ἕνωσις) in the *Mystical Theology* as both an unknowing (ἀγνωσία) and a knowing beyond the mind (γνῶσις ὑπὲρ νοῦν). In the *Celestial Hierarchy*, he claims the purpose of hierarchy itself is union and assimilation. John Saracen's new translation presented these tensions around mystical union studiously. What kind of union (*unitio*) occurs beyond the mind (*super mentem*) through an unknowing (*ignorantia*) or super-intellectual knowing (*cognitio superintellectualis*)? Thomas Gallus made sense of this ambiguity by appealing to the rhetoric of experience (*experientia*) and affect (*affectus*). Later in this chapter, we will see how he uses the rhetoric of "experience" and "effectivity" to depict the relation that emerges between the soul and the Word in mystical union.[2] In this section, I argue more explicitly that this rhetoric makes sense of the underlying ambiguity in Dionysius's account of the goal of mystical theology. For Gallus, Dionysius's description of mystical union as an unknowing knowing beyond the mind is best understood as a form of affection and experience.

---

2   *Effect* and *affect* have a common Latin stem from *ficio* ("to make" or "to do"). *Efficere* (*ex* + *ficio*) is "to carry out, to do completely," as the Word "carries out" or "effects" the exercise and experience of the soul in contemplative union. *Afficere* (*ad* + *ficio*) is "to do something (to one), to influence," as the Word "influences" or "affects" the mind in contemplative union.

Affectus

Gallus's two most significant innovations on Dionysian mystical theology are (1) his elevation of affect (*affectus*) to a privileged place in mystical union and (2) his angelic hierarchization of the mind.[3] Scholars have pointed to the influence of Augustine and Hugh on Gallus to account for the emphasis on affect. Augustine granted Latin readers a far more robust vision for the role of affect in relation to God than Dionysius, and Hugh—called by medieval readers the "other Augustine (*alter Augustinus*)"—had himself posited that one could love God more than one could know God.[4] These explanations are entirely plausible, but they leave the impression that Gallus's qualifications of Dionysian theology were attempts to conform it to established Augustinian habits of thought. Appealing to Augustine and Hugh does not make sense of how Gallus could reconcile affectivity with the rhetoric of mystical union in the Dionysian corpus. For Gallus, the Dionysian corpus begged for an explanation of mystical union as a matter of affect.

While Gallus distinguishes between two kinds of knowledge (*cognitio*)—one intellective and characteristic of the wisdom of the philosophers and one super-intellectual and affective, belonging only to the wisdom of Christians—both are founded on the efforts of the various other powers of the mind. Gallus does not distinguish sharply between pagan, intellectual wisdom and Christian, super-intellectual wisdom but "relativizes" them.[5] That is, intellectual knowledge—including that gained by collection, consideration, and ratiocination—appears to be a necessary but not sufficient precondition for affective knowledge.

Intellectual knowledge, however, is of two sorts, one active and one passive. The first active form of intellection (*intellectio*) is that gained by methodical processes of ratiocination. It is "composed from the consideration of created things.... For this reason the Apostle says in Romans 1:19: *what is known of God is manifest to them*. For what can be gathered from the preexisting knowledge of sensible things, is indeed known."[6] As Gallus

---

3   On the latter, see below, 154–57.
4   See Coolman, *Eternally Spiraling into God*, 17n75.
5   Coolman, *Eternally Spiraling into God*, 124–25.
6   Gallus, *Song Commentary III*, Prologue.A, 107: "*Duplex hic designatur Dei cognitio, una intellectualis que comparatur per considerationem creaturarum . . . Unde Apostolus*

describes in more detail in his treatise *The Spectacles of Contemplation*, the powers of sensation, imagination, and reason all take part in this active effort of collection (*collatio*), drawing together the images of sensible things into the mind, considering the causes of these things, and in turn reasoning even about the soul itself and to some extent its cause.[7] Generally, as one advances through these steps of contemplation, the baser, active powers of the soul gradually suspend (*suspensio*) themselves as higher powers take over.[8]

This first form of intellection, Gallus insisted, was thoroughly engaged by pagan philosophy. Gallus admired the extent to which pagan philosophers realized the potential of the intellect (*intellectus*) building on the foundation set by sensation, imagination, and reason. Yet he also believed it lacked the super-addition of grace given by the Word. On the one hand, Gallus realized, Plato was the one who had put forth the idea of eternal reasons, the archetypes of creation that Gallus held were contained in the eternal Word. Pagan philosophy was not only skillful at the methodical knowledge (*scientia*) that worked from the collation of created things but also went some way to intellectually intuit these principles of creation and therefore was able to know God, as Paul affirmed in Romans 1:19. In this way, Gallus could explain the virtuosity of pagan philosophy.[9] In this, Gallus was traditionally Victorine as Hugh of St. Victor a century before had explained the great extent to which secular letters achieve wisdom.[10]

---

ad Rom 1d: quod notum est Dei manifestum est illis. Notum siquidem est quod ex preexistente sensibilium cognitione colligi potest."

7 Thomas Galllus, *Spectacula Contemplationis*, in "*Spectacula Contemplationis* (1244–46): A Treatise by Thomas Gallus," ed. Declan Lawell, *Recherches de Theologie et Philosophie medievales* 76, no. 2 (2009): 249–85. The treatise's editor, Declan Lawell, describes it as largely derivative of Richard of St. Victor's *De Trinitate*.

8 For instance, sensation is suspended when the imagination is active, the imagination is suspended when ratiocination occurs, and so on.

9 He does not dwell on Paul's larger point in the first chapter of Romans that the possibility of this knowledge of God leaves the pagans "without excuse" for their ignorance and idolatrous practice.

10 As we saw in chapter 2, in his *Didascalicon*, Hugh uses two metaphors for the soul's condition, both of which suggest Hugh's fairly optimistic vision: (1) the *deformation* of the soul, which could be resolved by the disciplined training of the soul's powers with divine grace; but also (2) the *forgetting* of the truth, which learning could remedy. That is,

Nevertheless, Gallus's treatment of the angelic hierarchy of the mind hints at what he thought was lacking in pagan wisdom: a mental orientation toward the Word itself, eternally with and spoken by the God beyond being. The powers of the mind—sensation, imagination, reason, intellect, and affect—all work dynamically in the mental hierarchies of "Nature" and "Diligent Effort." However, Gallus stresses, only the intellect and the affect may continue beyond the highest order of "Diligent Effort," drawn by the Word beyond the mind into the hierarchy of "Grace." This movement from the mind's active effort to the Word's "effective" action is reflected in Gallus's use of the perfect passive participles *intellectus* and *affectus* for these powers. This knowledge or wisdom gained beyond the mind is received passively, not produced actively through collection, consideration, and ratiocination of sensible things.[11] For those engaged in Christian wisdom or mystical theology, intellection and affection beyond the mind, as we will see later in this chapter, are "effected" by the Word itself. In these forms of intellection and affection of the Word, sensation, imagination, and reason are obstacles that must be left behind.[12]

This reasoning qualifies the description sometimes made of Gallus as anti-intellectualist.[13] Gallus is less anti-intellectualist than super-intellectualist. While Gallus holds that knowledge drawn from created things must be removed from the mind, he also stresses both that this form of knowledge is foundational for Christian wisdom and that certain forms of intellection (*intellectio*) occur passively beyond the mind (*super mentem*). While the mind is suspended (*suspensio*) at the highest order of "Diligent Effort," the powers of affect and intellect both continue beyond the mind. As we will see later in this chapter, the Word and its *theoriae* play a significant role in determining

---

the pedagogical agenda of the Victorine School was to take advantage of the learning of pagan philosophy. Thus, Gallus, following Hugh, is optimistic about what pagan intellection (*intellectio*) achieves, even if he questions the failure of pagan philosophy to achieve affective or experiential knowledge of God.

11 For this reason, the first of the orders in the hierarchy of "Grace" is the "Thrones," which receive God.

12 Cf. below (159–60) the description of "unveiling of the mind" (*revelatio mentis*), one of the three principal exercises of the mind. The Song depicted the mind's baser powers as "little foxes," busy in the lower orders of the mind but obstacles to contemplation needing to be removed.

13 As proven by Coolman, *Eternally Spiraling into God.*

the shape of the soul's knowledge (*cognitio*) and affection (*affectio*) at this stage as the Word draws and transforms the intellect and the affect, and the soul "wanders" among the *theoriae*. That is, these forms of knowledge and affection do not "belong" properly to the soul but are rendered relationally as the soul and the Word meet. Suggesting how distinct medieval and modern theories of the soul and mind can be, knowing and feeling for Gallus are primarily matters of relation.

That said, Gallus affirms that the affect (*affectus*) knows God more intimately, intensely, and completely than the intellect (*intellectus*) for two reasons: first, God is beyond being and therefore beyond intelligibility; second, the affect is more receptive of the Word than the intellect. It is more capable of or open to receiving divine interventions. The affect alone can be drawn into the ninth and highest order of the hierarchy of "Grace," as the intellect—like the other, lower powers—is suspended. What is affect, and why can it proceed beyond intellect? The loving or affective union that occurs in this order is still a kind of knowledge (*cognitio*), though it is super-intellectual, the intellect having been suspended. Gallus draws the idea of the affect as a super-intellectual power from Dionysius:

> *Behold, he [Dionysius] ascribes a twofold knowledge (*cognitio*) to God: one from the mental collection of created things, which is intellective; the other from the experience of rays of eternal wisdom, which is beyond intellect and all being (*super intellectum et omne ens*). But consider which power of the soul it is by which this super-intellectual wisdom is perceived, from these words in the same [DN] ch. 7: "It is necessary to see that our mind has indeed a power for understanding through which it sees intelligible things, but it also has a union exceeding the nature of the mind through which it is joined to those things which are above itself. It is necessary to understand divine things according to this [union]," that is, to know them. Let us understand "union" to be the principal affect (*affectus*) of the soul by which we are joined to God.*[14]

---

14   Gallus, *Explanatio de Divinis Nominibus* 2, 126.
   As Gallus states, he is referring to a passage in chapter 7 (*Explanatio de Divinis Nominibus* 7, 370), which he glosses in the following way: "**Moreover** our mind has another

Here, Gallus claims the authority of Dionysius himself for describing two separate powers of the mind, one that knows by the intellect and one that knows by a union or the affect. Again, affective knowing is a matter of union with God, the mind being drawn beyond its own nature.

The super-intellectual knowledge attained by the affect is a superior form of knowledge. This is clear from Gallus's description of Moses's final ascent in the Dionysian treatise *Mystical Theology*. In Dionysius's description of Moses's ascent, he used almost all his primary terms for mystical union:

> **United,** *I say,* **to the entirely unknown,** *and this* **through familiarity with every knowledge,** *that is, through the love which effects a universal knowledge, through which also the union teaches all things (1 John 2g; John 14e: Whoever loves me will be loved by my Father, and I will love him and show myself to him), through which union to the divine spirit and to the Word containing all knowable things, he knows the Word itself and searches out the profound things of God (1 Cor. 2e).*[15]

Affective union, which is beyond the mind and beyond the intellect, nevertheless allows one to know the Word in a way intellection never could. This is because affect knows the Word in its eternal and super-essential simplicity, or, as Gallus puts it in the Song commentaries, knows the bridegroom himself rather than his multiple gifts.[16]

Is there a reason Gallus invokes affection and love at the height of mystical union? Although Dionysius makes references to the divine name Love and the "suffering (πάθος)" of Hierotheus (a proof-text Gallus wields adeptly), he does not make affection (*affectio*) or being affected (*affectus*) central to his mystical theology. Most readers of Dionysius conclude that he is concerned with knowledge (γνῶσις, *cognitio*), unknowing (ἀγνωσία, *ignorantia*), and union (ἕνωσις, *unitio*) but not affection. Why, then, does Gallus

---

power, namely **union**, the knowledge of which experience alone teaches, because it exceeds the speculative intellect more sublimely than the intellect [exceeds] the imagination and sensation."

15   Gallus, *Explanatio super Mystica Theologia* 1, 29.
16   See below, 163–66.

import the rhetoric of affectivity? Gallus's use of affect should not be thought of as an imposition on Dionysius's mystical theology. Rather, it makes some sense of the ambiguities inherent in Dionysius's depiction of mystical union. As should be clear by now, Gallus did not have antipathy toward knowledge, intellection, or even unknowing; indeed, he claimed that affection was a form of knowledge (*cognitio*). Nevertheless, something about the use of the rhetoric of intellection (*intellectio*) to describe the heights of Dionysian union was insufficient for Gallus.

The idea that the mind's affect could know God beyond the intellect addresses an infelicitous conception in Neoplatonic epistemology that it shares with much modern epistemology—the tendency to depict knowing on the model of vision. Indeed, there had been before Gallus and would be long after Gallus an Augustinian tradition of thinking about the knowledge of God in terms of a *visio Dei* obtained by the intellect. Neoplatonism at least since Plotinus had held that intellection requires both a knower and an object to be known, the kind of thing that exists and is intelligible. On the model of vision, intellection requires a distinct knower and object known. The "collection" and "consideration" of created things that to Gallus were characteristic of pagan philosophy worked on this model. As Gallus described, in the process of producing knowledge by method (*scientia*), the mind surveyed visible things with sensation and then reproduced them in images with the imagination. The picture that is conveyed in his treatise *Spectacula Contemplationis*, which stops short of super-intellectual affection in its account of the steps of contemplation, is of the knowing soul as a distant overseer of the created order, mentally gathering it all together.

Contrast this image with that of the Song commentaries, where Gallus consistently depicts the soul dispossessed and impinged on suddenly by the Word. This picture can be understood as encompassing super-intellectual knowing, unknowing, and union. As the soul knows (*cognoscere*) the Word beyond the mind (*super mentem*), it is no surveyor of the Word of God but dependent on its own ecstasy and the interventions of the Word itself. This kind of knowledge is intimate, not distant. For Gallus, affective knowledge works not on the model of vision but on the model of taste, touch, and smell, where there is some kind of incorporation or dissolution of the boundaries between the thinker and their object: "Moreover the rational mind has an eye, an ear, and a word or tongue for speaking in the intellect, in the affect [it has] touch, taste, and smell, through which it examines experientially *the profound things of God* . . . just as taste and smell examine the insides of bodies."[17] Just as the food directly affects (or "does something to") the senses, so does the Word of God in contemplation influence or intervene on mental processes otherwise seeming to belong to the knower. Though Gallus holds that something like this can occur to an extent with the intellect, he insists that something will be missed about Dionysian mystical union if one models it on intellection, which may be too closely associated with forms of mental collection, consideration, and ratiocination.

Of course, because Dionysius calls mystical union a "knowing beyond the mind," he does not describe it as a form of intellection either; he frequently advocates for "unknowing" (*ignorantia*). The rhetoric of affect is expansive enough to include unknowing as well. The "being affected" Gallus describes does not imply any kind of grasp on the one who is intervening in the mind. It is only when the active effort to understand (*intelligere*) the Word ceases that the Word draws the mind out of itself. Though Gallus insists the intellect is drawn on this ecstatic journey, he is equally clear that it finally fails where the affect continues. Just as Dionysius advocated for a knowing beyond intellect (γνῶσις ὑπὲρ νοῦν), Gallus's rhetoric shifts from understanding (*intelligere*) to knowing (*cognoscere*) as the mind moves ecstatically beyond itself. In this sense, affect "un-knows" as it suspends an understanding (*intelligentia*) that grasps an object of knowledge.

Finally, Dionysius's language of the union itself, along with his considerable treatment of the divine name Love, provided plenty of impetus for Gallus to turn to the rhetoric of affect, especially as it is understood as akin to taste, touch, and smell—the more intimate or interior senses. The rhetoric of union is one of intimacy, and while erotic intimacy is not the only form of intimacy, it is one that conjures union. While the etymological understanding of affect (*affectus*) as a "having been done to" resonated with Gallus, so did the more common association of affection (*affectio*) with love. Love was, as we have seen, the Dionysian dynamic that best described the relation between God and the created order.

---

17   Gallus, *Explanatio super Angelica Ierarchia* 1, 486–87.

Experientia

Just as the rhetoric of affect seeks to take advantage of tensions within Dionysian theology, so does the related rhetoric of experience (*experientia*). As the last few chapters have highlighted, special experiences of apparitions and union were central to Dionysius's conception of the theologian (prophetic or apostolic author of Scripture), even as these experiences are not taken to deny the influence of culture—the theological language and liturgy with which Dionysius was entirely concerned. Rather, the rhetoric of experience was, for Gallus, capacious enough to articulate the complicated and sometimes mysterious relation between the soul and the Word that emerges from the soul's double orientation, so to speak. The soul knows the Word both by its orientation to the created order—where the Word is incarnate—and by its orientation to its cause (the Word eternal). The experience was a basic theological category for Gallus, not because it referred solely to apparitions and ascents beyond language but because it could describe what was common to the soul's relationship to both the natural and the supernatural, the intelligible and the super-intelligible, the God present to being and the God beyond being. Gallus concludes that when intellection fails, experience remains.

Though Gallus's frequent use of the rhetoric of experience in his commentaries may lead one to think that he associates experience especially with the mystical, there are plenty of times in his corpus that he describes quotidian forms of experience. For instance, when fleshing out the divine name of Light, he tells his readers to think about what "we learn from our proven experience of vision (*per certam experientiam visus*)."[18] Elsewhere he talks about common experience: "We know sensible things naturally through the experience of the senses of the body."[19] Gallus even uses the term in discussing evil, which, because Dionysius held a privative view of evil, is "known through the experience of the failure, as it were, of the acuity of the understanding from the lack of an intelligible object, just as darkness is known by the failing of the exercise of keen eyes."[20] Finally, common, everyday experience ought to be frequently examined: reasoning powers "rise

---

18 Gallus, *Explanatio de Divinis Nominibus* 2, 139.
19 Gallus, *Explanatio super Angelica Ierarchia* 1, 494.
20 Gallus, *Explanatio de Divinis Nominibus* 4, 272.

up through the threefold operation of diligent effort: namely meditation or examination of experience, the resolved circumscription of meaning, and the free and commanding execution of the given meaning."[21] These examples show that for Gallus, experience was continuous and not reserved for mystical discourse any more than intellection. Experience instead encompasses all manner of thought and feeling.

At the same time, there can be no doubt that Gallus was thoroughly engaged in an analysis of experience in the soul's union with the Word. The following passage shows how this special experience is a super-addition to a broad range of experiences that are part of mystical practice:

> *But that stirring* (excitatio) *[of the mind] occurs by the exercise and manifestation of his invisible goods, most highly and universally desirable in human beings, by inspiration, by the lavishing (*largitione*) of manifold goods, by long-suffering expectation, by the exhortation of the scriptures and the doctors, by the consideration of their subtle works, by the contemplation of pure and profound things, and by the experiences of inward affection* (intime affectionis experientiis). . . . *For whatever is laudable and loveable in creatures is a participation of the true good and beautiful which is God.*[22]

This passage shows the integrated view of experience with which Gallus works. Gallus's theology of the Word ensured that all the soul's processes—from the consideration of created things, to the intellective contemplation of the *theoriae*, to the intimate affection with the eternal Word itself—were experiences of the Word.

It is necessary to understand this as the context for Gallus's descriptions of mystical experience of the Word, which though special and superior, does not occur outside the context of the Word's cosmic incarnation in creation, history, and sacred letters. The difference between these everyday experiences and the experience of mystical union to the Word is that, in uniting to the Word, one is drawn into an intimacy with the God beyond

---

21   Gallus, *Explanatio super Angelica Ierarchia* 10, 634.
22   Gallus, *Explanatio de Divinis Nominibus* 4, 243.

being and beyond intelligibility. Experience of the Word is a continuation of everyday experience, but in knowing the Word, one knows the beyond being source of all intelligible things, which is unintelligible: "For that union has a super-intellectual experience both in the journey of this life and in the homeland of the next."[23] For Gallus, Dionysian mystical union is with the Word that remains with God, the Word that contains the *theoriae*, and the Word that creates all visible, sensible things. That is, mystical union is with the Word *in toto*, so it necessitates a language for the realization of such a multifaceted intimacy.

> *Therefore this contemplation of holy things is understood as the affectual experience of profound and superintellectual theoriae. . . . But this knowledge of divine things is perceived by the Seraph of the mind, and it completes the best portion, which is Mary's (Luke 10g). . . . For no other method of knowledge (scientia) or knowledge (cognitio) of God is more perfect, whether in via with the status of travelers or in patria in the mode of things grasped.*[24]

In this passage, we see there are many methods of knowledge or experiences besides the affect's simple knowledge or experience of the Word. Though Gallus's understanding of experience as encompassing the entirety of the Word's actions is undoubtedly a modification of or an addition to the Dionysian description of mystical union, it is responsive to the three primary ways Dionysius describes the goal of mystical theology: a union, a knowing beyond mind, and an unknowing.

Reading the Word

In the Introduction, I described how my analysis of Victorine theology would draw from the attention to language that has become prominent in the study of Christian mysticism. Scholars examining mystical language analyze the ways mystical writings use language to incite certain modes of consciousness or experience. For example, as we saw in chapter 4, Dionysius's use of the

---

23 Gallus, *Explanatio de Divinis Nominibus* 1, 92.
24 Gallus, *Explanatio super Angelica Ierarchia* 3, 546.

dialectical tension *between* cataphatic and apophatic statements was a way to inculcate, exercise, or perform an awareness of "the God beyond being who is present to being" in a way a simple propositional statement could not. Chapter 4 also appealed to the language of hymning to describe Dionysius's understanding of theological language. These approaches to mystical language are closely related to rhetorical analysis in that they emphasize how language functions, though these approaches show that the reading or writing of a mystical text may have a wider range of outcomes than persuasion. To borrow a felicitous distinction from the scholar of ancient Greek philosophical schools Pierre Hadot, the use of language in Christian mystical literature both *informs* and *forms*.[25] The questions remain: What or who is formed? And how?

I also described in the Introduction how some of these approaches to Christian mystical language presume that these mystical uses of language do their work on the autonomous, self-governing mind of the reader. That is, in the example of cataphatic and apophatic language in Dionysius, this kind of analysis might suppose that the dialectical tension creates a new kind of mental consciousness or intellectual intuition in the reader's mind, some transformation of the reader as an individual subject or self.[26] I appealed to Constance Furey's injunction to scholars of religion to attend to the ways religious texts construct not only individual selves but also, and perhaps primarily, intimacies and relationships as particularly important for my understanding of the Victorines. Thomas Gallus was undoubtedly concerned with the formation—or, rather, reformation—of the mind when he calls the Song of Songs the "practical part" of Christian wisdom, but his notion of the mind implies neither an autonomous entity nor a primarily self-reflexive orientation. In fact, while he undoubtedly develops a complex psychology and theological anthropology, these terms are only useful insofar as we are able

---

25   See the essays on philosophy as a "spiritual exercise" in Hadot, *Philosophy as a Way of Life*.

26   Furey ("Body, Society, and Subjectivity") reminds us that not all religious texts are concerned primarily with the dichotomy between the self and society or the body and society. Rather, much religious literature—and here I include the Victorines—has as its objective the formation of a certain kind of intimacy or relation, not a certain kind of individual.

to avoid their modern association with autonomous, self-governing mental activities. What I describe in the rest of this chapter is how the Song commentary depicts a mind (*mens*) that is a locus of both natural and supernatural (graced) activities, a mind made up, as it were, of both intentional acts of the soul and impinging or influential acts of the divine Word. Thus, while the Song commentary performs a certain kind of practice of the soul, its critical locus is not on the soul or mind as a discrete entity but on the mind as a site of the soul's intimacy with the eternal Word. How can a text like the Song commentary perform such an intimacy?

A Victorine act of reading must start, as we saw in chapter 2, with the letter (*littera*) of the text.[27] In the next section, I show that Gallus indeed starts here, even though he moves swiftly to the spirit of the Song. Gallus's attention to the letter is important, however, because it is the foundation for his two major moves of spiritual interpretation of the Song. First, he understands the bride and bridegroom, the primary voices of the Song, as figures for the soul and the Word of God. The back-and-forth beckoning of the two voices spiritually represents the interplay of the soul and the Word in mystical union. Thus, I analyze Gallus's spiritual interpretation of the bride and the bridegroom theologically. Then Gallus continuously describes how these voices speak in the verses of the Song—either "experientially"

---

27 See ch. 2, 45–46. Remember that the term *littera* covers a broad semantic range—from the smallest orthographical marking to the whole of literature. Thus, it performs a great amount of work in the Victorine imagination, especially regarding the theory and practice of scriptural interpretation. Therefore, when I refer to Gallus's "literal interpretation," I mean to point to his attention to basic grammatical and literary features that must first be understood before one can move to a spiritual understanding.

The following passage from *Explanatio super Angelica Ierarchia*, 1, 493–94, supports the view that Gallus, like the other Victorines, presumes the theory of scriptural interpretation that insists on the distinction between the literal and the spiritual:

> **For the supremely divine ray . . . cannot illuminate us**, that is, shine on this mortal condition by radiating from above . . . **unless enveloped**, just as spiritual understanding is veiled by the literal sense, **by a variety of holy veils**, that is, by multiple sensible forms which appropriately designate celestial and divine things, veiled and hidden by unworthy things . . . **uplifting-ly**, that is, in such a way that the faithful and zealous are led through the consideration of spoken veils to the cognition and contemplation of celestial mysteries.

(*experientialiter*) or "effectively" (*effective*). This is key to understanding the intimate relationship between the soul and the Word, and a following section will tease out the implications of "how the voices speak" for Gallus's mystical theology. While Gallus's emphasis is on the "effective," grace-bestowing Word as the source of contemplative practice, molding the soul for mystical union, the roles played by the soul and the Word suddenly, subtly, and significantly shift at critical points in the text, where the soul itself becomes increasingly "effective" and comes to understand the Word as sharing in its "experience." Rehearsing the movement of Gallus's reading—from a thorough understanding of the letter to a discernment of the spiritual significance of the text—shows how Gallus's interpretation also performs the soul's intimacy with the Word. I will return to this last point in the conclusion, after I have rehearsed Gallus's major interpretive moves, both literal and spiritual.

Literal Interpretation

The Song posed a particular problem to its Victorine interpreter since only with a foundation in the literal should one seek a more profound spiritual understanding. How could an erotic love poem that made no mention of God or religious practice first be interpreted literally to the benefit of the reader? Indeed, Gallus neither spends much time on literal interpretation, nor is there any indication that he conceives of the Song as a report of actual events, like the historical books of the Old Testament.[28] Instead, he consistently interprets the bride and the bridegroom as spiritual figures for the soul and the Word of God—the central feature of his interpretation, which will be examined in the next two sections. While Gallus's ultimate concern is with a spiritual interpretation, he ensures the reader has first grasped the "letter" of the sacred writing. Before turning to an analysis of Gallus's spiritual interpretation, I will briefly rehearse his treatment of the letter of the Song, showcasing how he practices the Victorine program of reading.

When performing an initial literal interpretation of the Song, Gallus attends to three considerations: (1) grammar and syntax, (2) the basic

---

28 See chapter 2, 45–46, for a fuller treatment of the Victorine approach to the historical-literal sense.

meaning of lexical items, and (3) the text's form and structure. In order to perform the movement from word (*verbum* or *vox*) to thing (*res*)—the act of literal interpretation—Gallus frequently pauses to consider both the grammatical function of the word itself, examining the word's case, number, or tense to expound its literal meaning. For example, Latin's ablative case (*ablativus*), he writes, "is appropriate for pointing out essence." When the Song states that "flocks of sheep ascend from the washing with twin offspring," it uses the ablative case for "with twin offspring (*gemellis fetibus*)." Spiritually, this indicates that the "essence" of the soul's union to the divine Word (the "flocks of sheep") is in both loving and knowing.[29] One must first identify the ablative case and its use (its *literal* function) in order to most fully appreciate its spiritual significance.[30]

Beyond grammar, Gallus uses his liberal arts training to ensure that the Song's unfamiliar words indicating, for example, the flora and fauna of the ancient Near East are carefully expounded. When he comes across the word *nardus* ("nard"), he begins by identifying three of its characteristics: (1) it is a spikey herb, (2) it grows on high mountains, and (3) it is odorous.[31] By enumerating these characteristics, which may have been unknown to the average canon regular, who had never been exposed to a plant grown in the eastern regions of the Mediterranean, Gallus both acquaints the reader with an unfamiliar word and expounds its literal meaning, establishing for the reader an understanding of the thing itself. This literal interpretation in turn is a foundation for a spiritual one. While nard itself signifies contemplative

---

29   Gallus, *Song Commentary III* 4.B, 177.

30   As for other grammatical considerations, Gallus frequently comments on number with the adverbs *singulariter* ("in the singular") or *pluraliter* ("in the plural"), which he often takes to spiritually indicate the Word's simplicity or multiple efficacies, respectively. For example, verse 6:12, "may we behold you," is glossed with "the bridegroom puts himself in the plural because of the multiplicity of his inflowings" (*Song Commentary III*, 6.G, 214). For other examples of *pluraliter*, see also "ointments" and "rays," 1.B, 123; "storerooms," 2.C, 147; and "eyes," 7.C, 217. For *singulariter*: "oil" and "ray" 2.C, 147; "aperture," 5.E, 196.

Similarly, Gallus interpreted the past tense (*in praeterito*) in the Song's line "the vineyard was pacifying" to spiritually signify the certainty with which the bride or soul makes herself peaceful in contemplation (8.E, 229). See also 3.B, 168. Thus, a word's case, number, and tense should be discerned before advancing to its spiritual significance.

31   Gallus, *Song Commentary III* 1.M, 138.

knowledge coming from the divine plenitude, its characteristic spikiness signifies how the knowledge of invisible things, coming from the simplicity of the divine essence, is multiple, like thorns from a stem. Its lofty habitat signifies its reception from sublime *theoriae* or "spectacles."[32] Finally, its odor signifies a spiritual sensation of sweetness.[33] Gallus frequently uses this method of introducing a word with a brief literal exposition of three characteristics before advancing to its spiritual meaning. The Song was filled with unfamiliar words that had to be explained first literally.

Gallus's attention to the form and structure of the Song was also significant, though Gallus preferred the term *series* ("sequence") to describe the running order or course of the text—the text's surface, as it were.[34] For instance, in the prologue to the third commentary on the Song, Gallus writes that the practice or exercise of mystical theology can be discerned

---

32   On the *theoriae*, see below, 149–52.

33   Gallus, *Song Commentary III*, 1.M, 138.

34   If Gallus's careful attention to the words themselves is typical of a twelfth-century Victorine concern for the literal as a foundation, his attention to the form and structure of the Song is more typical of his early thirteenth-century milieu. As Alastair Minnis (*Medieval Theory of Authorship*) has shown, literary analysis taking place in the schools could be quite sophisticated and was changing due to the introduction of the fuller corpus of the works of Aristotle. Minnis's analysis shows that medieval commentators on sacred writings were attuned to the kinds of concerns we would characterize today as form and structure—that is, the basic outline of a text and the ways its parts hang together or its elements relate to one another. In the prologues of twelfth-century commentators, the term used for the text's form was its *modus agendi vel tractandi* ("way of guiding or treating"), while thirteenth-century commentators preferred to analyze the *divisio textus* ("division of the text"). While Gallus uses the older term *modus tractandi*, either ignorant of or, perhaps, avoiding the newer Aristotelian terminology, he nonetheless exhibits concern for how the text is divided up. When glossing the Dionysian corpus, the *modus tractandi*, or textual division, was easier to trace as Dionysius's "theoretical" treatises could be broken up into distinct units that covered particular topics or concepts. *On Divine Names*, for instance, proceeded name by name, with Dionysius treating each in turn. Divisions in the text were thus easily discernible, and the assigning of chapters, for instance, followed these topical divisions, at least in part. Thus, when Gallus describes the Dionysian corpus's *modus tractandi* in his prologues to each book, he briefly summarizes each chapter. In contrast, dividing up the text of the Song, a poem, was not as simple, but as I argue here, his use of the term *series* suggests Gallus was attentive to what we would call the text's form and structure.

"throughout the sequence of the entire book (*per totius libri seriem*)."[35] Elsewhere, "The entire course of love (*amoris cursus*) consists in a constant and continual summoning of the kind that is clear in the sequence of the book (*in libri serie*)."[36] To Gallus, the Song was clearly and for good reason structured by the back-and-forth beckoning of the voices of the bride and bridegroom. The structure itself performed the "course of love."

Other terms show up that confirm Gallus's attention to the structure of the text. For example, he points to instances of repetition in the sacred poem with terms like *geminatio*, *repetitio*, and *duplicatio*.[37] The text's repetitiveness has its own spiritual significance—the bride or soul must be continually renewed in the Word, so no purely linear narrative would be appropriate to the Song's subject matter. Gallus also remarks on the Song's *interpositiones* (parenthetical insertions or interjections), which signify how the soul is surprised suddenly by the Word.[38] Finally, Gallus's concern with the *consummatio* ("ending") of the text is another device in his conceptual tool kit for thinking about its *series* or sequence.[39] In sum, though Gallus does not write a literal commentary on the Song, his spiritual interpretation is performed as a careful elaboration on an initial analysis of the letter of the text, from the smallest semantic unit to the entire course of the text as a whole, even to its place within the whole of sacred literature.

I have begun this chapter with a brief look at Gallus's approach to the "letter" of the Song for two reasons. First, this reinforces the Victorine approach to sacred literature. Though Gallus is unquestionably more interested in contemplation and spiritual interpretation than the school's

---

35   Gallus, *Song Commentary III* Prologue.B, 107. Elsewhere, "the bride seizes these paths [of eternity] throughout the entire sequence of this book, with the bridegroom calling, illuminating, helping, supporting, embracing." 2.H, 155. Gallus also uses *series* to refer to the entire sequence of sacred writings, as in "Solomon's wisdom of Christians is touched on throughout the entire sequence of the scriptures and the books of the great Dionysius," 1.A, 122 Thus, just as *littera* could refer to everything from an orthographical marking to literature itself, *series* could refer to the running order of a sentence, the structure of the entire Song, or even the divinely arranged whole course of sacred literature.
36   Gallus, *Song Commentary III* 5.A, 190.
37   Gallus, *Song Commentary III* 3.A, 166; 4.E, 183; 5.G, 200.
38   Gallus, *Song Commentary III* 4.D, 180.
39   Gallus, *Song Commentary III* 8.E, 230.

historical-literalist Andrew of St. Victor, he remained thoroughly engaged with its pedagogical principles. Second, I take Gallus's foundational concern with the letter and "sequence" of the Song as an invitation to interrogate how he thinks about its structure or *modus tractandi*, how he divides the text, as it were. How does Gallus see the Song breaking down? How does a spiritual reading develop out of a thorough understanding of the letter and sequence of the text? What does he notice about its structure, the ways the elements relate to one another? How does the poem's *series* contribute to the practice or performance of the wisdom of Christians?

I identify two primary ways in which Gallus divides the Song. First, and more in line with traditional exegesis, Gallus treats the Song as a dialogue between the voices of different characters, primarily the bride and the bridegroom, whom he understands to be figures for the soul and the Word of God, respectively. While he does not, like some modern readers, explicitly read the Song as a drama, he consistently identifies who is speaking in the text, which contemporary scholars agree has a dialogic, if not a dramatic, form.[40] A second, more unique, mode of division Gallus showcases across the sequence of the text, however, comes from how these voices speak. He repeatedly describes the voices speaking with the adverbs "effectively" (*effective*) and "experientially" (*experientialiter*), as when he glosses, for example, "the bridegroom is speaking effectively here" and "this was said experientially by the bride." More will be said about what Gallus means by these terms. As we will see, these two ways to divide the text—between (1) the voices themselves and (2) their mode of utterance—largely overlap. The bride's voice most often speaks "experientially," the bridegroom's "effectively."

Yet Gallus's two ways of analyzing the sequence are not entirely identical, and this is, I take it, for a particular theological purpose, which comes to light when we think about Gallus's commentaries in terms of practice. The Song practices, exercises, or performs the unique relationship between the soul and the Word of God as they cooperate in the pursuit of a form of contemplative union, in which the soul is assimilated to the Word, and the Word is understood to be cozened or drawn by the soul. The sudden bouts

---

40   J. Cheryl Exum, *Song of Songs: A Commentary* (Louisville, KY: Westminster John Knox Press, 2005), 78.

of role reversal—when the bride's voice becomes "effective," and the bridegroom shares in her "experience"—are critical in Gallus's attempt to stylize the intimacy or relationship between the soul and the Word. In the rest of this chapter, I make this argument by treating the two major ways Gallus divides the text, first the distinct voices representing the soul and the Word and then how the voices speak (their modes of utterance), either "effectively" or "experientially."

Spiritual Interpretation: The Voices of the Song

The first way in which Gallus distinguishes the voices or utterances (*voces*) of the text is according to the characters to whom they belong, primarily the bride and bridegroom, or, in Gallus's spiritual interpretation, the soul and the Word of God. The Song itself invites attention to the voices in its dialogic form and its multiple evocations of the beloved's voice (*vox*), and Gallus is not the first to break up the text this way.[41]

The Voice of the Bridegroom

One of the two main voices of the Song belongs to the bridegroom, who spiritually signifies the Word of God, as Gallus makes clear early and frequently in the commentaries. Throughout the Song, each of the bridegroom's utterances to the bride spiritually signifies the Word's communication to the soul in the highest stages of contemplation. These utterances, as we will see in the next section, because they come from the Word itself, also have a direct practical influence on the soul. In chapter 4, I described some precedents for Gallus's theology of the Word (*Verbum*) in Augustine and Hugh of St. Victor. In this section, I further expound a few passages from the commentaries to show how Gallus adopts and adapts Word theology, especially by depicting

---

41 The bride and bridegroom appeal to one another's "voices" in 2:8 ("the voice of my beloved"), 2:12 ("the voice of the turtle dove"), 2:14 ("let your voice sound in my ears / for your voice is sweet"), and 5:2 ("the voice of my beloved knocking"). My attention to the centrality of voice in the Song and the Song commentaries surely owes something to the suggestion implied in E. Ann Matter's title for her definitive work on the Song's interpretation in the Middle Ages, *The Voice of My Beloved*. Though Matter does not explicitly treat the theme of vocality or utterance, it strikes me that the Song's insistence on the reader's or hearer's attention to it may have been part of what made it appealing to Gallus.

in detail how the Word contains *theoriae*, the eternal reasons of all things, which become "spectacles" to be encountered by the soul.

While Gallus does not explicitly rehearse Augustine's or Hugh's distinctions between the inner and exterior Word, his exposition of the union of the soul with the eternal Word in the Song suggests the analogy.[42] If Gallus's ideal of Christian perfection is union with and assimilation to the Word, how does this occur? Placed in the context of Augustinian theology of the Word, one can say Gallus reads the Song as exhibiting the practice that moves one from an apprehension of the exterior Word to union with the inner Word or, rather, an apprehension of the Word both incarnate and eternal. As we will see, the movement to union with the eternal Word occurs primarily through the mind's intellective and affective engagement in the *theoriae*, or divine exemplars contained in the Word.

The commentaries do not explain these issues systematically, but Gallus treats them occasionally as the bridegroom (the Word) communicates with the bride (the soul) in the Song. For instance, in one passage, we see the notion of the eternal generation of the Son or Word of God from the Father. When the bridegroom calls the bride "a sealed fountain (*fons signatus*)," Gallus glosses that the contemplative mind receives and gives wisdom from the Word of God. The Word itself is called in Scripture a "fountain of life, because it is the original Life and Wisdom." He adds, "'Fountain' in the singular rightly refers to the Word, in which the supremely simple, supremely multiple, and truly original gathering of the waters of saving wisdom exists . . . the Word from the Father. Therefore, by descending into human and angelic minds from the fullness of both this singular Fountain and this Sea, fountains arise in them."[43]

Here, for Gallus, the Song depicts the bride as a sealed fountain, poured into by the Fountain of the Word, itself sourced by the Sea of the Father.[44]

---

42   Consider also how the following statement seems to presume an understanding of the idea: "But the mental word forms the spoken words, because from the abundance of the heart the mouth speaks." Gallus, *Explanatio super Mystica Theologia* 1, 23.

43   Thomas Gallus, *Song Commentary II*, in *Thomas Gallus: Commentaires du Cantique des Cantiques*, ed. Jeanne Barbet (Paris: Vrin, 1967), 4.F, 97–98.

44   Evidence that this image was important to the Victorines can be found in Godfrey of St. Victor's didactic poem "The Fountain of Philosophy." Translated by Hugh Feiss,

In this Fountain or Word is gathered all the plans of Wisdom, just as the Word contains the eternal reasons for Augustine. By stating that this Fountain contains both "simple" and "multiple" gathered waters, Gallus evokes the distinction between the Word as united to its source (like a prelinguistic concept united to a person) and the Word as containing the various principles of creation (like an inner word or a plan of an exterior word).

Gallus also advances the Victorine notion of the manifestation of the divine Word in the incarnation, creation, and Scripture.[45] In his commentary on *Divine Names*, to Dionysius's statement that "the Word beyond substance completely and truly became a substance," Gallus adds, "This is the fact that the Word beyond substance became human."[46] Elsewhere, when Dionysius writes about how created things exhibit divine "harmony," Gallus adds, "The pagan philosophers have investigated this harmony with no little care, and it has been fulfilled in the incarnate Word, where the highest, lowest, and middle have been joined together in one person who is the plenitude of all beauty."[47] Here, Gallus describes the incarnate Word as the complete or perfect expression of the eternal Word while also suggesting its expression in the created order, the knowledge of which even pagan philosophy can attain.

Indeed, Gallus's cosmic Christology—his focus on all of creation in general and Scripture in particular as the manifestation of the Word—means he seldom attends to the Word incarnate in the suffering and saving Jesus Christ, the object of so much attention in mystical theology and devotion in the new religious movements developing at the same time he is writing. Instead, his consistent attention is on the more Neoplatonic Christian christological concern with the Word as the principle of creation and the Victorine concern with the Word as the originator of sacred literature. For instance, Gallus interprets a Dionysian reference to the divine art (*ars, techne*) with the gloss, "that is, . . . the Word of God, which is the most simple and most universal art of all things."[48] Elsewhere, he refers to the Word as "the principal

---

O.S.B., in Franklin T. Harkins and Frans van Liere, *Interpretation of Scripture: Theory* vol. 3 (Hyde Park, NY: New City Press, 2013), 371–425.
45   See ch. 4, 105–11.
46   Gallus, *Explanatio de Divinis Nominibus* 2, 148.
47   Gallus, *Explanatio de Divinis Nominibus* 1, 86.
48   Gallus, *Explanatio de Divinis Nominibus* 4, 309.

origin and fountain of all the words of sacred Scripture";[49] "The words of God shine from the Word of God."[50] Although John Saracen's translation rendered λόγος (*logos*) with *verbum*, while transliterating θεολογία with *theologia*, Gallus recognized the connection: "The Word of God (*verbum Dei*) . . . truly is theology (*theologia*), which incomparably exceeds everything created and existing."[51] What these passages suggest is that the Word in Gallus's commentaries is primarily the principle of creation and sacred writings, the primary media or vehicles for reformation of the soul. Gallus's modification of the Augustinian theology of the Word was thus centered on how one becomes united to the eternal Word through the inflowing of divine grace mediated in creation and Scripture to the soul's intellect and affect.

Following both the influence of the Dionysian corpus and the Song, Gallus's primary way of describing the goal of the soul's interaction with the Word is as a form of union and, less frequently, assimilation. Suggesting a desire for the inner or eternal Word, Gallus writes of "a uniting in the unity of the simple Word *in which are all the treasures of wisdom and knowledge* hidden."[52] Again, the invocation of both "simple unity" and multiple "treasures" suggests a union with the Word as both Augustinian prelinguistic concept (simple) and source of divine plans (multiple). Elsewhere, Gallus describes how the soul's nature is "united to the Word," even as the Word's "supereminence goes past those ascending to divine union."[53] As we will see below, Gallus's union to the Word respects the balance among what can be intellectually known, what can be affectively known, and what cannot be known of the eternal Word.

Before treating the implications of Gallus's identification of the bridegroom in the Song with the Word, one more point must be made about Gallus's theology of the Word. By far the most significant aspect of Gallus's treatment of the Word is his exposition of the character and role of divine exemplars, or what he more often calls, from the epistemic or experiential rather than the metaphysical point of view, *theoriae*. The best English translation of this word is "spectacles," but even the Latinizing John Saracen

---

49 Gallus, *Explanatio super Mystica Theologia* 1, 9.
50 Gallus, *Explanatio de Divinis Nominibus* 1, 75.
51 Gallus, *Explanatio de Divinis Nominibus* 1, 24.
52 Gallus, *Song Commentary III* 1.M, 139.
53 Gallus, *Song Commentary III* 3.B, 168.

transliterates θεωρίαι as *theoriae* in his translation, suggesting the Greek term is conceptually significant. While it is true to say the dialogic Song depicts the soul and the Word, it is more precise to say the Song treats how the soul traverses the Word's increasingly more profound *theoriae* in its practice of ever-more-perfect union with the Word. The practice of mystical theology, Gallus reasons, is largely about how one journeys in the *theoriae* in the quest toward more perfect union with the Word. These *theoriae* or exemplars are what we have already seen Augustine refer to as "eternal reasons," and Gallus says there are many names for them. Besides *exemplars* (*exemplaria*) and *eternal reasons* (*rationes eternae*), they can be called *ideas* (*ideae*), *archetypes* (*archetypiae*), and *efficacies* (*efficaciae*).[54]

In the *Divine Names* commentary, Gallus emphasizes how *exemplaria* are the causal principles of the world contained in the Word: "The eternal exemplars of all things that fall under the category of existence are in the eternal Word by nature, and all existing things are known and comprehended causally (*causaliter*) in those exemplars by glorified minds."[55] Gallus glosses Dionysius's own treatment of the *exemplaria*: "**We call the exemplars in God the reasons** of the Word, **substance-making**, that is, which make things subsist, exist, and have substance; **and pre-existing** in eternity before the creation of things, and also causally; **singularly**, that is, in the highest simplicity of the eternal Word, although their effects are uncountable."[56] That is, Gallus understands the Dionysian corpus to argue that *exemplaria* are the eternal reasons or causal principles contained in the eternal Word.

The *theoriae* show up throughout the commentaries. In one of his few references to himself, Gallus says in a prologue that he now writes a third commentary after having followed the "courses of the *theoriae* which superillumine the soul with understandings," a significant suggestion of the interdependence of scriptural interpretation and mystical union in the commentaries.[57] Given that the bridegroom represents the Word in the Song, many of the spaces, body parts, and possessions of the bridegroom figurally

---

54 For passages that have Gallus laying out the multiple possible designations for the *theoriae*, see *Song Commentary III* 4.D, 182; and *Explanatio de Divinis Nominibus* 5, 337.
55 Gallus, *Explanatio de Divinis Nominibus* 4, 185.
56 Gallus, *Explanatio de Divinis Nominibus* 5, 352.
57 Gallus, *Song Commentary III* Prologue.P, 109.

represent the *theoriae*. In fact, Gallus interprets almost any dalliance of the bride with multiple objects of some kind as the text's spiritual signification of the Word's *theoriae*. When the bride claims at 1:3 that the king has led her "into his storerooms," Gallus glosses: "In these storerooms, that is, the exemplars of the eternal Word, the bride is led forth in the highest hierarchy of her mind upward and deeply through unitive contemplation."[58] When the trope is repeated at 2:4, Gallus writes, "She says experientially: **he led me** through interior *theoriae* more profound than before, just as *Jer.* 3: *do not cease to go after* me, **into the wine storeroom**, that is, the Word containing all *theoriae*."[59] In unitive contemplation, the wayfaring soul gains access to and traverses the eternal reasons contained in the Word.

Examples can be multiplied. Vineyards are "the exemplars of the eternal Word, which are called storerooms above," Gallus writes, making a characteristic intratextual reference.[60] The golden bases, on which the bride says the bridegroom's legs rest, are "the super-eternally steady archetypes of the super-shining Word."[61] Pomegranates are "the exemplars of the eternal Word smelling sweet beyond the mind."[62] Finally, stones are "the indissoluble spectacles (*spectacula*) of the eternal Word, from which some special things ought to be chosen according to the experience of the contemplative soul, by which the mind may be exercised and carried up more effectively. [In this passage about stones] the angels invite the bride to attend to the special *theoriae* of the bridegroom."[63] This last quotation says explicitly what Gallus's identification of the *theoriae* throughout the sequence of the Song suggests: the practice of Christian wisdom is like a journey of the soul pursuing union with the Word by traversing the principles of creation.

One final passage on the *theoriae* of the Word helps to explain how Gallus sees them operating in the Song and, by extension, the practice of Christian wisdom: "For the giver of the Spirit and of spiritual charisms pours into the angels themselves all the *theoriae*, which will then be carried into the hierarchy

---

58	Gallus, *Song Commentary III* 1.E, 127.
59	Gallus, *Song Commentary III* 2.C, 147.
60	Gallus, *Song Commentary III* 1.G, 131.
61	Gallus, *Song Commentary III* 5.I, 203.
62	Gallus, *Song Commentary III* 4.G, 186.
63	Gallus, *Song Commentary III* 5.G, 199.

of our [mind] by the angels, and he both collects and prepares the multitude of these *theoriae* in himself with a simple Word like a fountain, just as infinite lines flow from a simple point in the center, *Div. Names* 2: *in whatever way*."[64]

The *theoriae* are the eternal reasons that, as contained in the Word, play a crucial role in the soul's union with and assimilation to the Word, both of which are, as we will see, attainable at least in part due to the intellect but especially the affect. By engaging with the *theoriae*, the soul knows the eternal Word itself. Yet it knows it only in the way one person knows the inner word of another. By grasping the meaning of the inner word of another, one knows that person intimately but not exhaustively.

The Voice of the Bride

Of course, the Song is not a treatise on the Word. Rather, as Gallus understands it, it is a practical presentation of the intercourse between the Word and the soul in unitive contemplation. As we saw in chapter 2, the reformation or restoration of the soul was a central concern of the Victorine pedagogy of sacred literature. Consequently, Gallus is thoroughly attentive to the soul and the way the Word influences the mind. His hierarchization of the soul, for instance, has been treated in most contemporary accounts of his work and is spelled out fully in his prologue to the third commentary on the Song.[65] Yet the aim of the work is not the reordering of a disorderly soul, needing for its hierarchies to be restored. Gallus's mental hierarchy is a kind of map or underlying structure of the mind, as it were, not an edifice built by contemplative effort.[66] Instead, Gallus's goal is implied in his phrase

---

64   Gallus, *Song Commentary III* 5.H, 202.
65   Gallus's hierarchized mind is central to the analyses of Bernard McGinn, "Thomas Gallus and Dionysian Mysticism," *Studies in Spirituality* 8 (1998): 81–96; and Coolman, "The Victorines."
66   At least Gallus seems to presume the existence of a hierarchically ordered mind already. There is no indication the hierarchical ordering itself is the result of prior contemplative effort akin to Augustine's pleas that God repairs "the house" of his soul (Augustine, *Confessions*, ed. Michael P. Foley, trans. F. J. Sheed [Indianapolis, IN: Hackett Publishing, 2006], 1.5) or Hugh of St. Victor's instruction to build an ark in the soul in which Christ might dwell, in his masterwork on contemplation (Hugh of St. Victor, *Noah's Ark*, in *Selected Spiritual Writings*, trans. a Religious of C.S.M.V. (Eugene, OR: Wipf and Stock, 2009; 1st ed. Harper & Row, 1962).

"infirmity of capacity" (*infirmitas capacitatis*).[67] That is, the mind, the highest part of the soul, is limited in its capacity to receive direct inpouring of the Word of God and needs to be exercised in contemplation toward a greater and greater reception. Because this mental hierarchization is well trodden in scholarship on Gallus but also critical to understanding the commentaries, in this section I will briefly describe Gallus's terms related to the soul that have some basis in the Augustinian and Victorine accounts before rehearsing Gallus's hierarchization of the soul. Finally, I will briefly comment on why the soul is so hierarchized.

Gallus follows Augustine and the Victorines with his interest in both the soul (*anima*) and the mind (*mens*). Augustine had held that the mind was the highest part of the soul, even deiform or trinitarian in structure. While Gallus at times seems to use the terms interchangeably, his preference is for the term *mind*. He tends to use *soul* instead of *mind* only when the Song or other sacred writing with which he is engaged has first used the term *soul*. That is, the mind, the highest part of the soul, is the primary object of Gallus's attention, but since the entire sequence of the Song portrays an exercise of the mind, which increases the soul's capacity for union with the Word, *soul* and *mind* become largely synonymous. Put another way, the Song commentaries treat the soul primarily in its highest mental activities: those of the intellect (*intellectus*) and the affect (*affectus*).

The result is a sophisticated theological account of mental exercise. While the commentaries exhibit a typical medieval mental vocabulary—imagination (*imaginatio*), image (*fantasia*), reason (*ratio*), knowledge (*cognitio*), and understanding (*intellectio*) all appear—the Song represents a Christian mental exercise that, thanks to divine grace, goes beyond the ordinary exercise of these powers, however diligently they may be exerted. Instead, the voices of the Song perform the drawing of the soul's affect (*affectus*) and intellect (*intellectus*) by the Word of God. More specifically, the Song's various encounters, movements, spaces, objects, and exhortations can be mined for spiritual insight into how the mind's affect and intellect are exercised in order to unite and assimilate the soul to the Word. Thus, Gallus's attention to the mind, affect, and intellect is due to the particular nature of

---

67 Gallus, *Song Commentary II* 5.B, 102.

the exercise discerned in the Song commentaries. Unitive contemplation of the Word culminates the disciplining of body and soul in the practice of religious life, especially the pedagogy of reading treated in chapter 2.

Gallus's major innovation with regard to the mind, however, was inspired by a short, enigmatic statement, largely ignored by other scholars of Dionysius, in the tenth chapter of *Celestial Hierarchy*. In it, Dionysius states, "And I may well add this, that the mind itself, whether celestial or human, has its own first, middle, and last orders and powers agreeing with each of the hierarchic illuminations."[68] With Dionysius's blessing, Gallus divides the mind into three hierarchies of three orders each and applies to each order one of the names of the nine orders of angels treated by Dionysius in *Celestial Hierarchy*. These orders are not faculties of the mind, nor are they checkpoints for an aspiring mind ascending upward. Rather, they provide something like a superstructure or map for the powers and activities of the mind, and especially the affect and the intellect. In general, they are arranged on a scale of the extent to which the activity that takes place in each order is attributable to, on the lower end, human effort or to, on the higher end, divine grace. For instance, Gallus says the lowest hierarchy of three orders is entirely of nature; the middle, of the cooperation of human effort and grace; and the highest, of grace alone. Again, this model of the mind is one that does not presume the autonomous operation of a self-governing individual but has room by design for the mind's "practice" to be "effected" or "carried out" by another.

Gallus's description of the mental hierarchy is clearly and prominently depicted in his prologues to both existing Song commentaries.[69] Starting with the lowest order of the "Angels," he begins to rehearse the lowest of the three hierarchies, the hierarchy of nature alone. In the angelic order are basic perceptions or observations of the world, without yet any judgment of these

---

68   Gallus, *Song Commentary III* Prologue.C, 107–8. Notice how consonant this verse would have been with Gallus's Augustinian instinct to already see the mind as deific or trinitarian. For Dionysius, a hierarchy is that which deifies and unifies to God.

69   Gallus, *Song Commentary II* Prologue, 66–67; SS3.Prologue.C–P, 107–10. The mental hierarchy's prominent display in the prologues, its uniqueness, and the thoroughgoing use to which Gallus puts it have all ensured it plays a key role in the interpretation of Gallus by nearly every contemporary reader.

observations, which begin to occur in the second order of the "Archangels." This judgment discerns whether what is observed is agreeable or disagreeable. In the highest order of the lowest hierarchy, the "Principalities," the mind either longs for what was judged agreeable or desires to flee from what was judged disagreeable. These are all basic operations that can and should be conducted well but which do not yet carry out any good.

In the middle hierarchy, where effort and grace cooperate, the fourth order of the "Powers" involves the initial activities of reason, intellect, and affect—mental powers that, applied to the judgments of the "Principalities," begin to orient the mind toward good and away from evil. In the fifth order, the "Virtues," natural force and the force of grace are added to the initial movements of intellect and affect in the "Powers." Finally, the sixth order, the "Dominions," culminates the mind's effort and with the command of free will suspends the intellect and affect "in order to receive divine interventions (*ad suscipiendum divinos superadventus*)."[70] Here, Gallus claims, the mind "is stretched and exercised (*extenditur et exercetur*) . . . to the highest limits of its nature (*ad summos nature sue terminos*)."[71] In the Song commentaries, Gallus hardly mentions the lowest hierarchy, and his infrequent treatment of the middle hierarchy is typically focused on the mind's act of suspension (*suspensio*) in the "Dominions."

Because the Song treats the "practice" of Christian wisdom, which goes beyond what pagan philosophers and the natural mind can know through their own diligent effort, the bride-soul and bridegroom-Word primarily encounter one another in the highest hierarchy of the mind, after the intellect and affect have suspended their own effortful operations and now operate "in excess" (*in excessum*) of the mind, as it were. Here, the soul's "suspension" does not mean the end of its "practice." Rather, Gallus's rhetoric becomes even more fervid when discussing the highest hierarchy. The lowest order of this highest hierarchy, the "Thrones," "receives divine interventions through excess of the mind."[72] The name *thrones* aptly represents the multiple receptive "cavities" or "capacities" of the mind for "the supersubstantial

---

70   Gallus, *Song Commentary III* Prologue.I–K, 108.
71   Gallus, *Song Commentary III* Prologue.I–K, 108.
72   Gallus, *Song Commentary III* Prologue.L, 109.

ray" of divine light. Thus, at the "hinge" between the "Dominions" and the "Thrones," suspension of the mind's greatest powers, intellect and affect, gives way to the reception of divine grace that heightens the activity of intellect and affect.[73]

The "Cherubim" are the penultimate order, which contains the knowledge (*cognitio*) of both intellect and affect as they have been drawn or attracted by divine grace beyond the mind. At this point, Gallus adds, intellect and affect have "walked together up to the final failure of the intellect, which is at the summit of this order."[74] Though intellect and affect are the two powers of the mind that can be drawn "in excess" beyond the mind itself, the intellect cannot be drawn as far as the affect.[75]

The ninth and final order, the "Seraphim," contains "only the principal affection, which can be united to God (*sola principalis affectio Deo unibilis*)."[76] This is the site of the mind's experiential or affective union with the Word, whom it "embraces" and in whose "embraces" it "is enveloped." Thus, while the mind's seraphic order is the site of most intimate encounter between the soul and the Word, the union that occurs there, in excess of the mind, is one Gallus stylizes as a relation modeled primarily on the most heightened moments of bride-bridegroom union in the Song.

As we will see, Gallus sees evidence of the angelic hierarchy of the mind and its operations spiritually signified in every chapter of the Song. In fact, Gallus's expansive description of mental domains allows for an allegorical reading of the landscapes and bodyscapes, as it were, of the Song. That is, if one of the primary features of allegory distinguishing it from metaphor or other analogous literary terms is that each element in a text has an alternative significance, then Gallus's hierarchization of the mind facilitates the deep and thorough exposition of the significance of each element of the Song.

---

73   I am indebted to Boyd Taylor Coolman's exposition of two major "hinges" in the mental hierarchy in Gallus's thought—between the "Dominions" and "Thrones," when the mind is suspended, and between the "Cherubim" and "Seraphim," when the affect proceeds beyond where the intellect can go. Coolman, *Eternally Spiraling into God*, 137, 143.
74   Gallus, *Song Commentary III* Prologue.M, 109.
75   I traced the reasons for this above, 133–34.
76   Gallus, *Song Commentary III* Prologue.N, 109.

Yet Gallus's hierarchization of the soul was, if he is to believed, something he had worked out early in his career, long before his extensive study of the Song. A more probable explanation for it is that it allows for a more sophisticated account of both human and divine operations and their effects on the mind in contemplation. As we saw in chapter 2, contemplation was always the end goal of the Victorine curriculum of sacred reading, and it is possible to read the development of Victorine literature as an ever-more-sophisticated theorization of the highest stages in that curriculum, culminating in Gallus's writings.

"The Voice of My Beloved"

As we have seen, the distinct voices of the bride and the bridegroom symbolically represent important aspects of Gallus's theology—the soul and the Word, respectively. As distinct as these two are, they share an important characteristic. In Gallus's interpretation, the complex geographical, corporeal, and natural objects and events belonging to both the bride and the bridegroom symbolize how both the soul and the Word invite a complex or multifaceted encounter with one another. The bridegroom's *theoriae*, represented variously in every chapter of the Song, become a complex landscape contained by the Word, in which the bridal soul can journey, becoming familiar, experienced. The *theoriae* lead the soul to increasingly more intimate encounters with the eternal Word. In turn, the bride's mental hierarchy provides the sites of divine encounter with the Word, who influences (literally, "pours into," *in-fluere*) the practice or exercise of the soul at every stage.

The way both the *theoriae* and the mental hierarchy mutually multiply or proliferate the two voices, as it were, has not before been noticed. On the one hand, one might interpret this multiplication or increasing complexity of both the soul and the Word as a practicality of spiritual interpretation. If the Song was to serve as a spiritual allegory for the soul and the Word, some sense must be made of its abounding images of flora and fauna, corporeal members and various utterances, military men and attending virgins. Perhaps Gallus spends so much time multiplying the soul and the Word in order to meet the demands of allegorical interpretation for each image to symbolize something.

158   *The Mystified Letter*

Applying Constance Furey's injunction to attend to intimacy and relation, however, helps us to see what else is going on here. Gallus's commentaries on the Song do not produce static characters, abstracted from their social environment. Instead, his interpretation of these characters includes their mutual imbrication or interweaving, which he sees at evidence in the Song, that is, the ways the characters' actions and intentions are attributable not solely to themselves. The *theoriae* and the mental hierarchies allow Gallus to theorize the ways that the mind is drawn and the Word condescends in contemplation—the ways each goes beyond, in excess, or even ecstasy, of itself. If the soul and the Word ought to be thought of in terms of relation, rather than as abstracted from one another, what kind of relation is it that Gallus performs in his interpretation?

Spiritual Interpretation: Effectivity and Experience

While there is a certain symmetry to the voices of the Song, Gallus typically describes these two voices, the bride's and bridegroom's, as speaking differently. The bride, he repeats, speaks "experientially" (*experientialiter*), the bridegroom "effectively" (*effective*). Despite the ubiquity of these terms in the commentaries, this has seldom been commented on.[77] Yet an analysis of the rhetoric of effectivity and experience reveals an understanding of practice and exercise that may be unfamiliar to modern readers because this practice is not performed through the effort of an autonomous individual. Rather, for Gallus, contemplative exercise is a matter of effected experience, dramatized by the utterance of the bride and bridegroom.

In this section, I begin by examining the rhetoric of *effectivity* in relation to the voice of the bridegroom before moving to describe the *experiential* voice of the bride. What might it mean theologically for Gallus to

---

77   This despite the fact that these terms are used more often than other major terms like *abundance* (*abundantia*), *ascent* (*ascensus*), *joining* (*coniunctio*), *excess* (*excessus*), *stretching* (*extensio*), *prayer* (*oratio*), *separation* (*separatio*), and *uplifting* (*sursumactio*). Contemporary analyses have largely ignored the adverbs *experientially* (*experientialiter*) and *effectively* (*effective*), focusing on nouns like *affect* (*affectus*), *angels* (*angeli*), *contemplation* (*contemplatio*), *hierarchy* (*hierarchia*), *intellect* (*intellectus*), *wisdom* (*sapientia*), *softness* (*suavitas*), *spectacles* (*theoriae*), and *union* (*unitio*) and verbs such as *embrace* (*amplexari*), *desire* (*desiderare*), *stretch* (*extendere*), *pour in* (*influere*), *suspend* (*suspendere*), and *lift up* (*sursumagere*).

call some of the Song's utterance "effective" and some "experiential"? In the final section, I show that Gallus's aim to perform the "practice" of experiential union leads to sudden slippages or shiftings between these typical relations. The ineffable *unitio experientialis* occurring between the bride and bridegroom both makes the bride's voice itself effective and even entices the bridegroom to seek the bride's experience.

"For the Bridegroom Speaks Effectively"

Over and over, Gallus writes that the bridegroom "speaks effectively." Because the bridegroom is spiritually understood to be the divine Word itself, when the bridegroom speaks, his "word is deed (*dictum est factum*)."[78] That is, his divine utterance brings about what it says. The speech that comes from the voice of the bridegroom is thus taken to be more effective than the bride's human speech because it is, in fact, the principle of everything effected. If, as we have seen, the theology of the Word stressed the causal activity of divine utterance in creating and ordering the cosmos, what does the bridegroom's voice effect in the Song? Gallus describes the bridegroom's efficacy primarily in relation to the bride, spiritually understood to be the soul. A careful analysis shows that the transformation of the bride effected in the Song occurs primarily through the bridegroom's effecting—or making efficacious—three "principal exercises of the mind": (1) *unveiling of the mind,* (2) *adapting it for union,* and (3) *most chaste prayer.* To say that "the bridegroom speaks effectively" in the Song is to attribute the experiential union of the bride to the bridegroom. Examples abound of the bridegroom effecting or making effective—Gallus subtly and significantly suggests both—each of the three principal exercises of the mind mentioned by Dionysius in a line from *Divine Names.*[79]

The unveiling of the mind (*revelatio mentis*) is an exercise in clearing away obstacles to experiential union, in the manner of Dionysian "unknowing." These obstacles are themselves lesser goods that range from desires for

---

78 Gallus, *Song Commentary II* 1.G, 76.

79 In *Divine Names* 3.1, Dionysius invokes what Gallus calls "the three principal exercises" as the means to the presence of the Good: *castissimae orationes* (πανάγναι εὐχαί), *mens revelata* (ἀνεπιθόλωτος νοῦς), and *aptitudo ad divinam unitionem* (ἡ πρός θείαν ἕνωσιν ἐπιτηδειότης).

worldly things to the rational speculations that provide the prerequisite steps of contemplation. Ultimately, following Dionysius, they all needed to be mentally removed. Regarding one passage (1:12) wherein the voice of the bride describes an especially intimate contact with the Word, Gallus states how union demands the removal of obstacles: "**He will abide between my breasts**, that is, as if joined breast to breast, that is, with the Word to the word, himself to me, he will rest so much more lingeringly with me as the stumbling blocks of separation are mortified more effectively (*efficacius*)."[80] Not only did this removal of stumbling blocks lead to greater unification with the bridegroom but it was also carried out by the bridegroom himself. The "hand of the lover excludes effectively (*efficaciter*) . . . it shuts out adulterous suggestions most effectively (*efficacissime*)."[81] That is, the Word removes or blocks out impetuses toward any goods but itself. The contemplative life sent the bride "on hard journeys, which, as she is more freely able, the bridegroom says effectively *that the obstacles are small.*"[82] That is, the Word minimizes or clears away the impediments to super-intellectual union, which were like veils that made possible the soul's earlier advancement.

The second principal exercise of the mind at work in the Song is adapting it for union (*aptitudo ad unitionem*). Under this broad category of the soul's transformation, Gallus describes moments when the voice of the bridegroom is said to effectively draw, dilate, beautify, and, of course, unify the bride. Let us look at an example of each way Gallus describes the adaptation for union and his attribution of each to the bridegroom's effectiveness.

The voice of the bridegroom, says Gallus, effectively attracts the bride, drawing and raising her to union, performing the very action he enjoins of her. Consider the following example, where Gallus glosses the bride's voice reporting the bridegroom's summons: "And by radiating so subtly to me, **my beloved spoke** by means of effect (*per effectum*): **arise**, that is, make me rise by unknowing (*fac me consurgere ignote*) higher than before in fervent affect (*affectu*) . . . and behold it signifies that she approaches continually

---

80	Gallus, *Song Commentary II* 1.F, 75.
81	Gallus, *Song Commentary III* 1.K, 136.
82	Gallus, *Song Commentary III* 2.H, 155.

through those ascents to a more familiar presence."[83] The bridegroom exhorts the bride to arise, raising her himself (*per effectum*). To drive home the point, when the voice shifts to the bridegroom's with "**arise**," Gallus's gloss remains in the bride's voice ("make me rise"). When the bridegroom speaks, it affects the bride. When the Word speaks, it affects the soul. Similarly, Gallus describes another imperative of the bridegroom as effective (at 6:12): "The bridegroom, compassionate to the fallen bride, effectively (*effective*) calls back to her, saying, **return**, from the lower hierarchies."[84] These two examples show that the bridegroom's exhortation of the bride signifies that the Word affects and attracts the soul. It carries out its own act of summoning.

The bridegroom, in turn, effectively incites the bride to draw and receive him as well, which Gallus finds in the Song's highly metaphorical language. On 2:1 ("I am the flower of the field"), Gallus glosses, "The bridegroom speaks effectively (*sponsus loquitur effective*): invite me, bride, to the flowery little bed, which indeed is decorated with flowers by me, and I stretch your little bed into the wideness of a field."[85] Clearly, this is far from a literal interpretation of this verse. It signifies that the Word incites the affected soul, transforming it by dilating or opening it up. When the bridegroom calls himself "the flower of the field," he "stretches (*extendere*)" the "flowery little bed" that Gallus had identified before as the "inner part of the mind," small because simplified, "in order that it might fit" the "immensity of the bridegroom."[86] This act of dilation of the mind is again carried out by the bridegroom. Gallus confirms this in the second Song commentary on the same passage: "But the bridegroom calmly lingering on the same bridal-bed and inflowing the more fertile fervors and splendors of lights, expands (*dilatat*) the bed itself, as it were, into a field and he speaks with the very effect (*ipso effectu loquitur*): **I am the flower of the field**, that is, I, expanding (*dilatans*) plentifully out of myself with your capacity for my magnitude [because the individual 'flower' is in the singular], fill you up with the

---

83 Gallus, *Song Commentary II* 2.D, 81.
84 Gallus, *Song Commentary III* 6.G, 214.
85 Gallus, *Song Commentary III* 2.A, 144.
86 Gallus, *Song Commentary III* 1.P, 142.

multiplex fragrance of sweetness."[87] This act of dilation is especially prominent in Gallus's commentaries on Dionysius. Notice that while the bride is often engaged in an exercise of stretching herself, here Gallus describes this as a function of the bridegroom's effective utterance. Just as the Word draws the soul, inciting desire and movement, it also stretches it for reception.

Gallus's most common use of the rhetoric of effectivity to describe the soul's adaptation for union occurs with the most frequent refrain of the Song, the bridegroom's proclamation "you are beautiful." For Gallus, the adaptation for union is primarily a beautification of the soul. For example, in the second commentary, "**Behold you are beautiful**. Therefore the bride filled with those splendors . . . is marvelously beautified by the bridegroom, whose word is deed. Therefore he effectively says (*effective dicit*) to her: **behold you are beautiful**."[88] On the same passage in the third commentary, "**Behold you are beautiful**. The bridegroom, having been made a bundle of myrrh and a grape cluster of cypress for the bride, speaks to her effectively (*effective ei loquitur*)."[89] Not only does the Word draw, dilate, and fill the soul with contemplative splendors but it transforms the soul aesthetically, making it beautiful in preparation for union.[90]

The passage 6:3–9, spoken in the voice of the bridegroom, is an encomium tracing the bride's physical features, one that incidentally echoes the bride's acclamation of the bridegroom's at 5:10–16. Gallus reads it as an extended description of the bridegroom's effective beautification of the entire mental hierarchy of the bride. It starts, "For the bridegroom speaks effectively: **Beautiful is my friend** by a beautifying (*pulchrifica*) beauty, *CH 7g: a beautifying and principle beauty* by which you will be effected (*efficieris*). . . . The bridegroom, having spoken effectively the foresaid things to the same bride, who rises by true unknowing and has been taken to the

---

87   Gallus, *Song Commentary II* 2.A, 77.
88   Gallus, *Song Commentary II* 1.G, 76.
89   Gallus, *Song Commentary III* 1.O, 141.
90   The beautification of the soul suggests that the Word may in turn be affected or enticed by the soul. Despite Gallus's identification of the bridegroom primarily with the eternal Word rather than with the suffering or incarnate Christ, he allows for the text's presentation of the bridegroom's passions. He is only sometimes anxious to qualify them, stating at times, for instance, that the bride's beauty can refer to the soul finding the Word beautiful.

Thrones, Cherubim, and Seraphim, adds effectively: **Your hair . . . like a flock of goats**."[91] Gallus refers the reader to his earlier gloss in his treatment of the bride's encomium (5:11) to remind the reader that hairs, "which are subtle and rise from the highest part of the head, signify the subtle, principal, and first inflowings of *theoriae* in the Seraphim of the bride."[92] When the bridegroom praises the various beautiful aspects of the bride, it signifies the Word's beautification of the soul: effectively drawing, dilating, and inflowing gifts of graces to it.

The same encomium sums up this effective adaptation for union, when the bridegroom acclaims, "One is my dove, my perfect one." The Song itself seemed to suggest that the perfection of the soul is in being unified with and by the Word. It is no surprise that Gallus adds, "Raising her and simplifying by leading up, he speaks effectively."[93] This is the summation of the bridegroom's effective work in transforming or deifying the bride through drawing, dilating, nourishing, and beautifying: "The highest perfection of the mind consists in the union beyond the mind (*unitione super mentem*) . . . whence, in the hierarchic operations, after purgation and illumination completing perfection occurs. . . . Therefore he says that his bride is perfect because of the union of the principal affection (*propter principalis affectionis unitionem*) by which she is supported and clings truly perfectly to him."[94] The Word is to be attributed with unveiling the mind and preparing it for experiential union, perfecting and uniting the mind to itself. The bridegroom's utterance effects or carries out these two exercises of the bride in Christian wisdom. Again, in the highest hierarchy of the mind, the soul has suspended itself, but its exercise continues, directed by the divine Word.

Finally, the most frequently mentioned of the three principal exercises of the mind in the Song commentaries is most chaste prayer. "Most chaste prayer," unlike "chaste prayer" and "more chaste prayer," begs for the bridegroom himself rather than his gifts. While it may be clearer how unveiling of the mind and adapting it for union are attributable to the bridegroom,

---

91 Gallus, *Song Commentary III* 6.B, 207–8.
92 Gallus, *Song Commentary III* 5.H, 201.
93 Gallus, *Song Commentary III* 6.D, 210.
94 Gallus, *Song Commentary III* 6.D, 210.

Gallus insists that even most chaste prayer is effected by him. An extended look at how Gallus glosses 2:14b in both commentaries will reveal that even the exercise of most chaste prayer is effected by the Word. First, the passage on which Gallus comments, spoken by the bridegroom:

> *Show me your face*
> *Let your voice sound in my ears*
> *For your voice is sweet*
> *And your face is beautiful.*

Gallus's sequential gloss on the first couplet divides the two lines. In both commentaries, Gallus claims these lines are effectively spoken by the bridegroom. For instance, of the first line, Gallus writes in the second Song commentary, "The bridegroom says effectively (*effective dicit*): **Show me your face**; that is, he presents me to himself and makes me present *with most chaste prayers, unveiling of the mind, adaptation for union, Div. Names* 3a; the face, the higher and more eminent and more beautiful part of the human being, signifies the order of Seraphim in which I am presented again to the bridegroom."[95] Notice that Gallus clearly attributes each of the three principal exercises derived from Dionysius to the bridegroom. Together, they make the bride present to the bridegroom. The soul is prepared by the Word for union with the Word, presenting the soul in excess of itself. In the third Song commentary:

> *To the mind of the bride, frequently showered with superbeautiful clarities and by this made more receptive of divine lights, the bridegroom radiates to her more clearly than usual, and this is what he says effectively* (effective loquitur) *to her:* "**Show me your face**. *I having been showered with supersplendent rays, I present your highest hierarchy, the Seraphim, to myself again, and I make it give service to me"; DN 3a: but then when we invoke it . . . we are present to him.*[96]

---

95   Gallus, *Song Commentary II* 2.F, 83.
96   Gallus, *Song Commentary III*.2.M, 162.

The first passage concisely sums up how the bridegroom speaks effectively by making the bride present through making her three principal exercises of the mind efficacious. The performance of these exercises is attractive and uplifting, bringing the soul before the Word. We have seen that the Word removes obstacles and transforms the soul for union, which occurs through the ecstasy of the mind in its highest hierarchy, the "Seraphim." But how does the bridegroom effect the bride's most chaste prayers, the voice of the bride itself?

Gallus's glosses on the next line of the couplet are again fairly consistent across the two commentaries and worth quoting at length. From the second commentary, "**Let your voice sound**, always renewed, rising, and louder. Let your voice sound more audibly and clearly **in my ears** so that I may hear you clearly, and you may progress. . . . The bridegroom says this entire thing effectively, as if it were very pleasing to him."[97] And from the third commentary, "**Let it sound**, that is, let him speak effectively to you; **let your voice sound** *of most chaste prayers, DN 3a*, **in my ears**, that is, 'it provokes me efficaciously (*efficaciter*) to hearing.' For he, the plenitude of largess and bountifulness, is provoked to hearing effectively, as long as he is asked greater things fittingly; but he is provoked to scorn, as it were, by asking for lesser gifts."[98]

Just as with the first line of the couplet, Gallus clearly labels this hortatory line from the bridegroom as itself effective, carrying out that which it says. For the bridegroom to effectively say "show me your face" and "let your voice sound" is for the Word to draw, beautify, and provoke the soul, making it present to the Word and supplying it with most chaste prayers, its voiced desire for the Word itself. In effect, the bridegroom gives voice to the bride.

Yet this passage also suggests that the effected voice of the bride—her most chaste prayers—also has become itself effective in that, in turn, it provokes the bridegroom to hearing. This dynamic, that the voice of the bride is credited to the bridegroom but in turn has effect on the bridegroom, echoes Gallus's emphasis on the effected beautification of the soul by the Word.

---

97   Gallus, *Song Commentary II* 2.F, 83.
98   Gallus, *Song Commentary III* 2.M, 163.

Being made strikingly beautiful, and being given most chaste prayers, allows the bride to in turn attract and affect, as it were, the bridegroom. There will be more to say about this below. For now, consider the following excerpt, which finishes up Gallus's gloss of the passage in the second commentary: "Therefore the bridegroom adds, **Your voice is sweet and your face beautiful**, that is, by which you are pleasing to me, and the effective request of your progress (*postulatio profectus tui efficax*), which is a cry (*clamor*), is pleasing to my hearing. That is, on account of my goodness it is pleasing to me, not because of your merit."[99]

This "effective request" (*efficax postulatio*) is never again mentioned in the Song commentaries, curious given the centrality of voice and most chaste prayer, as I have shown here. Yet this is because the voices of the Song, for Gallus, dramatize the effective utterance of the Word, which assimilates and unites the soul to God. The utterance of the soul is the cry of one drawn, changed, and effected by the practice of experiential union.

"Therefore She Speaks Experientially"

I have singled out examples of the bridegroom's effective utterance in order to analyze it theologically and rhetorically and to show how thoroughly the soul's exercise is attributed to the Word when considering the "wisdom of Christians." Yet, as we have seen, Gallus divides the Song as a dialogue in a sequence (*in seriem*) with the voices responding and beckoning to one another. As often as the bridegroom is said to "speak effectively," the bride is said to respond "experientially." When Gallus frequently glosses that the bride "speaks experientially," the soul (1) has been united to and affected by the Word, and so (2) responds with its own utterance, (3) meant in turn to affect the soul itself and others (even the Word), (4) even as it admits the inadequacy of its utterance to its divine referent.

Gallus employs the language of experience for both the union effected by the bridegroom and the bride's utterance that is evoked by it. We have already seen that the highest mystical union for Gallus is not intellective but affective and experiential. As we saw above, he justifies this by reference to Dionysius. For instance, "not knowing in a mirror *but suffering* (patiens)

---

99   Gallus, *Song Commentary II* 2.F, 83.

divine things, On Div. Names 2v, in an incomparably more sublime and excellent way, [the bride] experiences union and contemplates."[100] That is, in Dionysius's mystical knowing beyond mind (*cognitio super mentem*), the soul (bride) is said by Gallus to experience the Word (bridegroom). How does the soul "experience" the Word?

We have already seen that the three exercises of the mind effected by the Word leave the soul receptive of the Word's splendors or delights. The verse "Your name is an oil poured out" (1:2) was especially important to Gallus because it seemed to suggest the theology of the Word. His gloss on it in both commentaries helps to see how the theology of the Word fit with mystical theology. In the third commentary, Gallus glosses, "This nourishment [of oil/Word] does not occur through a mirror, but through the experience (*per experientiam*) of divine sweetness, since that taste and touch are not exercised through a mirror."[101] As the Song suggests, experience of union with the Word was more akin to tactile or gustatory encounter than visual or audial. Rather than the collection (*collatio*) and consideration (*consideratio*) of distant sights or sounds characteristic of the non-ecstatic, prerequisite steps of contemplation, it was an intimate and immediate "love" (*dilectio*) that transformed knowledge. In the parallel passage in the second commentary:

> "**Your name is an oil poured out**, *that is, knowledge of you, which I was able to draw up by experiences* (experientiis) *from your hidden place, is, as it were, an oil poured out—purging, illuminating, and healing my whole hierarchy. . . ." The bride speaks in the Thrones: your breasts, receiving wisdom, as it were, from the chest, just as the Thrones receive the royal visitations from above. She speaks in the Cherubim where she was lifted higher than the Thrones and more fruitful in experience* (experientia fecundior)*: fragrance of the best ointment. She speaks in the Seraphim: your name is an oil poured out. For that seraphic order, which is unknowing, learns of God without mediation.*[102]

---

100   Gallus, *Song Commentary III* 6.D, 211.
101   Gallus, *Song Commentary III* 1.C, 124.
102   Gallus, *Song Commentary II* 1.A, 69.

The Word pours into the soul, flowing into each of the orders of its highest hierarchy, and Gallus suggests the higher the excessive order, the more experiential is its encounter with the Word, the seraphic order being the order in which the soul meets the Word immediately and intimately, having removed all obstacles and having been prepared for union. Elsewhere, Gallus claims, "All the more profound stretchings, which are experienced in the practice of the wisdom of Christians, pertain especially to that [seraphic] order."[103] As the order of the "Seraphim" is the highest order in excess of the mind, it is the site of the most supernatural, graced encounter with the Word. If we were to map Gallus's rhetoric of experience, it is most frequent and most heightened here, even as it also pertains to the other excessive orders and the middle hierarchy, which is characterized by nature and grace.[104]

The constant reference to the bride's *experience* paints a picture of symmetrical contrast with the bridegroom: when the Word acts effectively—especially, as we saw, in the highest hierarchy of the mind—the soul is affected (*affectus*). *Experience* describes the impingement or influence of the Word on the soul that leaves its traces on the soul's entire cognitive apparatus, as it were: "The bridegroom is said to be **leaping on the mountains and hastening over the hills** because he impresses his vestiges to the receptive orders through unitive joining and experiential knowledge (*experimentalem cognitionem*), the orders which experience (*patiuntur*) divine things."[105] When the soul is affected in any of its parts by encounter with the Word, it is said to experience. However, since the primary affection occurs when the apex of the soul's affection is joined to the person of the Word, not just the Word's gifts, in the "Seraphim" of the mind, Gallus calls this *experiential union*.

This experience in turn evokes experiential utterance: "The bride, experiencing the secure rest provided for her by the bridegroom, speaks experientially."[106] Among the many instances where Gallus glosses that the bride is speaking experientially, he seems to suggest she is speaking *from* or *in response to* the encounter with the bridegroom in the "Seraphim" of the mind. That

---

103   Gallus, *Song Commentary III* 2.C, 147.
104   On the continuity of experience from nature to grace, see above, 136–38.
105   Gallus, *Song Commentary III* 2.E, 150.
106   Gallus, *Song Commentary III* 8.E, 229.

is, the soul speaks *out of, through,* or *as a result of* its union with the Word. This visceral kind of utterance is ambiguous. This is one of the reasons Gallus found the Song's poetics more appropriate rhetorically for expounding the wisdom of Christians than any other biblical book. Only a poetic use of language was appropriate for experiential union.

While Gallus often remarks on the ineffability of experiential union, as we will treat below, he also suggests that the experience of union with the Word compels the soul to speak, however equivocally. An extended treatment of a repeated motif in the Song shows how Gallus understood experiential utterance to arise from experiential union.[107] The phrase is found first in 1:3b ("The king has led me into his storerooms") and then echoed in 2:4a ("he led me into his wine cellar").

> **He led in**. *The continual variety of* theoriae *and the continual advancements of the bride lead her into experiential babbling (*experimentalem garrulitatem*), as it were. Therefore let it not be understood that she sometimes repeats the things said, but that she experiences (*experiri*) continual renewals, which is entirely familiar to contemplative minds, which have been exercised so forcefully and continually to the superior ray. Therefore she says experientially:* **He led me in** *through interior* theoriae *more profound than before.*[108]

Continually traversing the itineraries of the highest *theoriae*, the soul is led into a state of irrepressible talkativeness by its own spiritual exercise. "Babbling" (*garrulitas*) suggests the visceral nature of this utterance. It comes as the soul's irrepressible response to the Word, even as the soul is continually united to the Word to which it seeks to respond.

The participatory character of experiential union helps to explain this dynamic. As the soul experiences further participations in the Word, it passes

---

107 Notice in the following that, for Gallus, concerned with the sequence (*series*) of the Song, the repetition of the bride's voice has its own significance.

108 Gallus, *Song Commentary III* 2.C, 147. As recorded by the editor of the critical edition, one medieval manuscript has "*experientialiter*" here for "*experimentaliter*," perhaps a scribal error but also showing these terms could be used basically interchangeably. This supports my decision to lump them together under "the rhetoric of experience" and to translate each as "experience."

on what it has received, paradigmatically in utterance. Gallus writes, "Therefore she speaks experientially the participations which she receives from the plenitude of the bridegroom, according to her individual hierarchies and orders."[109] Again, Dionysius provides the backdrop. These participations *"are not known except insofar as they are participated in, On Div. Names* 2q."[110] Because experiential union describes this participation, the utterance evoked from it is said to speak these participations, pouring them out, as it were, just as they have been poured into the receptive soul.

While Gallus describes the visceral or irrepressible nature of the bride's experiential utterance, he also points to its function. Experiential utterance has its own effect on other contemplatives, on the soul itself, and even on the bridegroom. Although Gallus typically reads the Song as concerned primarily with the soul and the Word, he does indicate that experiential union should have broader social effects. For instance, at 1:5b ("The sons of my mother fought against me"), Gallus glosses, "**The sons of my mother**. These kinds of words of the bride are experiential (*experientialia*) and expressive (*expressiva*) of her state for the perpetual instruction of contemplative minds."[111] That is, among Gallus's readers, contemplative union engendered a pedagogical project. What one experienced ought to be passed on. A surviving collection of sermon notes by Gallus on "How the Lives of Prelates Ought to be Conformed to the Lives of Angels" suggests the application of Gallus's thought to an entire social order that mimicked the angelic—and, in turn, the mental—hierarchy.[112]

Yet in both Song commentaries, Gallus far more frequently claims that experiential utterance of the bride in the "Seraphim" of the mind is meant to transform the lower orders of the mind by passing on the participatory revelations in which the apex of the affection took part most fully. That is, it should affect the soul itself. We have seen this already when the bridegroom "effects" the transformation of the lower orders, but it is through

---

109   Gallus, *Song Commentary III* 5.H, 200–201.
110   Gallus, *Song Commentary III* 5.H, 200.
111   Gallus, *Song Commentary III* 1.G, 130.
112   See Thomas Gallus, "*Qualiter Vita Prelatorum Conformarite Debet Vite Angelice,*" ed. Declan Lawell, *Recherches de Théologie et Philosophie Médiévales* 75, no. 2 (2008): 303–36.

the experience of the bride that this is effected. For instance, remarking on her reception of the bridegroom, whom she calls her "bundle of myrrh," the bride says, "As it were, I distributed to my inferior orders from my plenitude, but nonetheless I firmly cling to the bridegroom to drink more copiously. Therefore, she speaks experientially: **My beloved is a bundle of myrrh to me**." We have seen some account of what this transformation looks like. Primarily, these orders are affected and dilated for greater reception of divine light and greater attention toward and pursuit of the beloved Word.[113]

This Word, however, is most frequently referred to by the bride as "him whom my soul loves."[114] Gallus reads this peculiar formulation as reflective of the fact that the soul, having been united to the Word experientially, has no appropriate language for or rational understanding of the Word. This reflects the influence of Dionysius's formulation of the God beyond being: "**Whom my soul loves**, yet unnameable, incomprehensible, supersubstantial, whom I know by the experience of intimate love alone, inasmuch as I participate, whom *you will know by* your *participation alone*, On Div. Names

---

113   As Coolman describes it, affective cognition "redounds to, that is 'flows down' to and is participated by the lower, intellective cognition." This same dynamic is true all the way down the mental hierarchic order, as it were. *Eternally Spiraling into God*, 24.

114   Besides 1:6, an extended passage, 3:1–4, translated in E. Ann Matter, *The Voice of My Beloved: The Song of Songs in Western Medieval Christianity* (Philadelphia: University of Pennsylvania Press, 1990), describes the bride's quest for "whom my soul loves":

> On my bed through the nights
> I sought him whom my soul loves
> I sought him and I did not find
> I will arise and go around the city
> through the streets and the courtyards
> I will seek him whom my soul loves
> I have sought him and I did not find
> The watchmen found me who guard the city
> have you seen him whom my soul has loved?
> When I had hardly passed by them
> I found him whom my soul loves
> I held him nor will I let go.

Similarly, the Song uses "beloved" or "beloved one" at 2:10, 16–17; 5:1–2, 6, 8, 10, 16; 6:–2; and 7:9–11, 13.

2, whom I can make known to no one except to myself loving you."[115] That is, the experiential utterance of the bride, which attempts to pass on her knowledge to others, cannot make others know the bridegroom. "Only those who experience (*experiuntur*)" the "apparitions of the divine lights (*divinorum luminum apparitiones*)," which occur when they are united to the uniting ray, can know the Word.[116]

In the bride's quest, wandering the streets of the city for "whom my soul loves," Gallus interprets the soul as exploring the multiple itineraries of the *theoriae*: "We call 'streets' the unitive superintellectual experiences (*experientias*) which *no one knows except who receives, Rev. 2*."[117] Each of these itineraries leads to the Word, so there is a sense in which Gallus draws on the multiplicity implied in these experiences to say that talkativeness (*garrulitas*) is appropriate for the union with the Word. United to the Word, one is also united to the multiplicity of experience that comes immediately from the Word. But no single expression will be adequate to the Word itself.

Given the emphasis placed on divine ineffability in the Dionysian corpus and the use of language to navigate that particular theological problem, it may not be a surprise to see that Gallus discerns that the voice of the bride struggles with a bridegroom who is ineffable and unintelligible. The soul may never appropriately speak of the Word. Most important to note, however, is how distinct Gallus's use of the rhetoric of experience is on exactly this point. So far, our description of the rhetoric of experience is not very distinct semantically from the ways the term is used today, even popularly, to describe one's individual encounter with the world that intimately transforms one and motivates a particular way of speaking. But Gallus ties "experience" to an encounter with that which is not rationally graspable.

"Rejoicing with the Grace of the Bridegroom"

So far, we have seen that Gallus typically describes the bride's utterance as "experiential," and the bridegroom's as "effective." That is, his division of the sequence (*series*) of the Song is primarily between the two voices—the bride or soul, who experiences the Word, and the bridegroom or Word, who

---

115	Gallus, *Song Commentary III* 1.H, 132.
116	Gallus, *Song Commentary III* 2.F, 153.
117	Gallus, *Song Commentary III* 3.A, 167.

is attributed with the carrying out of that experience. In the highest stages of contemplative union, the soul's practice is effected by the Word, who removes obstacles, adapts the soul for union, and provides the soul most chaste prayer. As mentioned above, the attribution of efficacy to the Word is pervasive. The soul, in turn and in the same measure, experiences union and speaks experientially.

Yet the transformation of the soul effected by the Word—the adaptation of the soul for union and the impact of experiential union—also results suddenly, subtly, and significantly in the soul's utterance becoming effective itself. As we previewed above, the soul's "effective request" (*efficax postulatio*) was "pleasing" to the Word, though, Gallus qualifies, on account of the Word's goodness, not because of the soul's merit.[118] That is, the bride's voice itself becomes sweet, inviting, or affecting thanks to its union and assimilation to the bridegroom. On the bridegroom's exhortation at (2:14), "Let your voice sound in my ears," Gallus glosses in the bridegroom's voice, "That is, it arouses me effectively and gets me to listen. For the plenitude of bounty and generosity is aroused to listen effectively, so long as it is asked suitably for greater things."[119] These passages suggest the most chaste prayer of the soul, effected by the Word, in turn, affects the Word.

The assimilation of the soul to the Word, and the soul's resulting efficacy, is depicted by Gallus's frequent evocation of the inflowing (*influitio*) of divine light and heat to the soul's intellect and affect, which occurs in its highest hierarchical orders and is passed on to its lower orders. In 5:5, the bride says, "I rose to open to my beloved / my hands dripped myrrh." Gallus glosses, "Therefore the bride, filled with copious lights, and inflowing generously from her plenitude to the inferior orders . . . speaks effectively and experientially: **my hands**, my hierarchic operations, **dripped**, through the divisions of graces they inflowed to the inferior orders, **myrrh**."[120] The continual inflowing of divine light, an important Dionysian image, provides a way for depicting the soul's own efficacy dependent on the Word's. The mind passes what it has received onto its lower orders, carrying out their operations.

---

118   Gallus, *Song Commentary II* 2.F, 83. See above, 37.
119   Gallus, *Song Commentary III* 2.M, 163.
120   Gallus, *Song Commentary III* 5.E, 197.

The soul even seems to effect its own contemplative exercise at times, somewhat at odds with Gallus's total attribution of efficacy to the Word. For instance, regarding the exercise of "unveiling of the mind" (*revelatio mentis*), we saw above that in the third commentary, Gallus interprets the line "catch the little foxes" to be spoken by the bridegroom and to mean that the Word effectively clears away the soul's worldly or intellectual cares in preparation for union.[121] In contrast, in the second commentary, Gallus attributes the same line to the bride, who "speaks effectively," when she says, "O attendants, **catch**, that is, beat down **the little foxes**, that is, deceitful and secret treacheries."[122] Again, the soul effects the exercise of its lower hierarchical orders ("the attendants"). The soul has become effective of its own exercise due to experiential union with the Word.

Examples of the soul's sudden bouts of efficacy throughout the Song could be multiplied.[123] What is important to notice is that, though Gallus discerned that the Word spoke with an effective mode of utterance throughout the Song, he also spots moments when the soul itself becomes effective because of its union with and assimilation to the Word. This means it begins to participate or cooperate in the operations of the Word. It joins the Word in carrying out its own contemplative exercise, and it entices and affects the Word itself toward union.[124]

This second claim, that the soul begins to affect the Word itself, is perhaps the more surprising theologically, and Gallus is indeed less inclined to bear out the implications of the Song's mutuality at this point. The Song's violent imagery of the wounding and striking of the bridegroom, though, suggested it. The bridegroom, for instance, is terrified by the bride. She is "terrible as a battle line drawn up from camps / turn away your eyes from me / for they make me flee" (6:3b–4a). Gallus, in a long digression, describes how the soul conquers its foe-lover bit by bit with multiple advances of the

---

121 See above, 159–60.
122 Gallus, *Song Commentary II* 2.F, 83.
123 See, for example, Gallus, *Song Commentary III* 1.G, 130; 3.A, 166; 3.B, 168; 5.B, 192.
124 Mutuality, reciprocity, or mirroring in the Song's structure occurs with important verbal echoes coming from the bride and bridegroom throughout, most notably chapters 5 and 6's respective encomiums on the two lovers.

cardinal and theological virtues. He ends his reflection with the following: "The bridegroom says to the sober bride: in order that you may seize heaven effectively (*efficaciter*) and violently, wound me, be strong against me!"[125] In another passage, Gallus writes that "this eye [of super-intellectual knowing] wounds the bridegroom with a wondrous sharpness."[126] Elsewhere, "the bridegroom shows effectively that the bride has penetrated the depths of God . . . by rejoicing together (*congaudendo*), he says to her, **you have wounded my heart, my sister,** by chaste love, **my bride**."[127] The wounding of the Word suggests both that the soul penetrates or becomes familiar with (gains experiential knowledge of) the Word and that the Word is affected itself by the soul.

It is possible that Gallus means the point of the Word's apparent affection is not that the Word "experiences" but rather that the soul comes to experience in the Word's sympathy with it. For instance, when the bride begs the "daughters of Jerusalem" to lead her to her beloved, Gallus discerns that the soul entreats the angels, "Lead me back to him by your upliftings and inflowings, in order that I may know through experience that he knows what I suffer, what I desire, **that I languish with love**."[128] Yet, at other places, Gallus is more explicit, appealing to the Dionysian position that God is cozened and drawn ecstatically by love.

> *This most chaste love is of such power that it arouses God to ecstatic love, according to* Psalm 8 *(I love those who love me). For this reason, in* Divine Names, *after the forementioned things are added, we ought to dare to say even this in truth, that even the very Cause of all things, by a beautiful and good love of all things, through an abundance of loving goodness, comes to be outside of itself.*[129]

The rhetoric of wounding and ecstasy surrounding the Word suggests a role reversal symmetrical to that of the soul's becoming effective. Is the Word affected? Does it experience like the soul?

125	Gallus, *Song Commentary III* 6.B, 207.
126	Gallus, *Song Commentary III* 1.O, 141.
127	Gallus, *Song Commentary II* 4.D–E, 95.
128	Gallus, *Song Commentary III* 5.F, 199.
129	Gallus, *Song Commentary III* 2.K, 159.

These questions are not taken up by Gallus, but our attention to Gallus's use of mystical language allows the subtlety of Gallus's presentation its due. What we can conclude is that Gallus attributes absolute efficacy to the Word and experience to the soul, even as he performs bouts of role reversal, most often with the soul becoming effective but also with the Word being enticed, penetrated, and drawn out of itself by the soul. In this way, Gallus has respected the sequence (*series*) of the Song, with its reciprocal mutuality, while drawing on Dionysius's ideas about the goal of mystical theology being union and assimilation.

Conclusion

When Gallus commented on the Song of Songs, he was reading the mystified letter. This chapter has traced the movement of interpretation from the letter (*littera*) of the Song to a deeper penetration of its spiritual meaning (*spiritus*). Gallus plumbed the depths of the Song multiple times, writing at least three sequential commentaries, because the Song's spirit was elusive and inexhaustible. The dialogue between bride and bridegroom provided an abundance of images for the ineffable and unintelligible mystical union between the soul and the eternal Word.

Reading and commenting on the mystified letter engaged the entire mental apparatus. The union with the Word was affective and experiential, beyond intellect. Reading transformed the soul, drawing it beyond itself, dilating and beautifying it, and ultimately making it an effective agent of its own spiritual progress. Gallus's Song commentaries are thus an appropriate place to draw together my analysis of the Victorine reading culture. Not only do they culminate the chronological course of the emergence of the mystified letter at St. Victor, as the last of the great Victorine texts, but they also exhibit how engaging with the mystified letter at St. Victor transformed and transported the reader, who was united to the source of the mystified letter, the Word of God.

6

CONCLUSION: READING THEN AND NOW

Toward a Theology of Reading

The primary goal of this book is to renew the practice of reading by retrieving a theology centered on the mystified letter. Theological retrieval draws from sources or "founts" of the past for renewal in and beyond the present.[1] The work of retrieval, though, does not simply plunge into the metaphorical waters of the past but collects, hauls, and distributes its wisdom to those who need it. The challenge of retrieval for the theologian is the long distance between past and present. This concluding chapter draws from my analysis of the mystified letter at the abbey of St. Victor in the twelfth and thirteenth centuries and applies its wisdom to our present circumstances. What would it take to retrieve the mystified letter, to slake our thirst among the dry and dull reading cultures of today? What can we draw from the reading culture at St. Victor and its theology of reading?

This book's theological analysis has shown that the letter was once mystified at the abbey of St. Victor when two strands of Christian theology came together—a theology of the letter (from Paul and Augustine) and a mystical theology (from Pseudo-Dionysius). The former established the letter as a central theological concept at St. Victor; the latter mystified it. That is, I have traced how Victorine theology developed to mystify the letter and create a flourishing reading culture. My analysis has focused on the significant impact of theology on the school's reading culture. Victorine theology—habits of reflecting on God, the Word, and the letter itself—invested both sacred and secular literature with a sense of ineffability and unintelligibility, wonder and awe. It created passionate and curious readers. The Victorines fostered reverence for reading as *the* practice that had an unspeakable capacity to inspire and transform.

---

1   See ch. 1, 7–11.

While my analysis has focused on how Victorine theology was instrumental to the formation of this reading culture, historians point out that Victorine life revolved around the practice of reading. At the abbey, reading was a monastic discipline, regular and orderly. It occurred during mealtimes in the abbey's refectory but also "through the delivery of sermons, conversations with novices during times like the 'time of speaking' or the 'time of conference,' teaching times with novices as part of their education in the order, or lectures that were open to external students."[2] At St. Victor, the practice of reading was both transformative and communal, and it was unceasing, a regular part of religious and academic life.

In our own time, the pillars of our reading culture—the Church and the academy—struggle to foster such an imagination around reading that can stimulate enthusiasm and awe, much less build up communities of readers. In the Church, reading is somehow simultaneously divisive and dull as a result of an inadequate imagination about the letter. If Scriptures are simply used for proof-texting and argument-winning, they become demystified blunt objects of harm but not tools of potential transformation. As a result, many in the Church become exhausted by reading or simply read to get by. In the academy, reading hardly fares better. There are too many pressures against reading, which reduce it to a technocratic task with no spiritual or socially transformative effects. Demoralized professors, exhausted administrators, and uninspired students try to salvage the transformative experience of reading but have dwindling resources, imaginative or material, to do so. Can the Church and the academy today retrieve the mystified letter? Moving from past to present, let's review our conclusions about the mystified letter at St. Victor and trace out how they can be a source of renewal for the reading cultures of the Church and the academy today.

Retrieving the Mystery of the Letter

The greatest insight into the Victorines' theological concept of the letter was its basic *mystery*. The theological analysis at the heart of this book has shown

---

2 Dale Coulter, "General Introduction," in *Spiritual Formation and Mystical Symbolism: A Selection of Works of Hugh and Richard of St. Victor, and of Thomas Gallus*, ed. Grover A. Zinn, Frans van Liere, and Dale M. Coulter (Turnhout, Belgium: Brepols, 2022), 23. Coulter draws his conclusions from the *Liber ordinis*, a guidebook for monastic life at St. Victor.

that Victorine theology *mystified* the letter, investing it with a sense of awe and wonder, unintelligibility and ineffability. A retrieval of the Victorines' approach to the letter must start with the letter's mystery, the foundation of any possible renewal of the practice of reading. This is a major challenge for both the Church and the academy today. Both contemporary reading cultures foster a sense of reading as mundane and technical. Reading has a finite end when it answers questions, resolves disputes, or completes a task. If anything, reading is often put to work *removing* mystery. What would it look like to retrieve the letter's mystery, inspired by the theology of the Victorines? Let's remind ourselves of how the Victorines did it.

We have seen how, even before the letter was fully mystified at St. Victor, the brothers were primed to imagine an elusive spirit attending the letter. From the very beginning, the letter was never just the letter but was potentially spiritual. Imbued with Christian Trinitarian theology, the Victorines sought the active Spirit of God in the world, and nowhere did they discern it so vividly as in reading the letter, where the Spirit was always close to but distinct from the letter, hovering above, around, and beneath it.[3] Paul's language distinguishing spirit from letter suggested there was always something more to the letter.[4] Reading drew one beyond or deeper into the letter. The Spirit rooted the reader who sought spiritual understanding in and beyond the letter. Far from humiliating the letter, making it lowly in contrast to its lofty spirit, the elusive Spirit of God elevated the letter, investing it with divine mystery. At St. Victor, there was a dynamic tension between letter and spirit, with the Spirit animating or enlivening literature and the practice of reading.

As our analysis showed, though, the letter's mystery was further helped along at St. Victor by the mystical theology of Pseudo-Dionysius.[5] The enigmatic theologian who wrote of "divine names" taught the Victorines to see the letter as a veil, covering over while making accessible the mystery that could not be spoken of. A Victorine translator like John Saracen might transform the letter, putting it into the Latin language, but that was like a stylist who dresses their model in silk after they have first been dressed in satin, a

---

3   Cf. Ps 33:6 and 2 Tim 3:16.
4   See ch. 2, 28–34.
5   See chs. 3 and 4.

similar fabric. The true beauty lay beyond the veil, but there was no perceiving that Spirit without the letter to style it. God or the Spirit lay beyond the letter, hidden and inconceivable. The Victorine might "unfold" the letter, writing commentaries on it, but the veil's folds were many, and while the commentator could get ever closer to the mystery beyond the letter, they could scarcely grasp it. By the time of the last great Victorine, Thomas Gallus, the visible letter had an "estimative relation" to the invisible thing it covered over.[6] Miraculously and mysteriously, the visible letter could "lift" or "draw" one beyond one's knowing powers to the letter's unknown, invisible referent, which nevertheless always remained a mystery, transforming the reader in the process.

According to Victorine theology, this "estimative relation" between the letter and its hidden object was established by God's providence through human writers, or the "theologians," as Pseudo-Dionysius had taught to call them. The writers of Scripture, or the theologians, drew from the creative and providential actions of God to speak of the mysterious Cause of all things. Their language was, Pseudo-Dionysius admits, entirely worldly, drawn from their own human experience. Because God's creative and restorative Word was involved in all worldly things, there was no worldly language entirely inadequate to who or what God was, as long as it was rightly understood to have a mysterious relation to that to which it refers. In a sense, all writers—both Christian and pagan—became theologians since every branch of the liberal arts investigates and speaks of God's creative works, as does Scripture especially. The letter—whether sacred or secular—represented God's loving providential plan, like a veil presents its wearer.

The Victorine reading culture therefore centered on the letter's ability to represent the mysterious generosity of God, the loving Creator and Redeemer. Far from being a practice that turned one inward, reading the mystified letter ushered one through creation itself and drew one nearer to its Creator. That is, reading drew one outward toward God's temporal actions in the world and in turn toward God in eternity beyond. While it transformed one inwardly, it directed one toward all in God's care and toward God's loving care itself. In this way, the letter's mystery reflected not

---

6   See ch. 4, 117–21.

just God's beyond-ness but also God's creative and redemptive abundance. Mystification of the letter served to respect both God's transcendence and God's plenitudinous presence.

It may be noticed here that Victorine theology provides one strategy of mystification for one possible medium of spiritual transformation. The Victorines use theology to mystify the letter in order to transform its readers. Other strategies may be used to mystify other media for other ends.[7] However, the Victorines' exposure to the theology of God's Word encouraged them to see the letter as the best medium and reading as the best mechanism of spiritual transformation for themselves and their community.[8] They reflect a long-standing religious fascination with the remarkable, and perhaps incomparable, ability of reading to marvelously transform the human person.

A Transformative, Communal Journey along the Letter

In addition to the veil of the letter, another powerful set of metaphors for the mystified letter at St. Victor depicted the reader on a journey along a path. As we have seen, Hugh of St. Victor cautioned those readers not to stumble along the path of the letter.[9] They should traverse the letter while remaining rooted in its spirit. The Spirit-filled reader avoided stumbling or veering off the path of the letter, even as they also avoided clinging too tightly to it as if paralyzed by the awesome journey ahead of them. Hugh's theology of the letter both studiously avoids the dangers of an unmoving literalism and embraces the letter as the best medium for spiritual advancement or transformation, that which guides and trains the reader who is learning to travel.

Likewise, Thomas Gallus has the reader wandering along the winding paths of the letter.[10] His metaphors are drawn from the vivid language of the Song of Songs. He analogizes the bride's wandering through the city streets in search of her beloved (3:2) by positing that the soul traverses the manifold

---

7 For an excellent example of scholarly analysis of secular mystification in the arts, see Kosky, *Arts of Wonder*.
8 See ch. 4, 121–24.
9 See ch. 2, 28.
10 See ch. 5, 150–51.

marvels of the Word, or the "courses of the *theoriae*," searching out the eternal Word Itself, her bridegroom. The reader ambles through the verses of the Song as they become more acquainted with the glorious landscape of the Word incarnate and eternal. That is, Gallus accepts and intensifies the Victorine conviction that the letter is the best medium of spiritual advancement and transformation. It guides the reader through the Word's varied topography, as it were, as the reader slowly and progressively transforms and enlivens in intellect and, more importantly, in affect.[11] As with Hugh, Gallus casts the letter as a path for transforming the reader. Very infrequently does he suggest the possibility of the journey's end, given his Dionysian commitment to the mystery of the God beyond being. The good of reading is not to reach the end but to slowly deify the reader, uniting them and assimilating them to God's Word or expanding their intellect and affect to receive the Word's gracious inpourings.[12] Again the path of the letter marvelously conditions the reader more than it conveys them to God.

In addition, the reader was never a lonely wanderer. The Victorine theology of reading stresses the importance of the reading community on the journey of the mystified letter. This is no surprise given that monastic reading was thoroughly communal. Yet it was also the Victorines' theology of the letter that reinforced the communal nature of the readerly journey. Following Augustine, the letter was a system of signs, arranged with care by God.[13] The Victorine community journeyed together—reading, commenting, translating—discerning the path God had laid out and relying on God's Spirit to guide their reading. Augustine had taught that not only is this system of signs carefully arranged by God but it also relied on human society since that is what established an accessible system of referents in human language. There was no traversing God's system of signs without being taught to speak and to read, without the ongoing fellowship created by a society's sharing of words. This ensured that reading was both mundane and miraculous at the same time, and it required that the reader journey with others, whether in the Church, the classroom, or the abbey's refectory.

11	See ch. 5, 150–52.
12	See ch. 5, 161–63.
13	See ch. 2, 43–47.

A reader was always simultaneously reliant on the grace of God and their readerly community.

In both the metaphors of the letter's journey or path and the optimism about the transformative power of reading done in monastic community, we can see the influence of monastic perfectionism at St. Victor. The ideal of perfection in medieval monastic cultures reflected an optimism about the human being's capacity to realize their own end or potential thanks to the guidance provided by the monastic community and the grace of God.[14] Monastic rhetoric of remarkable feats of seeking and striving, such as Hugh's injunction to "read everything," reflects the conviction that monastic effort, aided by divine grace, could realize spectacular results. Gallus's description of the soul's steady dilation, nourishment, beautification, and ultimate deification reflects the Victorine trust in the reader's spiritual advancement or transformation.[15] However, as these dynamic terms suggest, the Victorine believed that the pursuit of perfection was one thing while on the journey (*in via*) and another thing in the homeland (*in patria*), after the resurrection of the monk and their entrance into the kingdom of heaven. Notice that monastic perfectionism does not create hubris in the individual monk since it is scarcely realizable in this life, and it requires the grace of God and one's readerly community. The perfection of the monk was in their transformation as they read the mystified letter in their community.

Challenges for Retrieval

The Church and the academy today lack such enthusiasm for the capacity of reading to transform individuals and communities. These institutions too often demystify reading, reducing it to winning an argument or securing an advantage. In contrast, the Victorines centered their theology of reading on the mystified letter and formed a community that read the letter to transform itself. The transformation of intellect and affect, mind and heart, is echoed in the formation of readerly communities. If the Church and the academy are to advance their stated goals along these lines of intellectual,

---

14   It had roots in Jesus's injunction to "be perfect, therefore, as your heavenly Father is perfect" (Matt 5:48), as well as the Aristotelian concept of a "final cause."
15   See ch. 5, 161–63.

moral, and social transformation, they must move beyond demystified forms of reading directed toward securing the faith or a financial future. Neither dull literalism nor uninspired technocratic reading will impassion minds or renew societies.

I have argued that theology was instrumental to the mystification of the letter in the twelfth and thirteenth centuries at St. Victor. While I contend that the Victorine theology of reading can once again help to mystify the letter and renew our reading cultures today, there will no doubt be challenges. To close this book, I highlight challenges for the Church and the academy in retrieving the mystified letter.

If the Victorine case is any indication, the theology of God is central to the mystification of the letter, and the Church today risks worshipping a false god (as it always has). What my analysis of Victorine theology has shown is that the Victorines were animated by a view of the God of mystery who is passionate and loving.[16] When Church leaders choke God's passionate love and affectionate care for God's creations, the letter becomes withered and dry since it is a representation of or intellectual and affective medium toward God's loving care. A God without loving *pathos*—compassion and care—leads to a deadened letter. Therefore, while there may be benefits to theologies of God that stress impassibility (God's lack of suffering) or that emphasize other attributes like God's justice or reason, only theologies that reflect on God's passionate love will lead to transformative reading communities that engage with the letter's mystery.[17]

An inadequate theology of God results in many abuses of the mystified letter in the Church. For instance, too often Christian exclusiveness—rooted in God's impossible judgment—denies the potential of reading's transformative power outside the rigid letter of the Bible or the walls of the Church community. The medieval theology of reading explored in this book sees all writing—sacred and secular—as potentially guiding the reader toward the

---

16   See ch. 3, 80–81, and ch. 5, 172–76.
17   For an introduction to contemporary debates around the theology of God along these lines, see Thomas G. Weinandy, O.F.M., Cap., *Does God Suffer?* (Notre Dame, IN: University of Notre Dame Press, 2000); and Elizabeth A. Johnson, "The Crucified God of Compassion," in *Quest for the Living God: Mapping Frontiers in the Theology of God* (New York: Continuum International, 2008), 49–69.

loving Creator of all, whose Spirit animates all human inquiry and art. Too often, Bible reading is suspicious and paranoid, not attuned to the Spirit, who animates all of creation and society.[18] When the letter is mystified, it opens the potential of readerly communities to take on new texts and new readers as there is no limit to the theological attempts to represent God's loving care. The letter is the human attempt to stylize the mysterious God, who passionately creates and redeems the world. Far from diminishing the sacred letter, the secular letter enhances it or equips the reader for it. Likewise, including those often driven from the Church enhances or equips the Church to transform itself and society. At St. Victor, the mystified letter always expanded the boundaries of Christian reading.[19]

There are also considerable challenges to the academy retrieving the mystified letter. The academy's disinclination toward God talk and aversion toward mystery are obstacles to the transformative experience of reading. With fewer opportunities for students and researchers to engage in reflection on the ways religious communities speak and think about the mystery of God (theology), one powerful intellectual framework for reflecting on reading is lost. Scholars in religious studies and theology have long described this modern move away from mystery with the term *disenchantment*. Mystification is a remedy for disenchantment, but it requires openness to God talk and the human experience of mystery. Since mystery is always encountered due to cultural and linguistic practices of mystification, as this book's example of Victorine theology shows, the academic study of mystery can be done rigorously with a range of multi- and interdisciplinary intellectual tools.

---

18   On Christian conspiratorial reading and "textual hatred," see James Simpson, *Burning to Read: English Fundamentalism and Its Reformation Opponents* (Cambridge, MA: Harvard University Press, 2007). The mystification of the letter in some Christian reading cultures pushes against insistent claims about the letter's simplicity and clarity, which Simpson argues lead to psychological violence and paranoia, the conditions for religious fundamentalism.

19   For example, Hugh enjoins his readers to read all the liberal arts and even seems to push the boundaries of the canon of Scripture. See ch. 2, 42–43. Some scholars see Hugh's expanding canon as a curiosity, but given our study of the mystified letter, it should be clear why at St. Victor the boundaries of canon became fluid and dynamic as the letter's mystery pressed against its rigid establishment.

The diminishment of reflection on God talk, theology, and mystery in the academy leads, once again, to abuses of the mystified letter. As both theological education and the liberal arts have contracted, the academy is left with fewer resources, material and imaginative, for engaging with the letter. Without the letter's mystery, academic reading lacks enthusiasm and becomes a technocratic task—as anyone who has spent time in the classroom can attest. Without the mystified letter as a central theological or moral concept, it becomes less clear why reading is even important, and both educators and students often conclude it's not. Only by articulating reading as that which has the marvelous and mysterious power to transform persons and societies will it be possible to renew reading in the academy.

These present challenges are complex enough to demand multiple creative responses. By calling for a retrieval of the mystified letter in the Church and the academy, I do not advocate for a simple return to the medieval past or build up Victorine theology as the sole therapeutic remedy for renewing our reading cultures. As my analysis has shown, the mystified letter has many paths to renewing our minds, hearts, and communities. My hope amid these present challenges is that our reading cultures are renewed when we reckon with the potential of reading to transform persons and societies.

BIBLIOGRAPHY

Primary Sources

Andrew of St. Victor. *Expositio super heptateuchum*. Edited by C. Lohr and R. Berndt. Corpus Christianorum Continuatio Mediaevalis 53. Turnhout, Belgium: Brepols, 1986.

Augustine. *Confessions*. Edited by Michael P. Foley. Translated by F. J. Sheed. Indianapolis, IN: Hackett Publishing, 2006.

———. *De doctrina christiana*. Edited by Joseph Martin. Corpus Christianorum Series Latina 32. Turnhout, Belgium: Brepols, 1962. Translated by R. P. H. Green as *On Christian Teaching*. Oxford: Oxford University Press, 1997.

Cicero. *De Inventione*. Edited by Jeffrey Henderson. Translated by H. M. Hubbell. Loeb Classical Library. Cambridge, MA: Harvard University Press, 1949.

Godfrey of St. Victor. "The Fountain of Philosophy." Translated by Hugh Feiss, O.S.B. In *Interpretation of Scripture: Theory*, edited by Franklin T. Harkins and Frans van Liere. Victorine Texts in Translation, 371–425. Vol. 3. Hyde Park, NY: New City Press, 2013.

Hugh of St. Victor. *De sacramentis christianae fidei*. Edited by J.-P. Migne. Patrologia Latina 176. Paris: Migne, 1854. Translated by Roy Deferrari as *On the Sacraments of the Christian Faith*. Revised ed. Jackson, MI: Ex Fontibus Company, 2016.

———. *Didascalicon de studio legendi: A Critical Text*. Edited by C. H. Buttimer. The Catholic University of America Studies in Medieval and Renaissance Latin 10. Washington, DC: Catholic University of America Press, 1939. Translated by Franklin T. Harkins as *Didascalicon on the Study of Reading*. In *Interpretation of Scripture: Theory*, edited by Franklin T. Harkins and Frans van Liere, 61–202. Turnhout, Belgium: Brepols, 2013.

———. *Noah's Ark*. In *Selected Spiritual Writings*. Translated by a Religious of C.S.M.V. Eugene, OR: Wipf and Stock, 2009. 1st ed. Harper & Row, 1962.

Iamblichus. *Iamblichus: On the Mysteries*. Edited and translated by Emma C. Clark, John M. Dillon, and Jackson P. Hershbell. Atlanta, GA: Society of Biblical Literature, 2003.

James of Vitry. *The Historia Occidentalis of Jacques de Vitry*. Edited by John Frederick Hinnebusch, O. P. Fribourg, Switzerland: University Press, 1972.

John Sarracen. Latin Translation of *Corpus Dionysiacum*. In *Dionysiaca*. Edited by Philippe Chevallier. 2 vols. Paris: Desclée de Brouwer, 1937.

John Scotus Eriugena. Latin Translation of *Corpus Dionysiacum*. In *Dionysiaca*. Edited by Philippe Chevallier. 2 vols. Paris: Desclée de Brouwer, 1937.

Philo of Alexandria. *Philo: On Flight and Finding. On the Change of Names. On Dreams*. Edited and translated by F. H. Colson and G. H. Whitaker. Loeb Classical Library 275. Cambridge, MA: Harvard University Press, 1934.

Plato. *The Collected Dialogues of Plato*. Edited by Edith Hamilton and Huntington Cairns. Princeton, NJ: Princeton University Press, 1969.

Plotinus. *Ennead*. Edited by Jeffrey Henderson. Translated by A. H. Armstrong. Loeb Classical Library. Cambridge, MA: Harvard University Press, 1989.

Proclus. *Proclus: The Elements of Theology*. Edited and translated by E. R. Dodds. Oxford: Clarendon Press, 1963.

Pseudo-Dionysius. *The Complete Works of Dionysius the Areopagite*. Translated by John H. Parker. London: James Parker and Co., 1897–1899. Reprint Merrick, NY: Richwood Publishing, 1976.

———. *Corpus Dionysiacum I*. Edited by Beata Regina Suchla. Berlin: De Gruyter, 1990.

———. *Corpus Dionysiacum II*. Edited by Guenter Heil and Adolf Martin Ritter. Berlin: De Gruyter, 1991.

Thomas Gallus. *Explanatio in Libros Dionysii*. Edited by Declan Anthony Lawell. Corpus Christianorum, Continuatio Mediaevalis 223. Turnhout, Belgium: Brepols, 2011.

———. *Extractio ex Libris Dionysii*. In *Dionysiaca*. Edited by Philippe Chevallier. 2 vols. Paris: Desclée de Brouwer, 1937.

———. *Glose Super Angelica Ierachia*. Edited by Declan Lawell. Corpus Christianorum, Continuatio Mediaevalis 223A. Turnhout, Belgium: Brepols, 2011.

———. *Qualiter Vita Prelatorum Conformari Debet Vite Angelice*. In "*Qualiter Vita Prelatorum Conformari Debet Vite Angelice*." Edited by Declan Lawell. *Recherches de Théologie et Philosophie Médiévales* 75, no. 2 (2008): 303–36.

———. *Spectacula Contemplationis*. In "*Spectacula Contemplationis* (1244–46): A Treatise by Thomas Gallus." Edited by Declan Lawell. *Recherches de Théologie et Philosophie Médiévales* 76, no. 2 (2009): 249–85.

———. *Thomas Gallus: Commentaires du Cantique des Cantiques*. Edited by Jeanne Barbet. Paris: Vrin, 1967.

Secondary Sources

Aertsen, Jan A. "Platonism." In *Cambridge History of Medieval Philosophy*. Vol. 1, edited by Robert Pasnau, 76–85. Cambridge: Cambridge University Press, 2010.

Bagger, Matthew C. *Religious Experience, Justification, and History*. Cambridge: Cambridge University Press, 1999.

———. *The Uses of Paradox: Religion, Self-Transformation, and the Absurd*. New York: Columbia University Press, 2007.

Bryan, Jennifer. *Looking Inward: Devotional Reading and the Private Self in Late Medieval England*. Philadelphia: University of Pennsylvania Press, 2008.

Bynum, Caroline Walker. *Fragmentation and Redemption: Essays on Gender and the Human Body in Medieval Religion*. New York: Zone Books, 1991.

Carruthers, Mary. *Book of Memory: A Study of Medieval Culture*. 1st ed. Cambridge: Cambridge University Press, 1990.

———. *The Book of Memory: A Study of Memory in Medieval Culture*. 2nd ed. Cambridge: Cambridge University Press, 2008.

Coolman, Boyd Taylor. *Eternally Spiraling into God: Knowledge, Love, and Ecstasy in the Theology of Thomas Gallus*. Oxford: Oxford University Press, 2017.

———. *The Theology of Hugh of St. Victor: An Interpretation*. Cambridge: Cambridge University Press, 2009.

———. "The Victorines." In *The Wiley-Blackwell Companion to Christian Mysticism*, edited by Julia A. Lamm, 251–66. Malden, MA: Wiley-Blackwell, 2013.

Coulter, Dale. "General Introduction." In *Spiritual Formation and Mystical Symbolism: A Selection of Works of Hugh and Richard of St. Victor, and of Thomas Gallus*, edited by Grover A. Zinn, Frans van Liere, and Dale M. Coulter, 21–52. Victorine Texts in Translation 5. Turnhout, Belgium: Brepols, 2022.

———. *Per Visibilia ad Invisibilia: Theological Method in Richard of St. Victor (d. 1173)*. Bibliotecha Victorina XVIII. Turnhout, Belgium: Brepols, 2006.

Dailey, Patricia. *Promised Bodies: Time, Language, and Corporeality in Medieval Women's Mystical Texts*. New York: Columbia University Press, 2013.

De Lubac, Henri. *The Mystery of the Supernatural.* Translated by Rosemary Sheed. New York: Crossroad Publishing, 1998.

Dunn, James D. G. "The Letter Kills, but the Spirit Gives Life (2 Cor. 3:6)." *Pneuma* 35, no. 2 (January 2013): 163–79.

Edstam, Torsten. "From Twelfth-Century Renaissance to Fifteenth-Century Reform: The Reception of Hugh of St. Victor in the Later Middle Ages." Dissertation. University of Chicago, 2014.

Exum, J. Cheryl. *Song of Songs: A Commentary.* Louisville, KY: Westminster John Knox Press, 2005.

Fassler, Margot E. *Gothic Song: Victorine Sequences and Augustinian Reform in Twelfth-Century Paris.* 2nd ed. Notre Dame, IN: University of Notre Dame Press, 2011.

Frend, W. H. C. *The Rise of Christianity.* Philadelphia: Fortress Press, 1984.

Furey, Constance. "Body, Society, and Subjectivity in Religious Studies." *Journal of the American Academy of Religion* 80, no. 1 (2012): 7–33.

———. "Relational Virtue: Anne Bradstreet, Edward Taylor, and Puritan Marriage." *Journal of Medieval and Early Modern Studies* 42, no. 1 (2012): 201–24.

Golitzin, Alexander. *Mystagogy: A Monastic Reading of Dionysius Areopagita.* Collegeville, MN: Cistercian, 2013.

Greenblatt, Stephen. *Renaissance Self-Fashioning: From More to Shakespeare.* Chicago: University of Chicago Press, 1980.

Grundmann, Herbert. *Religious Movements in the Middle Ages: The Historical Links between Heresy, the Mendicant Orders, and the Women's Religious Movement in the Twelfth and Thirteenth Century, with the Historical Foundations of German Mysticism.* Translated by Steven Rowan. Notre Dame, IN: Notre Dame University Press, 1995.

Hadot, Pierre. *Philosophy as a Way of Life.* Translated by Michael Chase. New York: Blackwell, 1995.

Harkaway-Krieger, Kerylin. "Mysticism and Materiality: *Pearl* and the Theology of Metaphor." *Exemplaria* 28, no. 2 (2016): 161–80.

Harkins, Franklin T. *Reading and the Work of Restoration: History and Scripture in the Theology of Hugh of St. Victor.* Toronto: Pontifical Institute of Medieval Studies, 2009.

Hollywood, Amy. *Acute Melancholia and Other Essays: Mysticism, History, and the Study of Religion.* New York: Columbia University Press, 2016.

———. "Song, Experience, and the Book in Benedictine Monasticism." In *The Cambridge Companion to Christian Mysticism*, edited by Amy

Hollywood and Patricia Z. Beckman, 59–79. Cambridge: Cambridge University Press, 2012.

Johnson, Elizabeth A. *Quest for the Living God: Mapping Frontiers in the Theology of God*. New York: Continuum International, 2008.

Jones, John D. "The *Divine Names* in John Sarracen's Translation: Misconstruing Dionysius' Language about God?" *American Catholic Philosophical Quarterly* 82, no. 4 (2008): 661–82.

Knepper, Timothy D. *Negating Negation: Against the Apophatic Abandonment of the Dionysian Corpus*. Eugene, OR: Wipf and Stock, 2014.

———. "Not Not: The Method and Logic of Dionysian Negation." *American Catholic Philosophical Quarterly* 82, no. 4 (2008): 619–37.

Kosky, Jeffrey L. *Arts of Wonder: Enchanting Secularity—Walter de Maria, Diller + Scofidio, James Turrell, Andy Goldsworthy*. Chicago: University of Chicago Press, 2013.

Lamberth, David C. "Putting 'Experience' to the Test in Theological Reflection." *Harvard Theological Review* 93, no. 1 (2000): 67–77.

Lawell, Declan. "Affective Excess: Ontology and Knowledge in the Thought of Thomas Gallus." *Dionysius* 26 (2008): 139–74.

Leyra Curiá, Montse. *In Hebreo: The Victorine Commentaries on the Pentateuch and the Former Prophets in Light of Its Northern-French Jewish Sources*. Turnhout, Belgium: Brepols, 2017.

Lindbeck, George A. *The Nature of Doctrine: Religion and Theology in a Postliberal Age*. Louisville, KY: Westminster John Knox Press, 1984.

Matter, E. Ann. *The Voice of My Beloved: The Song of Songs in Western Medieval Christianity*. Philadelphia: University of Pennsylvania Press, 1990.

McGinn, Bernard. *The Flowering of Mysticism: Men and Women in the New Mysticism—1200–1350*. New York: Crossroad Publishing, 1998.

———. *The Foundations of Mysticism: Origins to the Fifth Century*. New York: Crossroad Publishing, 1991.

———. "Mystical Consciousness: A Modest Proposal." *Spiritus* 8, no. 1 (2008): 44–63.

———. "Thomas Gallus and Dionysian Mysticism." *Studies in Spirituality* 8 (1998): 81–96.

Miles, Margaret R. *A Complex Delight: The Secularization of the Breast, 1350–1750*. Berkeley: University of California Press, 2008.

Minnis, Alastair. *Medieval Theory of Authorship: Scholastic Literary Attitudes in the Later Middle Ages*. 2nd ed. Philadelphia: University of Pennsylvania Press, 2010.

Mousseau, Juliet. "Daily Life at the Abbey of St. Victor." In *A Companion to the Abbey of St. Victor in Paris*, edited by Hugh Feiss and Juliet Mousseau, 55–78. Leiden: Brill Academic, 2018.

Newsome Martin, Jennifer. "Only What Is Rooted Is Living: A Roman Catholic Theology of *Ressourcement*." In *Theologies of Retrieval: An Exploration and an Appraisal*, edited by Darren Sarisky, 81–100. London: Bloomsbury T&T Clark, 2017.

Olson, Paul A. *The Journey to Wisdom: Self-Education in Patristic and Medieval Literature*. Lincoln: University of Nebraska Press, 1995.

Perl, Eric D. *Theophany: The Neoplatonic Philosophy of Dionysius the Areopagite*. Albany, NY: SUNY Press, 2007.

Proudfoot, Wayne. *Religious Experience*. Berkeley: University of California Press, 1985.

Rist, John M. "Love, Knowing and Incarnation in Pseudo-Dionysius." In *Traditions of Platonism: Essays in Honour of John Dillon*, edited by John. J. Cleary, 375–88. Aldershot: Ashgate, 1999.

Rorem, Paul. *Pseudo-Dionysius: A Commentary on the Texts and an Introduction to Their Influence*. New York: Oxford University Press, 1993.

Scharf, Robert H. "The Rhetoric of Experience and the Study of Religion." In *Critical Terms for Religious Studies*, edited by Mark C. Taylor, 94–116. Chicago: University of Chicago Press, 1998.

Scott, Joan. "The Evidence of Experience." *Critical Inquiry* 17, no. 4 (Summer 1991): 773–97.

Sells, Michael A. *Mystical Languages of Unsaying*. Chicago: University of Chicago Press, 1994.

Shaw, Gregory. "Neoplatonic Theurgy and Dionysius the Areopagite." *Journal of Early Christian Studies* 7, no. 4 (1999): 573–99.

Simpson, James. *Burning to Read: English Fundamentalism and Its Reformation Opponents*. Cambridge, MA: Harvard University Press, 2007.

Smalley, Beryl. *The Study of the Bible in the Middle Ages*. 2nd ed. Notre Dame, IN: University of Notre Dame Press, 1964.

Stang, Charles. *Apophasis and Pseudonymity in Dionysius the Areopagite: "No Longer I."* Oxford: Oxford University Press, 2012.

———. "Negative Theology from Gregory of Nyssa to Dionysius the Areopagite." In *The Wiley-Blackwell Companion to Christian Mysticism*, edited by Julia A. Lamm, 161–76. Hoboken, NJ: Wiley-Blackwell, 2013.

———. "Writing." In *The Cambridge Companion to Christian Mysticism*, edited by Amy Hollywood and Patricia Z. Beckman, 252–63. Cambridge: Cambridge University Press, 2012.

Stock, Brian. *The Integrated Self: Augustine, the Bible, and Ancient Thought*. Philadelphia: University of Pennsylvania Press, 2017.

Tichelkamp, Craig. "Mystical Theology and/in Translation: Re-veiling the Latin *Corpus Dionysiacum*." *Medieval Mystical Theology* 29, no. 1 (Summer 2020): 41–53.

Turner, Denys. "How to Read Pseudo-Denys Today?" *International Journal of Systematic Theology* 7, no. 4 (2005): 428–40.

Valente, Luisa. "*Verbum mentis—Vox clamantis*: The Notion of the Mental Word in Twelfth-Century Theology." In *The Word in Medieval Logic, Theology and Psychology: Acts of the XIIIth International Colloquium of the Société Internationale pour l'Étude de la Philosophie Médiévale*, edited by T. Shimizu and C. Burnett, 365–402. Turnhout, Belgium: Brepols, 2009.

Webster, John. "Theologies of Retrieval." In *The Oxford Handbook of Systematic Theology*, edited by Kathryn Tanner, John Webster, and Iain Torrance, 583–99. Oxford: Oxford University Press, 2007.

Weinandy, Thomas G., O.F.M., Cap. *Does God Suffer?* Notre Dame, IN: Notre Dame University Press, 2000.

Williams, Rowan. *Why Study the Past? The Quest for the Historical Church*. Grand Rapids, MI: Eerdmans, 2005.

Wolfson, Harry A. "Negative Attributes in the Church Fathers and the Gnostic Basilides." In *Studies in the History of Philosophy and Religion*. Vol. 1, edited by Isadore Twersky and George H. Williams, 145–56. Cambridge, MA: Harvard University Press, 1977.

———. "St. Thomas on Divine Attributes." In *Studies in the History of Philosophy and Religion*. Vol. 1, edited by Isadore Twersky and George H. Williams, 673–700. Cambridge, MA: Harvard University Press, 1977.

Wolter, Michael. "'Spirit' and 'Letter' in the New Testament." In *The Spirit and the Letter: A Tradition and a Reversal*, edited by Paul S. Fiddes and Günther Bader, 31–46. London: Bloomsbury T&T Clark, 2013.

INDEX

abundance (*habundantia*): and God's communication, 104, 147n42; *hyperochic*, 96; of loving goodness, 175; plenitude and, 73n61, 78–81, 117; transcendence and, 16, 98, 181; trinitarian, 62n25, 70, 104

academy, 1–4, 9–12, 21, 178–79, 183–86

affect (*affectus*): and beautification of the soul, 173; and Christian wisdom, 131; and Dionysian unknowing, 135; etymology of, 128n2, 131, 135; and experience, 112, 137–38; beyond intellect, 114, 120, 129, 132, 156; and intellect, 16, 131–32, 147, 149, 153–56; and knowledge, 120, 132–34; mental power, 131; in mystical theology, 12; receptivity of, 132; in reading, 21, 183; and spiritual senses, 134–35; of the soul on itself, 166, 170–71; of the soul on others, 166; of the soul on the Word, 162n90, 166, 173–75; transformation of, 73n61, 182; and union, 113, 128–35, 152, 156, 163, 166; of the Word on the soul, 16061, 166, 168

affection: apex of the, 113, 168, 170; disordered, 39; of God, 68, 183; inciting the Word's, 175; of Jesus, 107; beyond the mind, 131–32; in reading, 17n25

allegorical interpretation, 46, 156–57

allegory, 41, 156–57

anagogy, 123

Andrew of St. Victor, 5, 26, 30n10, 46n39, 48, 145

angels: beyond being, 55; entreating, 175; figurative language for, 119; immaterial knowledge of, 89n18; invisible, 118; and human beings, 104, 120, 147, 152; and hymns, 90; mental hierarchy of, 20, 129, 131, 152, 154–55; as model, 170

anthropology, theological, 14n20, 20, 139

apophasis (negation), 15–16, 66n41, 91, 94–97, 139

apparitions, 87–88, 112, 136, 172

Aristotle, 120n105, 143n34, 183n14

assimilation: effected by the Word, 166; goal of hierarchy, 128; to God beyond being, 52, 90; and knowledge, 77; union and, 125, 145, 147, 149, 152–53, 173–74; to Word of God, 101n47, 124, 173–74, 182

attraction, 68, 156, 160–61, 166

Augustine: and affect, 129; on eternal reasons, 103n57, 148, 150; among "the Fathers," 42; influence of on Hugh, 22, 35, 47; on literature, 27, 36, 37–38; on rhetorical invention, 31n13; *Rule* of, 4, 34–35; at St. Victor, 178,

182; on soul and mind, 153–154; theology of the Word, 81, 98–101, 104–6, 109–12, 147; theory of signs, 36, 43–45, 50, 76, 82, 89n17; and *visio Dei*, 134
awe, 3, 7, 21, 177–79

babbling (*garrulitas*), 169, 172
beautification, 89n18, 160, 162–63, 165–66, 176
being: attraction of God to, 69; derived from the Good, 56; God as Cause of, 59, 67, 69, 75; God as end of, 67–68; incarnation to, 106–7; presence of God to, 69, 84, 88; theology of, 70; Word as cause of, 109. *See also* beyond-being-ness
Being (divine name): as beyond being, 60, 72, 73, 78, 92–93, 116; as Cause of being, 74, 78, 116; after *Good* and *Love*, 53, 65, 67, 72–74, 80; negated, 66; in Scripture, 72–73
beyond-being-ness: abundance of, 79; as cause of being, 79, 81; cause of God's ineffability and unintelligibility, 57–60, 72–75, 86, 94, 132; characteristic of God, 53–62, 70, 73–74; and divine names, 86–89; of the eternal Word, 98, 101–2, 104–5, 119n104, 131; experience of, 111; as Good and Love, 69, 80; and incarnation, 106–8; negation and, 95; in Platonic philosophy, 56–57, 69, 72, 74–75, 78; plenitude of, 78–79; vs. preeminent possession, 73n61; presence of God's, 65, 69, 78, 81, 92; providence and,

62–65, 120; at St. Victor, 70, 78, 81; signification and, 76; in Thomas Gallus, 70–78; vs. transcendence, 55, 79; trinitarian, 61–64, 71, 77, 79; veils upon God's, 90, 92, 124
biblical interpretation. *See* scriptural interpretation
body, 16–17, 19

canon, 42–43, 185n19
capacity, 75, 89, 153, 155, 161
cataphasis (affirmation), 15–16, 67, 91, 139
Cause: of being, 56, 67, 74–75, 78–79, 116; beyond being, 55, 59, 64, 78–79, 81, 118–19; as divine name, 116–18; eternal Word as, 136; *hyperochic*, 92; mysterious and unintelligible, 81, 180; overflowing with loving goodness, 68, 78, 175; in Platonist philosophy, 56, 69, 78; presence of God as, 78–81
Cherubim, 156, 163, 167
Church, 1–4, 46, 178–79, 182–86
cognition. *See* knowledge
Coolman, Boyd Taylor, 20n31, 38, 73n61, 79n80, 156n73, 171n113
commentary: and the course (*cursus*) of the letter, 41; on Dionysian corpus, 83, 127; Gallus as writer of, 83–84; at St. Victor, 4, 5, 36, 46, 48–49; on Song of Songs, 22, 127–28; writing as spiritual practice, 17–18, 48–49, 83–84, 140, 145; as unveiling, 180
communication: of the God beyond being, 80–81; human, 44, 76, 105, 108, 121; the Word's, 98–99,

101, 120, 121, 124
communion of saints, 10–11, 23
community, 1, 3, 5–7, 181–83
consciousness, 16–19, 138–39
contemplation: affective, 138; descent from, 49; elevation to, 90; experiences of, 101; intellective, 137; in mental hierarchy, 158; reading and the goal of, 35, 41–42, 121–22; steps of, 130, 134, 160, 167; unitive, 145, 151–54
course (*cursus*): of the letter, 21–23, 36, 41, 43, 143–44; of the *theoriae*, 83, 121, 150, 182
creation: and divine love, 68–69, 81; divine names drawn from, 94, 116; full of God's mystery, 82; God's difference from, 55; presence of God to, 53; and sacred literature, 45, 120; and secular literature, 39; Word's role in, 100–101, 105–11, 130, 137, 148–49

Dailey, Patricia, 16–17
deification, 101, 163, 182, 183
dilation (of the soul), 160–63, 171, 176, 183
Dionysius (Pseudo-Dionysius): in Acts of the Apostles, 51–52, 58–59; on affect and experience, 132–36; on the God beyond being, 53–62; on Good and Love, 65–69, 135; among the Fathers, 42–43; on hierarchy, 154; on mental exercises, 159–60, 164; on mystical theology, 128, 132–34; on providence, 62–65; at St. Victor, 14, 51–53, 70–81, 101–2, 124–25, 177–80; on theological language, 15–16, 82, 84–97, 139; Thomas Gallus on, 70–81, 83–84, 97, 101–25, 127–38; the "treasury of the Apostle," 52, 79; on union, 128, 132–35
discipline (*disciplina*): liberal arts, 41; mystical theology as, 15, 17, 18; reading as, 5, 40, 178; scriptural interpretation as, 45, 48
disenchantment, 185
divine names: division of, 53, 65–66; *hyperochic* and causal, 90–97; hymn the entire divinity, 63–64; providence as source of, 62, 64; at St. Victor, 179; theologians' apparitions as source of, 87; theory of, 90–97; "unfolding of," 54, 123. *See also individual divine names*
division (textual), 41–43, 143n34, 145, 172

ecstasy, 12, 69, 124, 134–35, 158, 175
effectivity, 140–41, 145–46, 154, 158–66, 173, 176
efficacy. *See* effectivity
emanation, 80–81
eternal reasons, 100–110, 118–19, 121, 130, 150–52
exercise: of the mind, 123, 131n12, 153–55, 157–67, 174; reading as, 17n25, 125; spiritual, 16n23, 139n25, 169
expansion. *See* dilation
experience: effected, 158–66; multiple registers of, 136–38; in mystical theology, 12–21; of reading, 1–2, 5, 178, 185; of the theologians, 69, 87n15, 101, 180;

and utterance, 145–46, 166–73;
  of the Word, 98, 105, 111–15,
  120–21, 137–38, 158–76
fountain, 147–49
founts (*fontes*). *See* sources
Furey, Constance M., 19–20, 139,
  158

generosity (of God), 173, 180
God: beyond being, 55–62, 70–78;
  bridegroom as allegory for, 41;
  Creator and Redeemer, 180,
  185; divine names for, 90–93;
  experience of, 127, 136–38; as
  Good and Love, 65–69, 80–81;
  hiddenness of, 11, 180, 182;
  hyperochic negation of, 93–97;
  ineffable, 180; mystery of, 12, 82,
  182, 185; mystical theology and,
  15–16; passionate love of, 175, 184;
  presence of, 78–79; providence of,
  62–65, 180; theology of, 52–82,
  177, 184; union with, 128–38;
  veils upon, 82, 85–90; Word of,
  97–124, 146–76. *See also* Trinity
Golitzen, Alexander, 61, 77n71,
  85n8, 87n15
Good (divine name), 53, 56–57,
  65–69, 72, 78–81, 87
goodness, 103, 107–8, 168, 173, 175
Gospel, 42–43, 104
grace, 130–32, 153–56, 172–76, 183

Harkins, Franklin, 38–39
hierarchy: angelic, 170; Jesus as
  hierarch of every, 107; of the
  mind, 20, 131–32, 152–57,
  162–63; purpose of, 128; receptive
  of the Word, 167–68

Hierotheus, 112–13, 133
history: God's Word/Wisdom
  reflected in, 39, 45–46, 105–11,
  120, 137; retrieval and, 8n8, 11;
  Scripture as, 45–46, 111
historical-literal interpretation, 45,
  46n39, 48, 141–46
Hollywood, Amy, 15n21, 17n25,
  18n26
Holy Spirit: manifested in God's
  temporal actions, 37; proceeding
  from the Father and the Son,
  75, 103; and reading the letter,
  28–34, 47, 124–25, 179–82; role
  of in retrieval, 11, 23; teaching
  the theologians, 114. *See also* spirit
  (textual)
Hugh of St. Victor: influence of,
  5, 51–52, 122, 129, 131n10; praise
  for, 26; theology of the letter
  of, 22, 28–50, 181–83; theology
  of the Word of, 101–2, 146–49,
  152–54
hymns: creation as a source of,
  110; divine names as, 62, 64–69;
  embracing the entire divinity, 63,
  116; of the God beyond being,
  84–93, 116; of Hierotheus, 113;
  of the procession of God, 60–61,
  116; as responses, 114; veils as
  image for, 97
hyperoche ("beyond-having"):
  characteristic of God, 85, 120;
  describing Dionysian prefixes,
  66; divine names as, 91–97; and
  negation, 93–97; theological
  language as, 111, 116–17

impassibility, 184
incarnation, 98–101, 104–13,

136–37, 147–48, 182
ineffability: corollary of God's beyond-being-ness, 53, 55, 59–61, 63, 72–76; of experiential union, 114, 159, 169–72; of God, 57, 94; of the Gospel, 104; of the letter, 177, 179; mystical theology reflecting on, 11–12, 81; mystification as inculcating, 3; reading and, 21; in Song of Songs, 111n78, 115; theological language and, 86, 119; of the Word of God, 100, 105, 120
Intellect (divine name), 66
intellect (*intellectus*): and affect, 113, 129, 131, 153–56; drawn beyond the mind, 135; failure of or suspension of the, 104, 119, 132, 136; inferior to affect, 120, 132–33, 156, 171n113; reading and, 21, 182–84; receptive of divine inpourings, 105, 113, 173
intellection: association with being, 57n10, 59, 65n38, 73–74; beyond the mind, 131; collection, consideration, and, 127, 129–30; distinct from knowledge (*gnosis*), 60n20, 61n22, 113n84, 135; of God's providential actions, 63; in Platonic philosophy, 57, 87n15, 134; sensible symbols used for, 90
intelligibility, 59, 65, 74, 136, 138. *See also* unintelligibility
intimacy: affect more capable of than intellect, 132, 135, 167–68; God's with creation, 65, 82, 97; in mystical theology, 18–21, 139–40, 158; between a prelinguistic concept and its speaker, 100, 103; between the soul and the Word, 98, 134, 137–38, 140–41, 146, 152; between a visible sign and its invisible referent, 118–19
invention (rhetorical), 31–32
Iamblichus, 87n15, 89n17

James of Vitry, 6, 25–26
Jesus Christ, 55, 84n5, 88n16, 100–101, 105–11, 148
John Saracen, 6, 51, 70, 128, 149–50, 179
journey, 42–43, 50, 114, 138, 151, 181–83. *See also* course (*cursus*)

Knepper, Timothy, 73n61, 91n25, 95–97
knowledge (*gnosis/cognitio*): affective, 120, 123, 133; distinct from understanding/intellection, 60n20, 61n22, 113n84, 135; experiential, 113, 168; God hidden from, 62; intellectual, 127, 129–32, 156; of invisible things through visible signs, 46, 76, 111; methodical (*scientia*), 134, 138; in Platonic philosophy, 56–57; super-intellectual, 119, 123, 127, 132–33, 167

language, 15–18, 90, 111, 117–20, 138–39, 180
letter (*littera*): definition of, 27; experience of, 20; expansiveness of, 40, 50; and the mystery of God, 185; mystification of, 4, 7, 52; metaphors for, 47, 122; as path, 181–82; sacred and secular, 185; and spirit, 28–34, 122, 140, 144, 176, 179, 181; as system of signs, 47, 50, 124, 182; as a

theological concept, 27–28, 34, 43, 47, 50, 186; as veil, 53, 84, 97, 124, 179–80; visible, 180. *See also* theology of the letter
liberal arts, 38–39, 110, 142, 180, 185n19, 186
Light (divine name), 55, 65, 93, 136
light, 47, 55, 58, 103, 118, 171–73
literal interpretation. *See* historical-literal interpretation
literalism, 32–33, 184
literature: or the letter, 27; mystification of, 4, 7; sacred, 36–43, 98, 104, 121–22, 137, 180; secular, 36–40, 43, 130, 180. *See also* Scripture
littera. *See* letter *and* literature
liturgy, 3–6, 15, 52–53, 82, 85–87, 112–13
Love (divine name), 53, 55, 65–69, 72, 80–81, 135
love, 86, 133, 144, 167, 175, 184. *See also* "Whom my soul loves"

McGinn, Bernard, 12–14, 16–18
memory, 26, 37, 39–40
mind (*mens*): affected by theological language, 16–17, 115–16, 123, 139; angelic hierarchy of the, 151, 152, 154–57; ecstatically drawn beyond itself, 110n74, 114, 116, 124, 135, 155–56; exercises of the, 125, 153, 159–66; forgetting itself, 39; of God, 103n57; God beyond the, 86; highest part of the soul, 153; knowing beyond the, 111, 114, 128, 131, 134–35, 167; powers of the, 129–31, 133; Seraphim of the, 138, 156, 168, 170; site of an inner word, 100, 103, 115; spiritual senses of the, 134–35; suspension of the, 131, 155–56; among the *theoriae*/exemplars, 147, 158; union beyond the, 132, 133; unveiling/removing obstacles from the, 117, 131; uplifting of the, 151; using material guidance, 85; Word's effect on, 140, 159–66
Moses, 55, 77, 133
mystery: academic study of, 185; affect more capable of than intellect, 129, 133–35, 166–67; beyond the letter, 46, 180; characteristic of union with God, 128, 137–38; cultural aversion toward, 185; divine names hymning God's, 79; of divine providence, 64–65, 120; experience or consciousness of, 12–17, 21, 114, 185; of God at St. Victor, 70–81; of God beyond being, 52–53, 182, 70–78; known through sensible/visible forms, 122, 124; of the letter, 4, 20–23, 81–82, 124–25, 176–77, 178–81; and practice, 128, 137, 143; scriptural interpretation and, 150; in trinitarian theology, 61–62; of the Word, 49, 137–38, 166–67
mysticism, 12–15, 112. *See also* theology, mystical
mystification: definition of, 3–4; of God, 16, 53, 82; of the letter at St. Victor, 6–7, 25–27, 50–52, 84, 177, 179–83; remedy for disenchantment, 185; role of liturgy and art in, 6n5; role of theology in, 7, 15–18, 138–39,

184; of theological language, 91–92, 98, 118–19, 138–39

Neoplatonists. *See* Platonists

Origen of Alexandria, 41, 42

Paul: and Dionysius, 43, 51–52; and the God beyond being, 55, 58–59; on the letter and the spirit, 22, 28–30, 32n14, 34, 49–50, 124, 179; on the visible and the invisible, 100n46, 110, 130
pedagogy, 4, 36, 41, 48, 121–22, 170
perfection: beyond intellection, 84–85; the Cause brings all to, 66–68; definition of, 42n31, 183n14; and the instability of present life, 49; as monastic goal of reading, 35, 43, 122n109, 183; Scripture and liturgy lead to, 86–87; Song of Songs and, 41–42; and spiritual progress, 28, 43; as union with the Word, 163
Philo of Alexandria, 57, 99
Plato, 56, 78, 130
Platonists, 37–38, 56–59, 74–76, 134
plenitude, 78–81, 104, 107–8, 170–71, 173, 181
Plotinus, 56–57, 64, 134
powers (divine), 55, 57, 63–65, 82, 88
powers (of the mind), 129–33, 154–56
practice: effected by the Word, 157, 173; medieval theory of, 158; in mystical theology, 15, 17n25, 18, 21, 143, 150; of reading, 1, 15, 40, 48–49, 177–80; Song of Songs

as, 127–28, 139–41, 145. *See also* exercise; discipline
prayer, 49, 159, 163–66, 173
procession. *See* emanation
Proclus, 56–57, 61n22, 64, 67n45, 68
providence, 53–55, 62–69, 84–88, 94, 100–101, 180
Pseudo-Dionysius. *See* Dionysius

reading: communal and inclusive, 182–83; demystified, 179; the first step to perfection, 35, 43; as a journey, 124; the letter, 179; spiritual practice of, 15, 48–49, 125, 176; theology of, 35–48; as transformative, 181–82; the Word of God, 111, 113, 121–22, 138–41. *See also* reading culture
reading culture: of Church and academy today, 1–3, 11, 21, 178, 183–86; definition of, 3; renewal of, 8–9, 11, 23, 177; of St. Victor, 5–6, 21, 25–27, 83, 176, 177–78
relation, 18–21, 118–19, 132, 139, 146, 158
renewal, 8–11, 29–30, 105, 177–79, 186
repetition, 144
ressourcement, 8
retrieval, 7–11, 23, 177–79, 183–86
Richard of St. Victor, 5, 48
Rule of Augustine, 4, 35n16

salvation, 14
scriptural interpretation: allegorical, 41, 46; anagogical, 123; and commentary, 48–49; historical-literal, 36, 45–46, 141–46; and invention, 31n13; at St. Victor, 4,

25, 124; and signification, 45–46; spiritual, 45–46, 121–23, 141, 146–58, 158–76; tropological, 46

Scripture, 29–30, 40, 42, 65, 86, 109–14. *See also* literature, sacred

sequence (liturgical), 4, 6n5

sequence (textual): 22, 41, 143–45, 166, 172, 176

Seraphim, 138, 156, 164–65, 163–68, 170

signification (theory of signs), 43–47, 76–77, 109–11, 117–21, 124–25, 182

simplicity, 86, 133, 143, 148, 150

sin, 14, 101n47

Solomon, 17, 41, 127

Song of Songs: commentary on, 83; literal interpretation of, 141–46; as the practice of Christian wisdom, 22, 127–28, 139; special place among sacred literature, 41; spiritual interpretation of, 105, 146–76, 181

soul: bride as allegory for, 140–41, 145–57, 159–76; deformation of the, 38; forgetting itself, 39; having knowledge of the Word, 136–37; inflamed or uplifted, 123; restoration or reformation of the, 36, 39–40, 50, 101; transformation of the, 16–21, 121, 183; united to the Word, 128, 137, 140–41, 157–58; wandering among the *theoriae*, 104–5, 132, 181. *See also* powers (of the mind); hierarchy, of the mind

sources, 7–9, 11, 177

spirit (textual), 27–34, 47, 50, 122, 176, 179. *See also* Holy Spirit

spiritual senses, 134–35, 143, 167

St. Victor (abbey school): characteristics of life at, 4–5, 35; commentary and translation at, 48–49, 51, 83; history of, 4; the mystified letter at, 6–7, 22–23, 28, 81–82, 124–25, 177–83; Pseudo-Dionysius at, 51–53, 70, 83–84; reading culture of, 5–6, 21, 25–27, 83, 176, 177–78; representative figures from, 5–6; theology at, 4, 22–23

subjectivity, 19–21

suspension, 130–32, 155–56, 163

symbol, 16, 53, 85–90, 111–12

theologians (writers of Scripture), 55, 84, 86–88, 110–16, 120–21, 180

theological anthropology. *See* anthropology, theological

theology: education in, 186; of God, 53–81, 184; historical, 8, 13–15; influence of on reading cultures, 177–78, 184; of the letter, 22, 28, 49–50, 82, 177; modern, 8–10; mystical, 11–22, 52, 82, 177, 179–80; of reading, 3; retrieval as a mode of, 7–11, 23, 177–79, 183–86; role of in mystifying the letter, 6n5, 7, 22–23; Scripture as, 86, 102n53, 116, 149; at St. Victor, 4, 22–23; systematic, 8, 14–15; of the Word, 181

theophany, 65n38, 84

theoriae (spectacles): as eternal reasons of the Word, 104–15, 149–52, 157–58; following the courses of the, 83, 121, 182; lead to babbling, 169; pouring into the soul, 163; represented in the

Song of Songs, 143, 151; union with the, 138; wandering among the, 172, 131–32. *See also* eternal reasons

Thomas Aquinas, 73n61, 117n97, 120

Thomas Gallus: as commentary writer, 17, 42, 48, 83–84, 127; following methods of St. Victor, 46, 140–45, 182; influenced by Pseudo-Dionysius, 52, 70–81, 102–24, 127–76; the last great Victorine, 5–6, 22, 127, 180; theology of, 20, 70–81, 98–124, 127–76

transcendence, 16, 53, 55, 79, 96, 181 *See also* beyond-being-ness

transformation, 1–3, 15–18, 159–60, 178, 180–83, 186

translation, 5, 6, 22, 51–52, 70, 179

Trinity: and beyond-being-ness, 61–62, 75, 77; Jesus and, 107; plenitude of, 70–71; and providential goodness, 67, 80, 103; theological signification of, 119–20

Turner, Denys, 87n15, 112

unfolding, 53, 90n20, 123, 180

unintelligibility: corollary of God's beyond-being-ness, 53, 55–57, 59–61, 63, 72–76; of God's presence, 88; of God's providence, 64, 81, 94; of the letter, 177, 179; mystical theology reflecting on, 11–12, 81; mystification as inculcating, 3, 81–82; of relation between visible sign and invisible thing, 119–20; of the Trinity, 61–62; of the Word of God, 111n78, 115, 172

union: adapting the mind for, 159–64; affective, 114, 129–35, 156, 166–67; central to mystical theology, 11, 14; experiential, 124, 136–38, 166–70; as goal of Christian life, 52; as a kind of knowing, 77, 124, 128; leads to effective utterance, 172–74; Song of Songs as allegory for mystical, 140–41; soul's capacity for, 153; the theologians' experience of, 111, 113–14; with Word of God, 42, 98, 128, 147, 149–50, 182. *See also* assimilation

unknowing (*agnosia/ignorantia*): and affection, 133–35; cloud of, 62; of God's beyond-being-ness, 59, 72, 74; and *hyperoche*, 91n25, 93–96; mystical union as, 128; in Platonic philosophy, 60, 61n22; scriptural roots of, 58–59; and unveiling of the mind, 159–60, 162

unveiling (of the mind), 159–60, 174

veil: as metaphor for the letter, 53, 81–82, 124–25, 179–80; Pauline use of, 29; placed upon God, 63n30, 97; theological language as, 86–90; unveiling of the, 65n38, 86, 92, 111, 122–23, 159–60

Victorines. *See* St. Victor

vision, 57, 85, 134, 136

voice (*vox*), 44–45, 100, 109, 140–41, 145–66, 172–73

wander, 83, 132, 172, 181–82

"Whom my soul loves," 77n70,

111n78, 115, 171–72
William of Champeaux, 4
wisdom (human): of Christians, 52, 127–31, 155, 163, 166–69; Dionysius as theoretical part of Christian, 127; of the philosophers, 108, 114, 129–30; received from divine Wisdom, 147–48; remembering one's innate, 39; retrieval of, 9, 11, 23, 177; Song of Songs as practical part of Christian, 127, 139, 155
Wisdom (divine): memory as a site of, 26; reading as pursuit of, 37–40, 50; as source of divine utterance, 104; spectacles (*theoriae*) of divine, 80; human wisdom received from, 147–48
wonder, 3, 21, 177, 179
words (*verba*), 44–46, 76, 101, 142–43, 182. *See also* signification
Word of God: bridegroom as, 146–52, 157–58; containing eternal reasons, 148, 151, 182; creating and restoring, 46, 180; effective utterance of, 159–66; eternal, 136, 148–49, 151–52, 182; as experiencing, 174–76; incarnate, 136, 148; and the letter at St. Victor, 97–124, 181; as origin of Scripture, 45, 149, 176; reading to know the, 49; and the soul, 20–21, 140–41, 145–46; soul's affection for, 131–35, 156; soul's experience of, 136–38, 167–72; soul's union with, 147, 149–50. *See also* theoriae (spectacles)
wound, 174–75
writing, 15, 16n23, 18, 114–15, 121, 124